MW00652048

DIVINE CURRENCY

Cultural Memory

in

the

Present

Hent de Vries, Editor

DIVINE CURRENCY

The Theological Power of Money in the West

Devin Singh

STANFORD UNIVERSITY PRESS

STANFORD, CALIFORNIA

Stanford University Press
Stanford, California

© 2018 by the Board of Trustees of the Leland Stanford Junior University.
All rights reserved.

No part of this book may be reproduced or transmitted in any form or by any
means, electronic or mechanical, including photocopying and recording, or in
any information storage or retrieval system without the prior written permission
of Stanford University Press.

Printed in the United States of America on acid-free, archival-quality paper

Library of Congress Cataloging-in-Publication Data

Names: Singh, Devin, author.
Title: Divine currency : the theological power of money in the West / Devin
    Singh.
Description: Stanford, California : Stanford University Press, 2018. | Series:
    Cultural memory in the present | Includes bibliographical references and
    index.
Identifiers: LCCN 2017038483 (print) | LCCN 2017041114 (ebook) | ISBN
    9781503605671 | ISBN 9781503604827 (cloth :qalk. paper) | ISBN
    9781503605664 (pbk. :qalk. paper)
Subjects: LCSH: Money—Religious aspects—Christianity—History of
    doctrines. | Economics—Religious aspects—Christianity—History of
    doctrines. | Political theology.
Classification: LCC BR115.W4 (ebook) | LCC BR115.W4 S56 2017 (print) | DDC
    261.8/5—dc23
LC record available at https://lccn.loc.gov/2017038483

Contents

Acknowledgments

This study explores money, which marks relationships of credit and debt and, hence, obligation. It is altogether fitting that I acknowledge the debts—intellectual, relational, and financial—that made this project possible. Special thanks go to Emily-Jane Cohen for her enthusiastic support and advocacy for this book from the beginning. My heartfelt thanks go to a dedicated and generous group of readers who offered substantive feedback on the entire manuscript: Ethan Fairbanks, Hille Haker, Dotan Leshem, Luke Moorhead, Michael Motia, Roberto Sirvent, and two anonymous reviewers.

Appreciation goes to my colleagues and students at Dartmouth College and Yale University for discussions and insights that shaped my thinking on these matters. Special thanks go particularly to Dudley Andrew, Christopher Beeley, Stephen Davis, Philip Gorski, David Singh Grewal, Noreen Khawaja, Kathryn Lofton, Dale Martin, Eliyahu Stern, Kathryn Tanner, Linn Marie Tonstad, Emilie Townes, Denys Turner, Miroslav Volf, Frederick Wherry, and Andre Willis. A special word of gratitude goes to the supportive conversation partners at the Yale Marxism and Cultural Theory Working Group, especially Michael Denning, Moira Fradinger, John MacKay, A. Naomi Paik, and Caleb Smith.

A number of interlocutors along the way have impacted my thinking as it relates to the themes explored in this project. I am grateful for conversations with Luke Bretherton, Elizabeth Bruno, Kati Curts, David DeVore, Nigel Dodd, Marko Geslani, Yvette Gomez, George Gonzalez, Philip Goodchild, Marion Grau, Michael Hollerich, Ana Ilievska, Karin Knorr Cetina, Kwok Pui Lan, Yii-Jan Lin, Vincent Lloyd, Charles Mathewes, Christina McRorie, David Newheiser, Kristine Olson, Hollis Phelps, Kathryn Reklis, John Roberts, Erin Runions, Raphael Sartorius,

Daniel Schriever, Daniel Schultz, Shauna Lee Sexsmith, Charles Stang, Michael Thate, and Kevin Wilkinson.

Research for this study was supported in part by Dartmouth College, Yale University, the Forum for Theological Exploration, and the Mrs. Giles Whiting Foundation, whom I gratefully acknowledge. A generous First Book Grant from the Louisville Institute enabled completion of this project, which was also recognized by the Manfred Lautenschlaeger Stiftung and the Forschungszentrum Internationale und Interdisziplinäre Theologie at the University of Heidelberg. Special thanks to Michael Welker and the Lautenschlaeger family for their support.

Finally, my deep gratitude for good humor and support goes to Marcelo Ramagem, Gopal Swamy, Kuo-Lai Wong, and the Singh and Thompson families. Special thanks go to Nicole March for being a force of overwhelming goodness and love in my life. Finally, thanks to my mother, Randal Joy Thompson, to whom this book is dedicated and without whom none of this would have been possible.

Introduction

It has become commonplace today to speak of a widespread, so-called faith and hope in money and markets. The ubiquitous power and influence of the economy appear to require, or at least inspire, religious language and invocations of the divine. Economic institutions may sometimes be described as "idols" or "demigods" dictating the lives and destinies of millions. Money is depicted as an object of "worship," as enthusiastic participants in the global economy prostrate themselves before the "altars" of capital, seeking economic "salvation." These are usually no more than passing allusions or fleeting attempts at evocative metaphor. But such ascriptions and the links they imply have long-standing foundations.

The tendency to highlight money's purportedly religious dynamics can be traced in part to the ways in which economic ideas and activity have actually interacted with religious thought and practice over the centuries in Western societies. This book initiates an investigation of these connections between money and Christian theology, following the intuition that the development of the economy in the West is marked by an ongoing relation between these two spheres. I claim that portrayals of monetary acquisition as a spiritual quest, or of economic processes and powers as infused with religious characteristics, are in part the result of concrete conceptual and institutional resonance between talk about God and the nature and uses of money.

Particular early Christian theological ideas incorporate and retain traces of monetary economy. Monetary language, concepts, and practices

Introduction

prove useful in clarifying and formalizing certain emerging and central theological claims. This infusion of monetary thought and practice into core Christian doctrine means that Christian ideas, practices, and traditions help to convey this theological and economic combination into new social and political formations and legitimate evolving customs and institutions of monetary economy. If money lends its logic to the structuring of theology, God-talk repays by offering its prestige and sacred power to the world of exchange.

This book, therefore, coincides with studies of the partially theological sources of the modern economy. It also participates in broader considerations of the theological heritage of modern politics and statecraft, for it is my assumption that money and economy cannot be adequately grasped apart from matters of sovereignty and law. This investigation demonstrates that these connections among monetary economy, politics, and religious thought and practice have been present since key "founding moments" of the Western imaginary.

Rather than attempting a wide-ranging genealogy or documenting the *longue durée* of theological economic development, I consider several ancient points of interaction or resonance between money and theology. Moreover, although Judaic and Islamic theological traditions also interface with monetary economy, and both should be considered significant contributors to Western legacy, I focus on Christian thought. Christian theology persists as a central authorizing discourse in the development of Western societies and self-understanding. My study adds an additional perspective to the growing body of literature assessing the residual yet persistent Christian theological legacy—both explicit and implicit—in modern politics and economy. Widespread social and institutional influence by Christianity began at least as early as the fourth century, and the discourses I consider took place in this formative period of Christian theology and empire.

Assessing these founding moments is not a "quest for origins" or for the "pure sources" of the nexus of money and theology. It is an attempt to shed light on elements relevant to one "moment of arising" of this conceptual ensemble.[1] Considering Christian theology's debt to monetary practice for many of its key concepts in their early manifestations does not necessarily convey a more authentic image of the connections I seek to highlight. It does, however, potentially enlighten genealogical analyses of Christian influence by considering periods that remain authoritative within Christian traditions themselves. Patristic voices, those of the so-called church fathers, are resources to which Christian thought has continually looked in its ongoing self-construction. These early theologies are persistently drawn upon in theological discourse and retain an authoritative aura due to both their primacy and their antiquity, as well as their conciliar—and, hence, political and patriarchal—ratification.

Revealing the links between money and theology from these beginnings of formal Christian theological expression demonstrates that money cannot be dismissed as a corrupting influence on such ideas but is a critical structuring principle in theological thought. In turn, theological discourse eventually comes to play a determinative role in politics and economic administration in Christendom, meaning that monetized theology lends its own types of direction and legitimation to this worldly sphere. The historical priority of the late antique fusion of money and theology means that certain conceptual figures have been and continue to be taken up and redeployed in theology and practice across the centuries. Such redeployment is always originary and not merely mimetic, and each instance requires its own analysis. Yet, unpacking something like the beginnings of a formal Christian synthesis of monetary logic and discourse about God and salvation can only be salutary for analyzing the development and impact of such tradition.

Religions of the market?

Contemporary appraisals of the purportedly religious character of money and markets in the modern West often appear impressionistic. At a popular level, some condemn the existential posture of subservience to the gods of finance. In many scholarly critiques based upon stable, external, and often vague definitions of what religion entails, we can find glimpses of an apparent religious structure to global economy or contemporary economic practices labeled as quasi-religious.[2] Yet, it is often unclear what work the labels do other than provide emotivist or intuitive grounds for critique.[3] We find sharp dichotomies and oppositional tensions drawn between religion and the economy from the start. To invocations of market religiosity are sometimes added specters of heresy or idolatry, and the necessity of ensuing condemnation is made to appear self-evident. After all, shouldn't we all seek to decry idolatry, whatever it is?[4]

These approaches tend to take the form of pure and objective critique from a religious or theological point of view. They often work from the premise not only that religion can serve as an obvious and fixed template for diagnosing contemporary economy, but also that theology provides the conceptual and ethical correctives to societal woes. Not only is the conversation frontloaded such that denunciation of the present economic order is inevitable, but the socioanalytic usefulness of construing particular economic practices as religious also remains unclear. The spheres of religion or theology, typically construed as distinct from the economy, can then supposedly be brought to bear in judgment upon economic arrangements as false or heterodox religions. Left unconsidered is the extent to which theology and broader religious discourse and practice may have in fact helped to construct the very systems and structures assessed and critiqued. Even further removed are inquiries about the ways in which theologians have relied upon economic concepts and tropes to develop and articulate their ideas.[5]

We gain more analytical purchase from attempts to assess the analogous structural relations between theological discourse and the economy proper. Informed by structuralist and poststructuralist sensitivities to the operation of sign systems, one can compare the conceptual economies of theology and money, for instance.[6] This approach recognizes that both systems set forth certain postures of exchange and make claims about value. The arrangement of a certain chain of signifiers in one system can be brought alongside that in the other, possibly shedding light on their respective functions through the work of comparative and contrastive analysis. For instance, the spiritual goods and exchanges taking place within the Trinity or between God and creation, as posited by particular modern Christian thinkers, can clarify and in turn be illumined by models of material economic or semiotic circulation.

What one often finds in such assessments, however, is the assumption of unidirectional influence between these disparate systems: the theological is still brought to bear as a corrective critique of the economic. The possibility that the influence works in both directions is rarely entertained.

Furthermore, when the move is made to cross spheres and use theology to judge the economic realm, little justification is given for the possibility of this transfer, which often appears arbitrary. A basis for conceptual mediation between distinct structural fields, one that would undergird the possibility of theology addressing the economy in the first place, is underdetermined. Finally, these approaches risk redeploying the ahistorical perspective of their structuralist predecessors, wherein sign systems are considered with little regard for their historical and material derivation. Freeze-frame snapshots of semiotic relationships are taken to imply that the relationships have always operated in such manner. Synchronic analysis means further that the possibility of *mutual* historical influence between these systems is, from the start, foreclosed.[7]

Money, incarnation, and God's economy

Insights on the nature and function of money afford additional opportunities for conceptual comparison between economy and theology. Money serves as a useful point of entry into such considerations because it brings to the fore questions about the materialization of transcendent value and the role of representation, issues central to debates about God's relation to the world, for instance; because it crystallizes certain relations of power, authority, and control present in economic exchange which are critical to discussions of divine sovereignty; and because it offers a discrete set of attributes to analyze within the expansive field of economics, providing a workable scope of inquiry.

Drawing on sociologies and anthropologies of money, I understand money to be partly explained as a sign and representation of sovereign power inserted into a space or territory to aid in the governance of subjects.[8] The images that money literally bears in so many of its historical manifestations are just one clue to its function as a stand-in or representative of the value system and modes of disciplinary enforcement of an authoritative, organizing center. While sovereign power (as centralized) cannot be physically present everywhere, money circulates as an extension of sovereignty, creating tendrils of control that penetrate the very exchange relations of subjects and eventually shape evaluations of reality and consequent communal formation. Money is also a mark of obligation to this power, for monetary economy is set into motion by taxation: minting authorities disseminating tokens of exchange also legislate the return of a portion of them to the governing center, and monetary tokens are given value in part by their ability to discharge this debt. Analyzing money thus requires consideration of relations of authority and hierarchy.

My inquiry began as an exploration of the conceptual parallels between Christology and monetary economy. Informed by the aforementioned approach of analogous structural comparison, I sought to elucidate what appeared as noteworthy correspondences between ideas of incarnation and a particular understanding of money. It first struck me that we could speak preliminarily and loosely of a type of *monetary incarnation*, where a distant sovereign power is made present by its image of value. This materialized representative of sovereignty becomes a central object of desire, imports a specific value-laden codification of reality, and shapes relations and communities by its standards.[9] I considered what dynamics might be elucidated by reading the operations of money through the lens of incarnation. In what ways might construing the incarnation of the Son of God in monetary terms reveal previously unnoticed aspects of divine economy? To answer this question, I considered similarities and divergences between the operations of money and the classic tale of God's incarnate image, a representation of worth and value on earth which aids in the consolidation of divine authority and shapes communities according to a divine standard of value.

I was spurred on by the striking language of money and value operative in Christian discourse—ascriptions of worth and treasure to Christ, for instance, not to mention the thoroughly economic terminology of "redemption"—yet I was concerned to avoid some of the ahistorical lacunae of the aforementioned structuralist approaches. I thus sought to examine in what ways the similarities between monetary and Christological incarnations were more than merely analogous. Did the striking conceptual resonances stem from actual historical links between these two economies? Could we posit more than a coincidental and allusive parallelism between money and Christ? I found the evidence to be overwhelming—so much so that this book barely scratches the surface of the intricate interpenetration of monetary and economic thought and practice, on the one hand, and Christian theological reflection and ecclesial formation, on the other. In an effort to initiate a much larger conversation that needs to take place about the long-standing relations between religion and the economy, my study makes broad conceptual claims while taking a few historical snapshots of the relationship in question.

In this study, I reconstruct an understanding of God as an economic administrator and of Christ as God's currency. I claim that this view of God is at work as a background assumption in patristic theological discourse and results from the influence of Greco-Roman economic administration and monetary practice in the wider culture. This model gives form and structure to certain logics operative in theological discourse that have been shaped by their early context and social sphere. The nexus of theology and monetary economy also creates the conditions of possibility for theology's reciprocal impact upon the economic sphere.

While this view of God as economist and as currency shows through at various points in patristic discourse developing in the third through fifth centuries, it remains largely unarticulated in systematic fashion. I seek to bring coherence to a diverse set of economic metaphors and images operative in early theology that have been conveyed into emergent Western tradition as certain strands of theology were construed as "orthodoxy," raised to prominence, disseminated, and enforced. My wager is that this monetized theology has lent itself over the centuries and in various permutations to the growth of economic thought and practice in society. My genealogical and archeological eye is on late antiquity, but the model has potential for critically elucidating various historical periods. To invoke the idea of divine currency is simultaneously to make claims about an implicit concept in early theology, to diagnose a paradigm that was conveyed into Western thought and practice, and to commend a framework for assessing the interaction between theological discourse and practice and monetary economy across Western history.

Genealogy, archaeology, and re/constructive theology

This study contributes to a theological genealogy of economy in the West. A full-fledged genealogy would require a multivolume work that traces the emergence and permutations of the ideas I survey as they shape

late antique, medieval, and modern society. I engage here in an archaeological retrieval of key founding tropes in the early Christian imaginary.
I do so fully cognizant that archaeological work, as situated *description* of
a perceived past, is simultaneously a type of construction and is, hence,
redescription. Just as the various quests for the historical Jesus have lent as
many reflections peering into the "well" of history, any attempt to con-
ceptualize the past involves projection.[10] The present is as much a consideration in any such endeavor as the past. I make no apologies for pursuing
questions about early Christian theology with concerns about contemporary global economy and the pervasiveness of modern money in view.
While a long road or, better, series of diffuse capillary trails would need
to be traced to show how such ancient ideas lead to the construction of
the present order, I aim to contribute to such work by reconstructing paradigms operative in the early fusion of theology, politics, and economy in
the West.

Operating at a broad discursive level in terms of theology, politics,
and monetary economy, the study claims that the characteristics explored
are observable in a variety of textual and historical instances. I do not
presume to provide a richly detailed historical account of early Christian
theology or society, nor do I hold that patristic thought is in any way
monolithic. My aim is to set forth a general conceptual edifice for thinking about the nature of monetary economy and theology's relationship to
it in the West. While locating the model in historical moments, the work
here is primarily theoretical. Naturally, certain aspects of my theorization
will require nuance and modification in light of more in-depth studies of
specific historical and cultural formations. Furthermore, while I engage
major voices in patristic thought, outliers and points of contention will
persist and can serve to sharpen and refine the model I contribute.

This book makes use of genealogical and archaeological approaches
as it navigates these interstices of theory and history. I understand genealogy to be a supplement to and not a replacement for more traditional
methods of historiography.[11] Genealogy challenges assumptions about the
historian as a fixed, sovereign subject and objective observer of the past.
It questions historical approaches that serve "as the handmaiden to philosophy," vindicating timeless truths rather than analyzing the past in all
its complexity.[12] Genealogy subverts the quest for origins, interrogating

the drive for an original, pure moment of a phenomenon, something untainted by materiality and change. Instead, it strives to highlight the diverse and often conflicting ensemble of elements associated with a certain manifestation of a phenomenon. This means examining how it takes on a specific formation and also what makes that formation work, what gives it efficacy and legitimacy in a particular epoch. Genealogy requires attention to sources and openness to the detritus of history, to elements and connections often deemed unworthy of consideration or inessential to historical understanding.[13] Yet, seeing genealogy as marking disruptions or discontinuities presumes a semblance of continuity and even narrative for it to problematize, which is why I understand it to function together with the work of the historian.

While genealogy as attention to the transfers and permutations of particular historical formations—as a "hazardous play of dominations"— retains a diachronic sense, I regard archaeology as a more synchronically attuned approach.[14] Archaeology moves sideways and within a layer being analyzed. It probes and illumines the connections and influences surrounding the object while acknowledging that object as porous. Rigorous archaeology means examining not merely a certain idea but also the material practices, institutions, symbolic media, and political and economic formations that experience, shape, and manifest it. In attending to the distinctive nature of the layer, it serves to fashion the moment of rupture or discontinuity even while contributing to genealogy, which asks how this discontinuous singularity is nevertheless transferred to a new context.

My project straddles the bounds of historical redescription and constructive theory, and is in this way re/constructive. I uncover what I claim are implicit theologies at work in patristic thought. These ancient thinkers make use of the nature and practices of money in the broader culture, employing them in a conceptual edifice upon which to construct images of and make claims about what God is like and how God acts. My tactics of salvaging such submerged conceptual debris are in part constructive, for I occasionally supply what is left unsaid and seek to provide a systematization to ancient ideas that is not immediately evident in their context. I do so not with both eyes on the past—as if that were even possible—but with one on contemporary concerns about the ways in which theological discourse has shaped and continually offers implicit legitimation to concepts, practices, and institutions that structure the present.

As a re/construction, my approach brings me alongside certain contemporary constructive theological or ethical projects that draw on a theological heritage to produce new paradigms for socioeconomic critique and action. Voices within the field of constructive theology usually advocate concrete political ends and lifestyle or policy modifications, enacting a theological vision within social, political, or economic spheres. They typically rehearse and problematize a particular social and conceptual challenge and then offer a theological response as the oppositional word of correction. This approach may also be termed homiletical, for it emerges out of a long history of Christian preaching and draws on the authority of Scripture and tradition to confront the world and exhort believers toward action. Yet what is needed, in my view, is more light on the realities to which such prescriptions seek to respond, greater self-reflexivity on their modes of response, and investigation of how their theological and ethical engagements may have already helped construct the circumstances against which they protest. I therefore seek to prioritize redescription and defer prescriptive remedies. This is not to pretend that redescription is somehow neutral, disinterested, or apolitical. It is, rather, to pursue both the immanent critique of theology and theology as immanent critique.[15]

Furthermore, most constructive, prescriptive theological responses appear to function hand in hand with the aforementioned tendency to posit sharp contrasts between theology and economy. I do not belabor such differences in this study; in fact, I take them for granted. Assuming that Christology and money are divergent spheres, that Christ does not equal money, I do not outline what might be termed "dis-analogies" or discontinuities between them. Not only is Christian rhetorical distance from wealth a well-worn path, but recent theological reflection has made much of the supposedly dissonant divine economy of gift and gratuity that stands at odds with monetary exchange. Finding such conversations overdetermined, I regard it a much more interesting and illuminating task to pursue affinities between monetary economy and theological discourse, considering the more counterintuitive and controversial points of commonality.

Finally, since constructive theological analyses of money and economy often exhibit a reactive concern to emphasize difference, my exploration of similarities may unearth submerged connections that kindle such anxieties. Might the modern need to drive a wedge so quickly between theology and the monetary economic realm stem in part from their close connection and the apparent scandal this would bring? It is precisely this reactionary response to ostensive scandal that we should resist, so that we might consider both the reasons why this close association is taken as problematic and also reflect on the obsessive need to cover it up. While my project builds toward points of connection and mutual influence, it also raises the question of whether intervention and praxis require the contrastive, oppositional stance that is the norm in prescriptive proposals. What might accepting money's influence on theology and theology's shaping of economic order mean for theological projects of personal, communal, and societal transformation?

Monetary economy as theopolitical

Two current conversations in which this study participates concern the theological backgrounds to modern politics and to the modern economy, respectively. These discussions have in many ways developed distinctly. This is partly the result of the conceptual and methodological rupture between politics and economics that characterizes much modern thought. It is also due to the dichotomous and at times oppositional construal of political and economic spheres in the work of these conversations' symbolic progenitors: Carl Schmitt and Max Weber. Schmitt's retrieval of a theological aura to modern politics and sovereignty in *Political Theology* was couched in a resistance to the encroaching economic sphere.[16] Politics as the offspring of the theological was championed against economy as the implicitly godless realm of "disenchantment."

Although the notion of economic disenchantment invokes Weberian thought, Weber is recognized as being an advocate of free-market principles, even if his sociology included important analyses of political economic power and domination, as well as critiques of bureaucratization. Weber's analysis of the relations between religion and economy, famously set forth in *The Protestant Ethic*, construes economy without significant reference to the political sphere.[17] The result is that both scholars bequeath a legacy of inquiry into *either* theology and politics *or* theology and economics.[18] Yet the interpenetration and mutual construction of political and economic realms, increasingly recognized in the scholarship, means that theological reflection must take both economics and politics as simultaneous objects of analysis, and that both must be considered in tandem for their influence upon theological reflection.

We can therefore speak of "theopolitical economy" to denote this ongoing interaction between theological discourse and the political and economic spheres. By theopolitics and the theopolitical I mean a "zone of indistinction" between theology and politics in the discursive realm.[19] This is both a conceptual and historical marker. Conceptually, we can speak of the ways that religious talk of the divine merges with language of rule, authority, and sovereignty attributed to emperors, kings, or the state, for instance. Historically, such a meshing has concrete manifestations and is perhaps more observable in the ancient world and in societies not subject to the religious/secular distinction that is characteristic of modernity. Yet part of Schmitt's contribution was an insistence that a theological framework remained relevant for assessing modernity's political formations, a claim taken up in debates about its theological heritage among thinkers such as Hans Blumenberg and Karl Löwith.[20] Schmitt's impulse was not so much an attempt to undo or reverse secularization as it was an acknowledgment of the secular realm's own genealogical relations to theology. The conceptual purchase of the idea of theopolitics, therefore, stems partly from the persistence of this interpenetration of spheres in modern and ostensibly secular contexts. Recognizing this enduring link is useful for elucidating sources of the influence and traction of certain economic and political ideas, drawing as they may from potent, if now implicit, theological concepts whose effects continue in transmuted form.[21]

By monetary economy I mean the systems of relations and corresponding institutions, practices, and legal frameworks that enable exchange with monetary standards, accounts, and tokens. I reject the popularized view that money is a tool created spontaneously and merely to minimize frictions in trade that arise naturally and inevitably out of bartering economies. The most robust historical, sociological, and anthropological work on the matter recognizes this position as untenable. Rather, as introduced above, money is a tactic of sovereignty, an established system of abstract accounting with attendant symbols and tokens, one that ties spaces of economic production and exchange to channels of indebtedness to and commerce with governing powers. Money is an enforced set of proportions and terms of exchange, one that is quite often imposed and that necessitates hierarchy. Money brings sovereign categories of value into exchange relations, formalizing and quantifying a narrow set of patterns of production, reciprocity, and consumption. To the conceptual coercion sovereign power conveys through money by demarcating reality according to its arbitrary codifications, it supplements the material violence seen in punishments for counterfeiting, coin clipping, or tax evasion, for instance. The monetary circuit has always been vigorously policed. A more thorough analysis of monetary economy thus calls for attention to the political realm and to dynamics of sovereignty and administrative governance, particularly in the West with its specific theological, political, and economic heritage.[22]

The idea of "the West" itself operates as a general conceptual construct in this study. To demarcate the West geospatially appears futile in light of the colonial legacy and the globalization of forms of political economy associated with Europe. As Moira Fradinger remarks in her trenchant analysis of violence and political formation in Western tradition, "The 'West' has always had porous borders, though culturally construed as having an identity on the basis of establishing its 'other'—a Eurocentrism that has been thoroughly deconstructed throughout the twentieth century."[23] For Fradinger, however, the West persists as a useful placeholder for "a political tradition of thought that became dominant within the geopolitical space of the European capitalist colonial powers born after the fall of feudalism."[24] The West indexes a constellation of geographic, political, economic, and theoretical formations in Europe that makes use of a fictional heritage in the classical world. Such resources were drawn upon in the process of forming oppositional nation-state and ethnic groups as well as through confronting and colonizing cultural others. In fact, monetary economy and the rise and spread of capitalism are deeply tied up with this colonial project.

It is a particular irony that the region that would become Europe—long considered a cultural and intellectual backwater by classical and late antique civilizations—should, through a remarkable history of rhetorical reversal, construe Greece, Rome, and early Christian empire as forebears.[25] Such a site must be thoroughly provincialized in order to contextualize its universalist claims and clarify its dissimulation of these self-constructed origins.[26] In turning to Greco-Roman and early Christian sources, therefore, I consider enduring authoritative loci in the West's self-fashioning. These theological and symbolic sources combine with the operations of economy, which itself becomes central to Europe's development. My interest is in the conglomeration of late antique thought and practice that was conveyed to emerging European societies in Christian theology, pastoral practice, and imperial administration. My suspicion is that the monetary economic theological tropes and correlated ecclesial practices that I uncover remain hard at work in various phases of the West's development.[27]

Sovereignty, governmentality, and divine *oikonomia*

Examining the complex developments of economic reason and monetary power in the West has brought me into extended conversation with the work of Michel Foucault and Giorgio Agamben. Foucault's own genealogy of aspects of Western society looked to Greco-Roman and late antique thought for points of discontinuity with later formations in medieval and early modern society. His retrievals simultaneously suggest moments of prefiguring, when practices and mentalities in the ancient world can be glimpsed as echoes in modernity. My study converges, in particular, with Foucault's examination of "governmentality," a term denoting the new focus on governmental reason and the tactics for demarcating and managing populations and nurturing the biological lives and conduct of citizens that emerges in the sixteenth century and influences modern statecraft.

Foucault suggests that Christianity, with its "utterly new" ensemble of pastoral power, provided a kind of "prelude" to techniques of governance adopted and disseminated in early modernity.[28] He focuses less on the symbolic, theological, or conceptual systems at work than on diverse practices and techniques—an important genealogical corrective to historiography done as mere intellectual history. Yet Foucault does recall the image of the divine shepherd that informs practices of pastoral oversight and governance. At a very general level, God depicted as the nurturing caretaker of a flock resonates and correlates with pastoral management of a congregation. One might trace the permutations of this ensemble of strategies and techniques associated with this theological trope as it influences the political sphere. Specters of pastor and shepherd lurk behind— but do not lead to in simplistic linear fashion—the modern governmental state as disciplinary caretaker of its subjects and populace.

A central theme in Foucault's genealogy is the transformation in the West from more centralized modes of sovereign rule to diffuse and decentered techniques of governance. We can no longer locate power and control in a single center of agency, and the methods of oversight have shifted from a punitive authority over life and death to immanent and internalized strategies that shape and direct life. A major source of this change and contributor to the rise of governmentality is "the introduction of economy into political practice."[29] Although Foucault gestures toward economic themes and practices in pastoral governance, he stops short of a full elaboration, leaving unanalyzed the economic dimension that connects the early Christian imaginary and pastoral power with economized, early modern government.

Agamben takes up the problem and seeks to challenge and supplement it. A central claim of his genealogical work is that the tensions between sovereignty and economic governance, which for Foucault rupture in the sixteenth century, are present from the beginnings of Christianity.[30] Furthermore, these distinctions between sovereignty and governance can be seen in Christian models of God worked out in early Trinitarian debates. Moving beyond Foucault's passing references to the divine shepherd, Agamben makes theology a key object of analysis, for its language documents a site of extensive theorization around the political implications of transcendence and immanence. For Agamben, the rupture of sovereignty and governance stems from their peculiar and unstable union in Christian ideas of the godhead, seen in the monarchy of the Father and the delegated government of the Son, a discursive articulation always already bound up with political reflection on tactics of rule and administration drawn from the wider culture.

My project engages as well as challenges and supplements these approaches. I find salutary Agamben's focus on a type of continuity that allows for in-depth exploration of potential links between late antique Christian thought and modern developments. The possibility is arguably present in Foucault, despite his reception as a theorist of discontinuity. Agamben's study draws out this element and sets it in the context of an extended reflection on early Christian thought in light of contemporary questions of sovereignty and governance. His inquiry also demonstrates that the complex and ambivalent relationship between sovereign reign and government can be discerned in a host of contexts across a broad temporal spectrum. His purpose is not to claim a unified and stable figure over time, but rather to limn the space of a series of conceptual transformations and developments. His work also converges with contemporary concerns about theopolitics and theology's relation to modernity, showing this relation in ancient contexts.[31] Agamben demonstrates that the theological and political have been informing one another all along. Within the dyad he makes space for economic considerations.

Agamben makes space for economics, yet his inquiry stops short of assessing *actual* economic dynamics or the operations of economy proper and money itself in the theological and political concepts he explores. Working within one archaic valence of economy (*oikonomia*) as government and management, Agamben provides little analysis of how the ensemble of factors he uncovers is related to concrete economic factors such as the exchange and circulation of material goods, resources, and money. This is not an ancillary concern, for *oikonomia*, I will argue, primarily indexes the management of actual resources and even money with an eye toward profit, gain, or growth and retains such traces in its figurative employment. Furthermore, as I will show, ideas of money, resource management, exchange, and even coin minting continually inform models of divinity, visions of divine reign and governance, and, by extension, theopolitical considerations of sovereignty and administration.

My study serves to carry certain of Agamben's insights about divine and earthly government forward into a discussion of economy proper.[32] Addressing matters of actual economics returns us to concerns raised by Foucault about the influence of the economy upon governmental reason and models of statecraft. That modern government and politics find themselves in continual confrontation with economic factors and concerns is, as I will show, part of an ensemble that has operated in Western thought and practice at least since late antiquity. The concrete management of bodies, resources, and money, so central to modern governmentality, has as one precursor the inclusion of such a material focus in early Christian articulations of God's economy and work in redemption. Again, modern problems are not simple repetitions of ancient ones. But, like the theopolitical model of sovereignty and governance explored by Agamben, the patristic schema I retrieve of God as an economic administrator accomplishing redemption through Christ as currency is useful in analyzing ancient, medieval, and modern contexts. It fills out the picture we have about the West's theopolitical heritage by incorporating indispensable consideration of money and the economy.

Using money as a central object of analysis also helpfully straddles the poles of sovereignty and governance.[33] Money as a sign and representation instituted by sovereign power is simultaneously a central means of governance. Bureaucratic administrations rise up around monetary circuits, and calculative techniques of oversight work to support taxation, facilitate measurements of economic metrics, and inform analysis of market dynamics, for instance. Examining the monetary influence upon doctrinal formation takes us to the heart of government, where money as an instrument of rule, administration, and conquest informs ideals of God the Father as a reigning sovereign who delegates administration of the *oikonomia* to the Son as a governor, and of Christ as a payment within this economy that secures divine victory and extends God's reign over creation.

Of homology, metaphor, and resonance

In pursuing affinities between monetary practice and theological articulations at certain moments, I seek to move beyond the study of analogous concepts to claim that historical interaction and mutual shaping of fields has occurred. The relation between theology and money can therefore be described as homologous, exceeding analogy and involving historical relations and moments of coemergence. Homology is a term derived from the admittedly problematic discourse of genetics, and by its use I intend none of the reductionist (and often racist) claims of pure identity, fixed ancestral lineage, or bloodline that are sometimes associated with its deployment in the sciences.[34] Instead, I regard homology as a useful correlate to a genealogical approach. Homology as I use it posits that similarities between two fields can be understood not merely as coincidentally analogous and thematically or structurally similar but as partially the result of actual historical and conceptual interaction between the two spheres.

While homology as used in the natural sciences generally infers a common ancestor from which two distinct species are said to descend, the application is more flexible in our conceptual and discursive context. Resisting the essentialist quest for origins while employing homology means that similarities between fields signal a horizon of confluence that is always receding. Like the time before the rupture of religion and politics, this horizon invokes what has been called a "prehistory," that which is inaccessible to historical thought, yet which enables and grounds historical analysis of particular phenomena.[35] To speak of theology and monetary economy as homologous highlights the ways language about the nature and function of money is taken up by theology to crystallize theology's unique concepts. It is also to signal the ways theological language about debt, payment, and exchange is imported into descriptions of what money is or should be like or how it is deployed.

Homology acknowledges that both implicit and explicit linguistic and conceptual influence have taken place, while forestalling claims of origin. In other words, I do not argue that theology simply derives from the monetary economic realm, operating as a superstructural screen for a more primary or ontologically foundational economic base. Neither is monetary economy simply an incarnation of a preceding theological reality. The intermeshing that I highlight points to a horizon of union between money and theology that recedes from grasp and yet that can be posited. Put differently, the dialectical influence between money and theology is ongoing, and to claim one as originary disrupts what is meaningful about this mutual relation and falsely arrests their continual movement.

In addition, talk of homology invokes the literary critical approach known as "new economic criticism," whose methods inform how I read theological texts in relation to economy.[36] New economic criticism examines texts with attention to the economic context of their production as well as the operation of metaphorical or symbolic economies within the literary field itself. Textual criticism "is predicated on the existence and disclosure of parallels and analogies between linguistic and economic systems."[37] It also posits homologies in which the coordinate operations of particular material and literary economies portend a common, usually symbolic-economic influence. Light can be shed on the meanings in a text when its economic context is considered, even as internal symbolic economies, or "tropic exchanges," within the text are elucidated with economic paradigms.[38] I attend to monetary economic traces in theological texts, evidence of contact with or influence by broader economic dynamics taking place in the context of discursive production. I also delineate textual economies, ways in which networks of exchanges of metaphors and symbols contribute new cognitive content and theological meaning. I suggest further that part of the work of the texts in question is to shape economic postures and practices. The network of relations is vast and complex, and I outline what I take to be several crucial and determinative links.

As we consider homologous relations, we should recall that metaphors matter. Indeed, metaphors function as one key site of homological fusion between theological and monetary registers. Studies have repeatedly demonstrated that linking terms through metaphor contributes to actual conceptual content.[39] Metaphors are neither vacuous redundancies nor merely ornamental language; they create and enhance systems of thought. They leave lasting cognitive links in discourse, upon individual bodies, and within collective conceptual frameworks. Metaphors are essential meaning-making tools that often couple mental processes with material or physical experiences. A concrete set of attributes is applied in a figurative arrangement, often through disjunction and dissonance, with a new relation or set of associations coming into being. Metaphors bring out previously unseen aspects of the metaphorically depicted object and transform how it is interpreted and understood.

Metaphors can thus contribute to a legacy of substantive linkage and potent affinity between disparate discourses and objects. Metaphors linger, ossify, and become embedded in social understandings and resultant institutions. Once a metaphor has become fully entrenched and assumed within a framework of thought, it may sometimes be described as dead. A dead metaphor fails to provoke as it once may have, for its dissonance has been absorbed through repeated use, yet the linkages it facilitates persist and serve the conceptual structure.[40]

Thus, as I will explore, importing monetary and broader economic language into theology informs theological systems in unique and substantive ways. To speak of Christ metaphorically as currency and coin, for instance, is to ascribe to Christ key attributes of monetary economy in ways that establish elements of Christ's identity. These attributes in turn become footholds and bearing points for subsequent theological formulations and expanding networks of doctrinal claims. The monetary metaphor may thus come to inform the logic of the entire system. As a central building block of the broader edifice, the metaphor may even be forgotten or dismissed. This can be seen in the way the metaphor of redemption, used to speak of salvation, can be repeatedly invoked in Christian context without awareness of its thoroughly economic derivation and sense. The term continues to operate in a system of relays of meaning that may reactivate this economic reference in ways that go unnoticed.

Inasmuch as the sources of metaphor imbue a particular concept with their material or affective characteristics, slippage and reciprocal influence can occur. When they do, the sources of metaphorical ascription may in turn be shaped by the concept to which they have been related. As Kathryn Tanner notes, "The *simple fact of use* in discussion of divine matters, for example, may give the stamp of approval to the social and political practices to which reference is made."[41] In our case, it is possible that money, as a source of theological metaphor, may take on a sacral hue and heavenly aura in its affiliations with the identity and work of Christ. The form this influence takes is at least twofold. At one level, money is associated with the identity and work of God, and this association serves to provide a sacred weight and spiritual authority to money as a type of implicit legitimation. At another level beyond simple endorsement, the associations may provide new models for deploying money after divine patterns, modifying economic administration in the process. While such influential patterns emerge explicitly in Christian ethical exhortation on the godly uses of money, perhaps more significant are the tacit models provided by the cosmic acts God accomplishes through divine economy. The pastoral practices of imitating Christ and his redemptive economic management develop into institutionalized channels and official roles. The spiritually figurative and theological uses of money may thus double back upon the monetary economic world to shape new economic practices, whether in the church, the Christian empire, or, eventually, post-Christian society at large.

Finally, I have also spoken of resonances that exist between forms of political economic thought and practice, on the one hand, and theological discourse, on the other. Resonance invokes a sonic metaphor to describe the relationship.[42] Agamben claims that analogy—and, in my view, homology even more so—challenges logical dichotomies between distinct conceptual spheres. It does so "not to take them up into a higher synthesis but to transform them into a force field traversed by polar tensions, where (as in an electro-magnetic field) their substantial identities evaporate."[43] Not unlike Agamben's "electro-magnetic field," the relations I explore are those whose mutual impact might be glimpsed, if fleetingly, but whose actual relational structures we can never posit as stable in order to demarcate and fix.

The notion of resonance has been notably deployed by William Connolly in his exploration of the affinities between capitalism and American evangelicalism.[44] By "resonance" Connolly means to indicate the similar affective postures or "spiritualities" and modes of acting in the world engendered by these two systems of thought, feeling, and practice.[45] The term "resonance" speaks to the links we infer must be there to govern analogous patterns of response and action, such as those between pundits of neoliberal economic policy and subjects within the evangelical church in the United States. Yet Connolly's intervention remains gestural at the level of demarcating resonance. One senses with him that the affinities are there, and that his intuitive associations are probably correct, but one cannot get a picture of how the relation operates or where it comes from.

Resonance has effects as one object vibrates with another, yet the manner of impact remains almost imperceptible. Lines between what is proper to one field and another become blurred as what is properly within one is moved by the other, yet remains distinct. When I compare monetary economy, with its attendant formations of sovereignty and government, with theological models, I mean by resonances trace presence of one system within the other, as well as the implicit effects of one upon the other, effects whose lines of causality and fixed structures of relation are elusive, constantly receding from the observable horizon. Similar to an imprint—the stamp, seal, or coin impress—resonance speaks to the mark that is left by the other, yet expresses it in dynamic fashion.

"Divine currency" as a theological concept resonates with the operations of monetary economy, sovereignty, and governmental administration. In various ways, each sphere vibrates with the other, but we cannot posit origins or definitive causalities without fixing the movement falsely. Such imposed stabilization may nevertheless be useful heuristically in moments of analysis. I seek greater specificity than Connolly in demarcating such resonance by showing the direct linguistic, metaphorical, and conceptual interchange among monetary economy, doctrinal formation, and emerging forms of pastoral economy and imperial administration. It is this robust basis of theological, practical, and institutional interrelation that makes later affiliations such as those marked by Connolly possible in the first place, as this early fusion of Christian thought and practice with monetary ideas and institutions continues as a fund on which to draw in creative redeployment across the centuries.

Plan of the book

The argument and evidence proceed cumulatively, with opening chapters descrying glimpses of monetary economic and theological resonance, building toward more explicit forms of linguistic and conceptual interchange between the two registers. The first chapter sets out governing conceptual frameworks and begins our exploration of how the incarnation and divine economy resonate with money and economic administration. Drawing upon and amending Agamben's study, I recover the ancient traces to *oikonomia* that signal the management of concrete resources and money and highlight valences that invoke an economic aim toward profit, gain, or victory. I show that a discussion of ancient *oikonomia* must incorporate its operations in household economies, the financial and administrative governance of cities, and God's providential management of the goods of creation. The concept of *oikonomia* also invokes God's strategies for profit and victory in the work of salvation. I call upon Eusebius of Caesarea as one key ancient witness— and a founding theologian of Christian empire—who will accompany us throughout the study. I examine his assertion that God timed the incarnation to align with the heights of the Roman Empire's political and economic unification in a way that discloses divine realities. According to Eusebius, the consolidation of empire in all its social, political, economic, and infrastructural elements demonstrates the monarchic reign of God and signals what God's economy is like. His work suggests a latent fusion between theology and political economy.

The second chapter turns to consideration of the divine operator behind this *oikonomia*. I assert that we must supplement the vision of God as shepherd, recalled by Foucault as influencing the praxis of pastoral power, with that of the heavenly economist. A vision of God the Father delegating to the Son the administration of cosmic goods and blessings informs and empowers the pastoral economy of souls and of church resources. The Son as a steward and administrator provides a template for many of the transformations in late antiquity, as bishops emerge as protectors of the poor, attuned to flows of money and to ecclesial fiscal needs, and as the first Christian emperor imports such resource-oriented administrative virtues into the state apparatus and its policy. The divine economist operates behind and informs the initial glimmers of governmental power in late antiquity, as the state adopts attitudes of concern for the needy and for overseeing a flock of citizens.

In the third chapter, we take a closer look at how Emperor Constantine, according to Eusebius, manifests a divine pattern of just and redemptive economic administration. In fulfilling the heavenly template of reign and economic government, Constantine becomes a model for all of what God is like. Attending to themes left largely unaddressed in scholarship on Eusebius, I show how the bishop demonstrates keen attention to the emperor's money and economic administration. Money aids in Constantine's rule even as it demonstrates and communicates his character. In contrast to tyrants and their economies, Constantine displays just and generous disbursement of wealth, unmastered as his soul is by riches. Because of the attributive economy between God and emperor, Constantinian economic administration reveals divine management, and the ways the emperor uses money show how the Logos, as divine steward, administers the goods of creation. His example brings to center stage a consideration of the uses toward which God puts divine wealth and resources. This calculated use of wealth recalls the purposive and strategic nature of *oikonomia*, aimed as it is toward salvation, and turns our study to a focus on the work of redemption.

Chapter four carries the exploration forward to questions of salvation and to an important ancient idea of Christ as currency. I show how broader political economic practices of minting coins to demarcate the accession of a new sovereign ruler appear in Christian discourse about the arrival of the divine king. Just as new coins are issued to proclaim a new emperor in Greco-Roman contexts, certain patristic thinkers present redeemed humans as newly reminted or restored coins, which are evidence of the inbreaking kingdom of God. Such language coincides with an implicit understanding of the divine Son as the numismatic stamp that imprints the image of God on humanity. I claim that the Son's role here implies that incarnation is the materialization of this paradigmatic impress in the form of the chief coin of God, sent to regulate and correct the human economy. Humans as coins, tarnished and marked through improper use, are reminted and renewed by the presence of the ideal standard, Christ as the coin of God. In reconstructing an implicit and thus far unrecognized theology of divine currency, I also suggest how this theology lends a grounding structure to many claims about redemption in patristic thought, and how it may be theopolitically efficacious in the administration of empire.

Chapters five and six turn to Christian soteriology, showing to what ends Christ as God's currency has been deployed in formative doctrines of salvation that make redemption and ransom central themes. To talk of salvation as ransom or redemption is to make monetary economic exchange a primary locus for conveying what God accomplishes in saving humankind. This reveals that theories of *oikonomia* must recognize some form of economic transaction as centrally operative in achieving divine purposes. Gregory of Nyssa's narrative of a ransom exchange between God and Satan draws on the logic of debt and moneylending as well as ideas of political contest between competing monetary sovereigns. God offers Christ to the devil as compensation to discharge humanity's debt, which has led to its enslavement. What appears at first blush to be divine acquiescence to satanic demands reveals itself to be an act of conquest by God. Divine deceit and trickery have generally been the focal point of discussion around accounts such as Gregory's. Through a novel interpretation of his ransom narrative, I claim that such deception is merely a subset of the larger point: it is through monetary economy, an economy rife with struggle and power imbalances, that God accomplishes redemptive ends. Satanic territory is colonized through the power of debt and by economic annexation. Divine gratuity and superabundance in this monetary scenario are, in fact, also acts of aggression.

As monetary dynamics provide an explicit scaffold for soteriological claims, so God's activity, portrayed as unswervingly good, implicitly valorizes these economic practices in the world. Payment serves divine conquest and resonates with practices of the Roman Empire that draw new lands into its imperial territory by economic means. The link provides clues as to how monetary and broader economic practices may gain a spiritual aura, and how the state's use of economy to regulate bodies and populations acquires a layer of sacred prestige. God's deployment of economy to overcome enemies, provide abundant and eternal life, and manage the community of the redeemed resonates with ostensibly secularized state economic programs and policies that secure state rule, while also stewarding and extending the lives of the governed.

In what ways might the understanding of God as a sovereign economic administrator, accomplishing salvation through Christ as currency, be operative behind key institutional formations and cultural values in late antiquity that are transmitted to the West and proliferate in the Middle Ages? How might this divine model relate to shifting understandings of the nature of value, credit, and exchange, particularly during the Reformation, which has been recognized as pivotal in the political and economic development of the West? In what ways does it inform the introduction of economy into political reason and practice in early modernity? How might the implicit framework serve to ground the much-touted "divinity" of today's global economy? In initiating this retrieval of theological concepts that are operating behind economy, this study asserts that we cannot be satisfied with considering the links and interactions between such theology and ancient society. We must also examine the ways it has been conveyed to the complex and ambivalent development of Western theology, as well as major traditions of governmental administration and economic thought in the modern West, haunted as they may be by this specter of divine currency.

Incarnation and Imperial Economy

The Christian doctrine of incarnation tells the tale not simply of divine condescension to and proximity with creation but of God's governance of the world and oversight of redemption. The incarnation makes the sovereignty of the transcendent God over creation meaningful in its manifestation, proclamation, and actualization within the immanent and material sphere. As such, the incarnation presents a series of conundrums, conceptual and abstract as well as practical and political. Just as it proves challenging to imagine, for instance, the singular God as simultaneously transcendent Father in heaven and materialized (yet still transcendent) Son on earth, the long history of incarnational thought reveals sites of contention around what this mode of immanent rule means for Christian allegiance to earthly forms of power. Questions also emerge concerning what cues, if any, political rulers and institutions should take from the new models of governance implied in incarnation. For the forms of power and government displayed in incarnation provide archetypes of leadership and authority in the political sphere as well as within a new institution, the *ecclesia*, which constructs its own politics. Such theorizations of incarnational governance take place both when the church, as a persecuted, marginal community, confronts Roman imperial authority, and when the church, legitimated as the official religion, assumes the voice of power. The church thus takes certain cues from, comes into conflict with, offers support to, and serves as an exemplar for the wider regimes of political rule and government within Greco-Roman society.

The notion of economy (*oikonomia*) proves central for early Christian theorists because it enables them to make sense of and articulate the incarnation. Not only does it provide conceptual space for expressing the fusion of transcendence and immanence, as well as differentiating members of the Trinity, but it lends political and practical help in conveying relations of rule and representation as well as obedience and submission. *Oikonomia* deals in matters of governance by aiding such thinkers in working out how the Son might serve as delegated representative of the Father on earth while remaining coequal in divinity and power. This is why Giorgio Agamben, in seeking to explicate the sources of governmentality and its relation to forms of political sovereignty in Western tradition, is drawn back to classical Greek and ancient Christian understandings of *oikonomia*. Limning its various semantic transformations is critical to his project of uncovering sources of political and governmental power in the present. Agamben's intuition is correct that this term not only serves as a major conceptual apparatus for making sense of incarnation but also encodes notions of rule and economy that will be significant for how political and governmental power develop in the West.

At the same time, most early Christian thinkers consistently portray incarnation as soteriological, as tied to matters of salvation. Incarnational economy occurs for the sake of redemption. As we will consider, a primary aim and outcome of the incarnation is prominently characterized as a type of exchange, payment, or other transaction, as Christ is offered for humanity's debts of sin. The proximity between these two distinct ideas—incarnational economy as governance and incarnational economy for the sake of payment or exchange—has received surprisingly little consideration and requires exploration, for the resonances are not incidental: *oikonomia* does not merely designate management or administration but, as I show, primarily designates the stewardship and oversight of material resources and even money, always aimed toward gain and betterment.

Agamben does not explore the links between the ancient notion of economy as government or administration and ideas of resource management, exchange, value, monetization, and profit orientation. Using *oikonomia* for his purposes of exploring the spheres of political sovereignty and governmental rationality, he delimits the term primarily within the realms of political and divine governance and of economy as administration and management. What he neglects are the connections between *oikonomia* and the actual objects of its management such as bodies, money, and other resources, and the persistent role of profit seeking and utility maximization in such administration.

A fuller consideration of these heretofore neglected elements provides important links between ancient and modern ideas of economy, attuned as the latter often are to matters of money and resource exchange. The broader context of meaning also draws attention to the operations of economy proper—or material economy—both in forms of political governance and in Christian ideas of incarnation that shape and are in turn shaped by such political practices. When the theopolitical undertones to incarnation as a framework of governance and rule are examined in light of economy proper, the site of political economy itself becomes relevant. In the doctrine of incarnation, themes of political rule and government combine with the language of resource management, payment, and exchange. Such a nexus is precisely what has been considered under the rubric of *governmentality*: the irruption of economy into political practice as a distinct form of power enabling political governance through economic logic.[1]

To be sure, ancient *oikonomia* and modern economy are distinct concepts. A long series of permutations and redeployments have taken place in the shift from one to the other. In response to initial construals of simplistic correspondence between ancient and modern ideas of economy, the pendulum in scholarship on economic history swung far to the other side, emphasizing ancient *oikonomia*'s distinctiveness from modern economy. The reality, as is often the case, is somewhere in between. Important distinctiveness notwithstanding, ancient notions of economy include a fundamental reference to properly economic concepts and objects, providing a link between archaic understandings of economy as management and modern inflections of economy as exchange of goods and money, interest in efficiency, and aim toward gain. There exists a rich historical linguistic context to ancient *oikonomia* that unites ideas of administrative governance, profit motive, and money management as well as persuasion and even deceit for the sake of vindicating the economy.

This spectrum of *oikonomia* helps to illuminate diverse talk of God as sovereign king, administrator, governing steward, and even a type of payment in a redemptive exchange. It also helps to build a much richer and more robust case for the contributions of Christian thought to governmentality than what Agamben provides, given his lack of attention to the economy proper that informs both such Christian thought and, eventually, governmental reason. Money as a central trope in economy and in governmental administration emerges as a concomitant structuring principle for Christian thought in this area of incarnational governance, further suturing these apparently disparate spheres. The lacuna in Agamben's study thus leads to a consideration of the financial and profit-oriented valences to *oikonomia*, and of the ways this fundamental semantic range retains influence in theologically figurative depictions of divine government and redemption.

Eusebius, the bishop of Caesarea, is centrally important to such considerations. Until the last several decades, the intellectual contributions of Eusebius and his impact on Christian tradition were downplayed by modern scholars due to his biased reception as a semi-Arian as well as his apparent proximity to the emperor Constantine.[2] More recent scholarship has done much to undermine the legitimacy of this negative portrayal, recenter his influences upon emerging orthodoxy and vindicate the enduring mark he left on patristic thought. What this means, in part, is that his clear impact on what has come to be called political theology cannot easily be separated from orthodox Christian thought, despite the unease of some about such imbrications. This founding thinker of Christian empire provides an enduring theopolitical template for rule in both Eastern and Western forms of Christianity. Beyond patristic thought, the Eusebian specter lingers in medieval Christendom, such as in the Investiture Controversy and in debates about the scope of papal and imperial authority, and retains sway in modern models of political sovereignty.[3]

As I show, the material and monetary undertones to *oikonomia* reveal themselves as Eusebius claims that Roman imperial integration evokes divine realities. Roman political and economic unification, standardizations in currency and commerce, and pacification through both military presence and exchange practices prepare the world to apprehend the incarnation of Christ. What is more, these political and economic realities correspond to and proclaim theological attributes of divine unity, monarchy, and economy.

The divine act of incarnation is characterized by Eusebius as an economy and functions centrally in the economic governance of creation. Opening up the financial traces in *oikonomia* thus attunes us to the monetary economic forces at work in forging a set of fundamental and enduring claims about divine sovereignty over history and about God's nature, identity, and work in redemption. It opens the door to considering how money operates in the logic and conceptual structure of key points of doctrine at formative moments in the Christian tradition, doctrine that will in turn have wide-ranging sociopolitical impact in the Western imaginary and its institutional legacy.

Financing economy

Agamben's *The Kingdom and the Glory* seeks to unearth sources of the productive tension between political sovereignty and governmental administration that exists in Western political thought and practice. His study turns to the particular ways in which Christian theology and ecclesial institutions contributed substantively to this legacy. Taking up the specter of economy that haunts discussions of biopolitics and governmentality, Agamben undertakes a detailed exegesis in its ancient context, as *oikonomia*. Agamben's wager is that this notion of *oikonomia*, which proves central in emerging doctrinal discussion about Trinitarian differentiation as well as the identity of the Son, provides a conceptual and practical linchpin in the development of ideas of political governance in Western tradition.[4]

Crucial to Agamben's retrieval and application of the term to notions of government is the basic sense of the word, which, in most ancient Greek and later biblical contexts, denotes a kind of management, arrangement, or administration. Its initial sphere of application appears to be the *oikos*, or household, and pertains to the management of the relations and stewardship of the resources in this domain. A particular ordering (*taxis*) of the relations between master and slave, parent and child, and husband and wife, for instance, is sought in order to achieve harmony and maximize the good. Economy involves the proper ordering of relations, roles, and resources in the interest of the thriving of the house. This fundamental notion of purposive management and administration, applied initially to the household, enjoyed a range of other, often metaphorical applications. The arrangement of speech could demonstrate rhetorical *oikonomia* in the interests of persuasion, for instance, as the stratagems of a doctor or teacher in reaching intractable patients or students reflected such economy. In all denotations, "the awareness of the original domestic meaning was never lost."[5]

Almost immediately, however, and definitively in the Hellenistic age, *oikos* as the domain of application becomes conflated with the *polis*. Aristotle's stark opposition of these spheres, which is absent in Plato, is overcome by later writers who describe the *oikos* as a smaller-scale *polis*, and vice versa. The language of comportment of rulers in the practice of governance speaks of their appropriate *oikonomia*, and discourse on monarchy is definitively linked with the domestic sphere of the household, paralleling the household role of the *despotês* and, later, the *paterfamilias*, or head of the family.[6] What this means is that language of *oikonomia* is no longer formally relegated to the domestic sphere—if it ever was in any absolute sense—and moves within the wider discourse of the political.

Agamben's interest in the nature of political rule and forms of governance leads him to a focus on *oikonomia* as practice but causes him to overlook many of the objects of its practice that give it precise meaning and remain as concrete traces amidst metaphorical application. Also downplayed is *oikonomia*'s strategic and purposive nature, aiming at forms of profit, gain, and victory. From its inception, *oikonomia* is tied to the management of material resources in the household and money outside the *oikos*. The term includes a strong emphasis on pragmatic, even shrewd, business practices. Such resonances persist, meaning that concrete economic and even monetary valences continue to give significance to the figurative deployments of the term.[7]

The connotations of aiming for victory and gain in *oikonomia* are so resonant that economic business practices and military strategy are sometimes linked.[8] The term will remain useful in the language of military organization and strategy through Roman times, indicating the governance necessary for an efficient and expedient conquest. It will also refer specifically to the apportioning of the spoils of battle.[9] Thus, not only is there a shared usage of the term to apply to management of business and military practices, but specific links are also made between the transferable skills that exist in such fields, employing tropes of gain and profit more broadly. The implicit ideas of conflict, struggle, and aggression toward which *oikonomia* might be aimed are also significant.

Xenophon's immensely popular *Oeconomicus* depicts household management as aimed toward the flourishing and increase of estates. In the text, Socrates praises household management as a virtue to be sought but admits that he himself has little practical advice to give about it, claiming, "for I myself never possessed the tool of money, so as to learn, nor did any one else ever provide the opportunity for me to administer his wealth" (Xenophon, *Oeconomicus* 2.13).[10] Socrates assumes that money is included in those goods integral to prudent household administration as perhaps even the chief tool for the right measure and apportionment of accounts and direction of other resources. Money is deemed necessary to an understanding of *oikonomia*, and the use and increase of wealth remain central to its operations. For Xenophon, it is a commonplace that *oikonomia* aims at the profit and increase of the house using all tools necessary, including—perhaps especially—money. This understanding remains constant and increases in popularity, much to the horror of a later philosopher like Aristotle.

Despite his well-documented suspicion, Aristotle thought money had a legitimate and integral role to play in household management. It is not money's place in *oikonomia* that he contested but the disproportionate role it plays and its displacement of the true good toward which economy should strive. If anything, money should be subordinated to a pursuit of the highest good. Money must remain in the service of use-value, as a means to an end, and not become an end in itself as unbounded accumulation. In his day, "living well" had come to connote excess and luxury, and his aim was to reclaim a more philosophical frame for the good life, for, "while Xenophon put forth a simple manual of advice on what was a growing topic of practical interest in his day . . . [and] saw estate-management as aiming at the *increase* of estates . . . Aristotle, distaining [sic] the emphasis on piling up money, views it [i.e., *oikonomia*] more as the art of providing sufficient for comfortable living."[11] In aiming to stem the tide of excessive profit seeking and increase in mercantilism, Aristotle resisted the tendency for money to color the whole of what defined *oikonomia*. He nevertheless recognized its necessity and usefulness. Furthermore, his interventions did little to arrest the growing popular association between *oikonomia* and money making (*chrêmatistikê*), and the two regularly coincided.

Despite its pseudonymous claims, the posthumous work entitled *Economics* does little to continue Aristotle's warnings about accumulation. Instead, it resumes the pragmatic, handbook tone of Xenophon's earlier treatise. Money remains a central tool of economic management. In its sections discussing *oikonomia* as political governance of the state, "the financial emphasis is foremost in the illustrations cited."[12] The text also addresses divine administration, signaling the development in Hellenistic thought of an understanding of economy as reflective of a deeper, providential ordering of the cosmos. This expanded application is of course significant for early Christian discussions of God's ordering and managing of the world as a kind of economy.[13]

In the Roman era, the Epicurean student of Zeno, Philodemus, would make points reminiscent of Aristotle about proportionate living and a shunning of excess in his *Peri Oikonomias*. The popular-level "perversion" of *oikonomia* called for a philosophical return to a balanced meeting of legitimate needs and circumscribed wants.[14] This philosophical antipathy to the incursion of monetary values suggests the consistent and growing associations over time between *oikonomia* and profit-oriented money management, as well as the ongoing—and perhaps futile—attempts by philosophers to resist such conflation. In my estimation, an overreliance on the idealistic philosophical dichotomy between *oikonomia* and *chrêmatistikê* has led much modern scholarship to downplay the legitimate inclusion of monetary matters within *oikonomia* and to miss the everyday blurring of the two spheres in the ancient and late antique worlds. Furthermore, early Christian thinkers were not simply reading the elite philosophical discourses of thinkers such as Aristotle, but they also incorporated the widely held cultural beliefs that *oikonomia* included, perhaps as a central characteristic, the prudent and strategic use of financial resources for gain.

Increasingly, then, and remaining through the Christian era, *oikonomia* has applications specifically linking it to "business arrangements," "commercial, financial negotiations," dispersing funds or "the direct administration of a fund," "a market for wares," and the fiscal responsibilities of civic or private treasurers or stewards.[15] The emphasis on prudence, good judgment, and justified shrewdness and deceit also looms large. This range of significant applications is left unaddressed by Agamben and becomes a conspicuous omission in light of his desire to forecast modern economy with insights from the ancient world. While the conceptual distance between ancient and modern understandings of the economy is important, his focus on economic administration by divine or earthly powers would be augmented by attending to the objects of such administration—namely, goods, bodies, and money. Money's centrality in applications of *oikonomia* points to its potential function as a structuring principle in such circuits of exchange and management.

As Agamben recounts, only in later technical discussions of the divine relationship to and governance of creation does *oikonomia* takes on additional Christian theological nuance, when it is applied to God's own administrative activity in dispensing redemption and used to describe aspects of God's internal identity. Although less of a focus for Agamben, *oikonomia* also became central to doctrines of the incarnation, which work out a sense of God's full material presence and the redemptive purposes of God's manifestation on earth and in the flesh. Christian reflection sought to make sense of the incarnational claim that somehow God was present in Christ in a complete sense while remaining transcendent and reigning in heaven. While undertaking direct intervention and immanent activity in the flesh, God remained supreme and singular, one king and ruler in heaven, alone worthy of all honor and obedience. God persisted as radically transcendent and distinct from creation while being fully identified with humanity and walking among them. Such was the tension, or polarity, that called for reconciliation and adequate articulation.[16] *Oikonomia* served as a central conceptual device—or *dispositif*—for construing unity of being in the godhead in conjunction with a diversity of persons, relations, and activities. It also became determinative for terminologically precise debates about God's relation to the world in incarnation and activity in redemption. In both doctrinal cases, Trinitarian and incarnational relations, matters of sovereignty and governance were negotiated.

Figurative and metaphorical transferal is never clean or devoid of traces of concrete meaning. Indeed, the very point of metaphorical application is to retain such literal, material signification in new, incongruous, and disruptive arrangements of semantic and conceptual meaning.

Without this dissonance, the productive tension between the literal trace and the figurative ascription is lost, and the metaphor is devoid of significance. Attention to this financial backdrop to *oikonomia*, therefore, will illuminate the economic themes present in theology, as well as the properly economic ends toward which political theology will eventually be deployed. Furthermore, the genealogical links between ancient *oikonomia* and the rise of modern economy may be traceable in part to the Christian vivification and indirect sacralization of monetary dynamics attributed to a cosmic level.

Profit, surplus, and strategy

Even as *oikonomia* comes to denote God's identity in the work of redemption, the backdrop of fiscal management and profit seeking remain. Since the goal, return on, or profit motive of divine *oikonomia* is nothing less than the salvation of the world, a variety of suspect means are legitimated in the service of the most noble of ends. "If God reveals his salvational plan and intends it to be effective, its economy will make use of all the means familiar to a father in order to bring back his wayward son, all the subterfuges of the doctor to heal the patient despite himself, all the seductions dear to the teacher who must make the most difficult knowledge loved."[17] *Oikonomia* as strategy, persuasion, and control must therefore be kept in view. Strategic silences, apparent deception, and guile are valid elements of an economy, given its benevolent ends.

Rhetorical parsimony relates to a valence of economy that persists in current usage, that of a conserving gesture in the interest of profit. In both ancient and modern definitions, one demonstrates economy or is economical when one spares the use of goods (or words) or is selective with their employment.[18] This definition is quite possibly retained from *oikonomia*'s original domestic context and the management of goods and resources in the interest of household flourishing, for the "semantic field is from the outset tied as much to material as to symbolic goods . . ."[19] The notion of profit thus becomes explicit in such usage, for the aim and goal toward which persuasive representation and tactics of guile and deception lead is that of some gain, reward or improvement.

As Marie-José Mondzain notes in her significant study of *oikonomia*: "In the Classical authors, economic discourse is closely linked to a consideration of profit and utility. Consequently, the issue is not only one of rationalizing the operations relating to goods and people and defining an estate, but of optimizing expected benefits as well. This optimization can be thought of in quantitative terms (increase in wealth) or in qualitative terms (procurement of well-being or the approach of sovereign good)."[20] While money, for most classical philosophers, should not characterize ideal relations within the household, *oikonomia* could involve prudent money management outside the *oikos*. Money is necessary for domestic flourishing, and skillful household administration is concerned not only with nonmonetary goods but also with this central medium of exchange. Politically, economy includes methods leaders have "employed or cunningly devised in order to provide themselves with money."[21] A strong material and utilitarian sense thus remains ingrained in economy, one that assumes monetary dynamics.

Regardless of the object of its management, whether money, goods, relations, words, images, or arrangements of power and subjection, *oikonomia* retains notions of interest and calculation, of the striving for increase, gain, or amelioration.[22] *Oikonomia* "therefore concerns an ensemble of means implemented with an immediate material end in mind," a valence retained in patristic sources, "although in unprecedented scope, because it is the whole of providential nature, the incarnational plan, and the strategic adoption of means to ends that will be subsumed by the selfsame concept."[23] Thus, the purposive, strategic, and profit-oriented nature of *oikonomia* remains in discourse about God's management toward salvation and governance through incarnation.

Dotan Leshem's recent addition to studies of *oikonomia* clarifies that a focus on surplus and growth also takes center stage in the Christian era.[24] Divine economy is distinguished from classical notions of economy through the excess and openness invoked by its linkage with the eternal God, as well as with an eschatological trajectory that places the disciple on a path toward apotheosis. This openness and eschatological orientation are distinct from the typically cyclical, closed systems of the ancients. Themes of profit or yield on strategic investment come to the fore as they are deployed in a spiritual register of journey toward God and heavenly treasures. When the horizon is eternal, the prospects for growth become limitless and the boundaries between an economy of endless gain (*chrêma-tistikê*) and one of philosophical and spiritual maturity may become elided despite the opposition maintained by classical and Christian authors.[25]

Such themes associated with economy proper need to be considered together with the theopolitical context that Agamben retrieves. As he recounts, *oikonomia* conveys that the monarchy of God the Father corresponds to the site of political reign, while the Son and, in a less articulated sense, the Spirit indicate elements of governmental administration. Because these are united in the single being of God, however, sovereign power is itself "structurally articulated according to two different levels, aspects, or polarities: it is, at the same time, *dignitas* and *administratio*, Kingdom and Government."[26] Christian theology thus bequeathed to the West, as part of its inherited "governmental machine," a unified rupture of elements in political power and authority, the aporias of which continually plague the actual praxis of such authority in time and space. The sphere of sovereignty is made manifest with a praxis that executes the laws of the sovereign and manages its space through economy. Such administration makes present the transcendent sovereign, paradoxically making its absence present while permitting its distance to remain.

Oikonomia's mediation of divine distance and presence via incarnation is why analysis of incarnation's relation to governance must include attention to monetary economy. Monetary economy is one crucial element of governmental administration: it is a tool of order, discipline, and representation, and it signifies an intervention of sovereignty as it reaches out into its sphere of rule. If the Son signifies governmental authority and agency, then the systems and structures under the administration of the Son include money. What remains is to draw out the links between the Son and money. To the language of gift, value, and treasure traditionally ascribed to Christ, as well as to the discourse of payment and ransom in relation to redemption, we should add the apparatus of economic governance. In other words, given the broader theopolitical context of the Son marking a sphere of economic management of resources aimed at profit, the wide-ranging associations between Christ and various economic terms in Scripture and tradition are unsurprising and are given new depth of meaning.

Expressions of Christ's value or descriptions of the exchanges that take place in redemption thus operate within a larger theopolitical and economic framework and are not merely ad hoc embellishments and exclamations of praise. Statements extolling Christ and God's kingdom as a gift, payment, lost coin, pearl of great price, or treasure may be not simply metaphors of value but signifiers of a system wherein God reigns and manages through economy, an arrangement and administration of valuable goods in the service of divine sovereignty. Furthermore, claims about Christ being a compensation or ransom for sin invoke not merely isolatable ideas of divine goodness, grace, and generosity, but an entire network of rule and authority that is carried out in part through economic administration.

What remains to be considered in a subsequent chapter are the convergences between calculation, payment, exchange, strategic deceit, and vindication of sovereign purposes that come through in talk of God's dealings with the devil. As Gregory of Nyssa infamously suggested, at the heart of God's salvific economy occurred a duplicitous exchange, in which God gave Christ to the devil as a payment in exchange for debt-enslaved humanity.[27] Strategically and with guile, God withheld crucial information about the true identity of Christ, and the nature of the economy was such that the devil was unable to retain ownership of what he was paid and was consequently overthrown. Humanity was set free for renewed relationship with God, and Christ returned to his rightful place at the right hand of the Father. Concern about Gregory's theory from his contemporaries had little to do with the subterfuge and trickery undertaken by God but was more a protest at the thought of the devil as a worthy exchange partner for the divine. As we will see, Gregory vindicates his narrative by invoking the aggressive power dynamics of monetary economy to set forth a vision of divine conquest over the satanic adversary.

Incarnation and imperial unification

Incarnation initiates *oikonomic* thinking within Christianity. It requires novel conceptualizations of the deity—as both transcendent and immanent, fully divine and fully human, eternal yet present in history and subject to temporality. Because of the divine historical presence manifest in the incarnation, new dimensions of form, order, and meaning to history are also introduced into Christian reflection. Fate is demoted as providence assumes center stage; fixed cycles are disrupted with eschatological horizons and orientation toward future change, growth, and fulfillment. History as such becomes a source of revelation: not only does God's work in the world reveal what God is like, but God's appearance in material historical form sacralizes and sacramentalizes this sphere. The tokens, signs, practices, institutions, and other attributes of the human realm thus become semiotically significant and offer themselves as conceptual building blocks for Christian thinking about the godhead.

The early church father and bishop, Eusebius of Caesarea, provides a central model of the incarnation as divine government, as determinative of historical meaning and orientation, and as intermeshed with political and economic realities. He is thus a key Christian theorist of divine *oikonomia*, arguing that history manifests the guiding, purposive hand of God—a perspective most thoroughly developed in his influential *Ecclesiastical History*. Such a heavenly economy is thoroughly enmeshed with political and economic realities on earth. Indeed, per Eusebius, Roman imperial *oikonomia* reflects and reveals the heavenly economy above. Incarnation serves as the linchpin and critical juncture point where providential and redemptive economies coincide, for God's management of the world and of history is for the purposes of salvation. Incarnation reveals the nature of divine government. In its coincidence with Roman political and economic realities, incarnation also demonstrates that divine *oikonomia* retains overtones of both of political governance and monetary economic management of lives and resources.

Eusebius is an emblematic and frequently critiqued case of the synthesis between theological and political concepts in emerging Christian thought. The majority of patristic thinkers arguably appear influenced by their contemporary political ideas and institutions. Yet, in Eusebius, we are provided with an apparent validation and endorsement of the fusion between theology and politics.[28] The bishop's theological project coincides with a founding moment in the Western imaginary: the advent of the first Christian emperor. In his pronouncements about this monumental transition, Eusebius bequeaths an influential template for ensuing models of state legitimation through theological discourse. In contributing to a theological history of the church and empire, Eusebius focuses not only on the circumstances associated with Constantine's rise to power but also on the ways in which preceding political realities reveal God's hand at work. The figure of Caesar Augustus and the rise of Roman monarchy in particular play a decisive role in Eusebian theology. Not only does Augustus prefigure or serve as a type for Constantine, setting into motion what Constantine as antitype fulfills, but the Roman Empire at the height of power also reveals divine realities.

Eusebius asserts that God's timing of the incarnation providentially coincides with Roman imperial zenith. Unification, peace, and stability under Augustus represent the ideal time for divine self-manifestation. Furthermore, these characteristics of Roman imperial unity and governance reflect the nature of divine identity, oneness, and reign. Eusebius's striking claim here invokes both metaphysical and political economic realities, while highlighting their coimplication. Eusebius makes conceptual links among incarnation, divine economy, and the political and economic structures of empire.

Eusebius, like Origen before him, comments on infrastructural advances made by the empire.[29] He is attentive to the details of institutions and everyday practices around Roman ascendancy. The rise brings practical benefits such as ease of movement, communication, and consequent evangelization. Yet, for Eusebius, these benefits are secondary to the point that God is sovereign over historical and geopolitical events and has ordained and facilitated Rome's ascent to power. What is more, the very character of the godhead is revealed by these dynamics on the ground, dynamics that include money and its effects.

Eusebius's invocation of the significance of imperial unity and power for God's self-revelation requires consideration of the Roman situation. Money operated centrally in the development and extension of the empire, influencing its institutions, exchange practices, and attendant sociocultural dimensions.[30] Taxation and redistribution of money and material resources were driving forces for Roman imperial expansion. These practices also extended administrative networks both geographically and in complexity. The Roman Empire developed an elaborate bureaucracy extending throughout its territories.[31] Bureaucratic channels were a central device for the collection of taxes as well as the administration of justice.

What may have begun as a domestic image of rule by the emperor and his family grew increasingly complex through layers of attendants, emissaries, and administrators, as well as an unprecedented set of resources to manage.

While monetization was certainly uneven among provinces, the empire itself was highly monetized in terms of its official identity.[32] This means that salaries and payments were monetarily quantified and that most transactions were denominated in terms of money.[33] The later empire in particular saw greater levels of bureaucratization, monetization, and imperial administrative presence. Indeed, "*money*, not land, emerged as the general form of wealth," influenced in part by the Constantinian reforms in coinage and the monetary system.[34] Money increasingly came to characterize the relations between imperial officials, ossifying bureaucratic identities. Salaries helped define roles and offices. Payments also progressively moderated means of institutional access such that relations between officials and subjects became increasingly mediated by money.[35]

As imperial borders advanced through military conquest, monetary habits were in turn disseminated.[36] It was the norm in the ancient Mediterranean world that the spread of money was tied to military expansion. Many scholars suggest that the employment of mercenaries was a primary motive for the development of coinage in ancient Greece.[37] This practice was certainly extended in the Roman Empire with its occupying forces. Coinage was lightweight, portable, and marked by symbols of allegiance to its issuing source. As armies became nationalized and professionalized, monetary payments were standardized. Military presence led to soldiers imposing the tokens of exchange issued from their commander-in-chief. Local populations under occupied power would be required to accept the tokens and render goods and services to the soldiers. The populace could later offer a portion of these tokens back in tax tribute. In the interim, such coins would circulate among the people and increasingly permeate the exchange relations of the governed. The tokens were rendered valuable primarily because of the tax and tribute requirements. Transactors sought tokens in order to have something to render unto Caesar. The presence of coinage did not eliminate tax and tribute payments in kind for those who did not possess the necessary amounts of currency. Nevertheless, such commodity payments increasingly came to be denominated by the governing money standard, and many subjects were drawn into trade relations for the sake of acquiring money to pay taxes.[38]

While wars certainly did not cease under Roman rule, increased military presence could be marshaled ideologically into an image of peace and stability. To the peace achieved through the threat of violence, we can add the stability that comes with a unified measure of exchange and common currency.[39] While diversity of Roman provincial coinage existed and served as a point of contestation and assertion of local identity, regional differences gradually declined such that a unified, symbolically transcendent coinage came to circulate in the later empire.[40] Even as some measure of local diversity persisted, pundits and politicians regularly proclaimed the ideal of a single Roman coinage and a unified set of weights and measures.[41] By the time of Eusebius's later writings, the empire under Constantine enjoyed the introduction of the gold *solidus*. This unified currency provided relative economic stability as well as an increased sense of monetary integration across the empire.[42]

There is great symbolic and rhetorical significance, therefore, to the coordination of the incarnation with this political and economic context. In refuting charges of falsehood and sorcery concerning Christ, Eusebius turns to evidence of the power of God present in Christ's manifestation. A key aspect of such witness upon the stage of world history is the rise of Rome. Eusebius proclaims:

For His wonderful sojourn among men synchronized with Rome's attainment of the acme of power, Augustus then first being supreme ruler over most of the nations . . . And no one could deny that the synchronizing of this with the beginning of the teaching about our Savior is of God's arrangement, if he considered the difficulty of the disciples taking their journey, had the nations been at variance one with another, and not mixing together because of varieties of government. But when these were abolished, they could accomplish their projects quite fearlessly and safely, since the Supreme God had smoothed the way before them, and subdued the spirit of the more superstitious citizens under the fear of a strong central government. (*Demonstration of the Gospel* 3.7)[43]

Here we see a concern for practical barriers that might hinder the spread of the gospel. Such obstacles are also sociopolitical, stemming from differing cultures and political systems. Their removal proclaims the power and authority of God, a power that is manifest in "a strong central government."

Furthermore, Roman unity demonstrates the truth of the sovereign unity of God. Rome's rise is not simply the outcome of divine will but a manifestation of the harmony that is fundamental to the godhead. As Erik Peterson asserts, Roman unity is for Eusebius also a metaphysical claim.[44] Eusebius proceeds:

> For consider, how if there had been no force available to hinder those who in the power of polytheistic error were contending with Christian education, that you would have long ago seen civil revolutions, and extraordinarily bitter persecutions and wars, if the superstitious had had the power to do as they willed with them. Now this must have been the work of God Almighty, this subordination of the enemies of His own Word to a greater fear of a supreme ruler. (*Demonstration of the Gospel* 3.7)

Eusebius claims a correspondence between polytheism—acknowledging a multiplicity of gods and powers—and political turmoil and chaos. Stability and imperial unity are found in acknowledging the reign of the one, true God. For Eusebius, as for many thinkers in the Greco-Roman world, correlations could be drawn between monotheism and monarchy, with the existence and power of a single divinity justifying and supporting the centralized imperial ruler, and vice versa.[45]

Money remains an implicit yet real presence in the factors pertaining to God's timing of incarnation. The material institutional as well as ideological unity, stability, and peace Eusebius cites are not simply the result of political programs or military might but also everywhere the effects of economic integration.[46] These factors provide a subtext to Eusebius's broader claims about Roman triumph and divine manifestation. Given the residual presence of financial and monetary economic logic in *oikonomia*, it is no surprise that a thinker like Eusebius would be led to remark on the economic context of divine manifestation.

Eusebius brings themes of imperial unity and divine purpose together in a telling passage, delivered as part of his sermon dedicating Christ's sepulcher. Later appended to his Constantinian oration, the sermon augments expression of the sovereignty of God over the emperor's reign and over Constantine's benefaction for the churches. Eusebius returns to the topic of the Roman Empire's coincidence with incarnation as expressed in his earlier apologetic works. Monotheism and monarchy, as well as spiritual and imperial victory and unity, are linked: "For while the power of Our Savior destroyed the polyarchy and polytheism of the demons and heralded the one kingdom of God to Greeks and barbarians and all men to the farthest extent of the earth, the Roman Empire, now that the causes of the manifold governments had been abolished, subdued visible governments, in order to merge the entire race into one unity and concord" (*On Christ's Sepulcher* 16.6).[47] Eusebius emphasizes the peace and relational interconnection that result from both spiritual and political economic unity. It is under Constantine that such links came most fully into view.

Having reviewed the diversity of peoples conquered by Rome and exposed to the gospel, Eusebius proclaims it a miracle and proof of divine power that all are able to dwell together in unity. It is a unity marked not merely by tolerance but by a deep spiritual connection revealing, significantly, a familial relation under the fatherhood of God and ordered within one house: "all acknowledged each other brothers and discovered their related nature. All at once, as if sons of one father, the One God, and children of one mother, true religion, they greeted and received each other peaceably, so that from that time the whole inhabited world differed in no way from a single well-ordered and related household (*mias eunomoumenês oikias sungeneias*)" (*On Christ's Sepulcher* 16.7).

Deftly and within the course of a few sentences, Eusebius weaves together spiritual, political, and economic unity with terminology of the family and household. The Christian empire is a household (*oikos*), one family with one head, the *oikodespotês* or *paterfamilias*, God the Father. Invoking a long tradition of household order and resource management operative in notions of *oikonomia*, Eusebius extends this domestic vision over the entire Roman Empire.[48] This signals the importance of economic factors in Roman imperial consolidation. God is here the Father and ultimate authority over the imperial house with its various roles, relations, and stewardships. Such relations do not necessarily simply connote the fraternity of familial intimacies but also include the place of slaves in an ordered household economy. God's *oikos* must be reflected in an earthly *oikonomia*, even as the rule of God as Father coincides with the rule of the one emperor and *paterfamilias* of the empire. As we will see, it falls to the

Son as the Logos, the governor of the Father, to be the chief administrator (*dioikêtês* or *oikonomos*), who oversees and manages resource and power allocations.

Eusebius builds a bridge between Augustus and Constantine, for what Augustus begins, Constantine brings to fulfillment.[49] The peace and stability initiated under the Roman Empire of Augustus, which made possible the manifestation of the single Christian God in incarnation, come to fruition in the alignment of empire and deity when Emperor Constantine formally submits to God in professed Christian belief. In the Augustan moment of Roman imperial zenith, money contributed to bureaucracy, expanding channels of communication; it spread with military presence, imposing security on new territories; it created new markets for commodities, bringing roads, transport improvement, and other infrastructure; and it united regions in mutual interdependence, bringing stability through common exchange practices and accounting measures. From the historical vantage point of the intensification of such economic integration under Constantine, Eusebius projects such realities back upon the advent of Augustus, discerning truths about the divine plan. The Augustan moment represents many things; most certainly these include the social, political—and, as we now begin to glimpse, theological—impact of monetary economy and its related administration.

Taxation, governance, and divine solidarity

Augustan monetary economy provides one of the determining channels for the birth of Christ, one that remains symbolically central to Advent narratives. Money requires and engenders various techniques for monitoring, measuring, and cataloging people and productive forces within a territory. Among these techniques, census bears particular significance as one of the "enumerative strategies" of empire in managing bodies and subjects under centralized power.[50] It represents a long-running and nascent form of biopolitics, providing rudimentary statistical information in the interests of state tabulation and control. Indeed, census numbers bodies for several reasons, the most important of which is taxation.

The tax circuit gives value to money, and the power to tax reflects sovereignty.[51] Without taxation, money as we understand it would not exist. The imposition of taxes renders monetary tokens meaningful and valuable. As noted, monetary tokens have typically been disseminated via occupying military forces or civil servants, as signs of ruling power imposed upon the populace in exchange for goods and services. The state as guarantor declared that it would accept these arbitrary tokens back as a way for its subjects to discharge their debt of economic fealty. In so doing it established a monetary circuit, an ebb and flow of tokens that marked relations of credit and debt within a territory. Taxation established the decreed exchange proportions, indicating the abstract value of money, as the state declared other acceptable means of in-kind payment in terms of their equivalences with the money standard.[52]

The Augustan census, which drove Joseph and Mary back to Bethlehem (Luke 2:1), was decreed in the interests of imperial finance.[53] The star under which the Messiah was born marks the crucial interface between state and populace that drives monetary economy at its very heart. Symbolically, then, the labor pangs that brought Christ into the world stem not only from a people under foreign occupation and oppression. The incarnation, that moment of material connection between the realm of divine sovereignty and the immanent, governed sphere, also coincides with a key moment of exchange between imperial sovereignty and its subjects, as measures are taken to extract monetary value from those ruled.

Just as Caesar Augustus works to draw up resources via monetary economy, arranging bodies and ordering lives according to his sovereign plan, the divine sovereign grants a credit to the world, carrying out an alternative and wider-ranging plan or *oikonomia*. The tax census sends Mary to Bethlehem, and the Son enters the world under the sign of money and bureaucracy. Money and Christology are thus implicitly linked through the historical operations in the economy surrounding Advent. From circumstances preceding his birth until the thirty gold pieces that betrayed him, or even beyond that to the cross, his death, and a cosmic payment we have yet to explore, Christ's life is monetarily marked—indeed, bookended.

Ancient accounts corroborate this surprising association. In critiquing Eusebius's correlation of incarnation and empire, Peterson notes with dismay the view's widespread acceptance among many church fathers. He cites three sermons by John Chrysostom where the "golden-mouthed" preacher reflects on the providential events surrounding the birth of Christ. In his *Address against Jews and Pagans* 3, Chrysostom highlights the time of incarnation as coinciding with Roman dominance over the Jewish people. More specifically, "the time he was born and that first assessment [tax census] took place when the Romans had become the masters of the Jewish people."[54] He explicitly links the timing of incarnation with the timing of taxation, and suggests that a tool of monetary economy is evidence of sovereign domination.

In his *Homily on Matthew 2:11–15* 8.4, Chrysostom notes in passing that "Augustus assisted [or ministered to] (*hypêreteitai*) the birth in Bethlehem by his decree of the census."[55] Here as well the coincidence of Roman imperial power with the appearance of Christ is traced to the specificity of the census decree for poll-tax purposes. Augustus himself is an agent or even midwife of sorts, facilitating the location- and time-specific birth details of Christ in fulfillment of prophecy. Through tax census, the emperor unwittingly cooperates with a divine plan and aids in the birth of Christ.

Finally, Chrysostom sets the events into theological perspective in his *Homily on the Birthday of Jesus Christ* 2: "Augustus did not get the idea of promulgating this decree from his financial department (*oikothen*) or from his own initiative, rather it was God who moved his soul, so that even unwittingly he would assist the coming of the Only-begotten One."[56] Here again we find the idea of Augustus's tax census decree as centrally significant in orienting the time and place of the incarnation. To this is added the understanding that it is God who orchestrates these events. God is the sovereign agent over the monetary economic act that arranged the time and place of the savior's birth. God works through an emperor's financial administration. Given the theological attention paid by Eusebius to the significance of earthly events as disclosing divine truths, we are certainly invited to speculate as to why God chose to coordinate incarnational circumstances in such a way. Why mark the arrival of the Son into the world under the auspices of imperial taxation?

One striking answer is offered by Paulus Orosius in his *History against the Pagans*. This disciple of Augustine, writing in his own way to defend Christians against blame for Rome's decline—as his master did in *City of God*—develops in book six of his *History* what Peterson calls "an entire Augustus theology."[57] For Orosius, the significance of census itself explains God's timing of incarnation. Census as imperial demarcation is a manner of categorization and identification, and to the peace and stability brought to the entire world by Rome is added unity as symbolized in census recording. The tax census has an equalizing and totalizing function of including "the names of all."[58] To be co-opted by the census and consequently taxed marks one's belonging to the empire. Furthermore, such numbering and taxation are facts of human life.

As Orosius proclaims, the Son becomes visible at the time of tax census "for in the census list all men were entered individually, and in it the very Maker of all men wished to be found and enrolled as a man among men" (*History against the Pagans* 6.22).[59] To be included in the census is thus, for Orosius, a profound marker of divine solidarity with the human race. Since all must undergo taxation (indeed, as we say, it is one of life's two great certainties, along with death), what better way for God to show true humanity than to be "entered in the Roman census list immediately after . . . birth"?[60] The commonality of taxation plays a critical role in species identity and is also, according to Orosius, a marker of true Roman citizenship. Census and taxation provide the basis for his striking claims about human nature, political unification, and divine solidarity.

As Peterson paraphrases, Christ "wished in the first instance to belong to [the Roman empire], when he came, in order to be named a Roman citizen through the 'acknowledgement of Roman taxation.'"[61] Christ identifies not only with humanity but also with Rome, which becomes symbolic for Christian empire. The timing of incarnation, then, reveals a truth about divine identification with humanity, facilitated through tax census as part of Augustan monetary administration. As a tool of monetary economy, as well as one of the oldest biopolitical technologies, tax census plays a providential role in the Son's manifestation. According to Orosius, God acknowledges the validity and immutability of these practices by embracing them in the act of becoming flesh, choosing them as critical identity markers of human solidarity. God, in effect, affirms such biopolitical cataloging as evocative of human identity, choosing self-disclosure according to the constraints of such numbering and taxation as a way to declare God's humanity.

From one perspective, Roman taxation is a burden, albeit one that appears necessary for the discipline and order it brings, which in turn help humanity apprehend higher-order truths of divine unity and governance. From another vantage point, incarnation brings blessing and removal of the burden of sin. The two economies are not radically counterposed, however. Rather, through correlationist theology, an imperfect earthly model (tax census) is depicted as fulfilled in the divine dispensation (incarnation): the divinely ordained census becomes a temporal mechanism for the incarnation, and taxation gestures toward hidden truths about the divine economy and the savior that are revealed at Advent. Neither merely happenstance nor extraneous, the Augustan tax census is a *theological event*, and monetary economy is, yet again, identified with divine economy. Just as Christ's birth in a manger has been used to reflect on divine humility or solidarity with the poor, for instance, so tax census, as one of the many signs and symbols attendant to the birth of Christ, can be interpreted theologically.

Following Eusebius, such early theology construes a number of aspects of monetary economy as aiding divine manifestation. Money undergirds and is in turn empowered by a notion of territorial and ideological unity. Unity is forged by undertaking exchange with the same tokens of power, according to the standards of measure and value decreed by this sovereign account. Not only do common institutions and structures emerge in support of such a system, tying people together practically, but a base-level common identity can be accessed through sharing the same monetary tokens.

Furthermore, the ease of interface and sense of mutual dependence that result from being interwoven within the same sovereign economy promote a modicum of stability and mitigate, so the story goes, a propensity to internecine war. To partake of exchange under one centralized ruler is to be of the same "house," within the same "family," with exchange tokens literally bearing the image of this political economic "father." Ideological unity and peace are both the result of and serve further to entrench the centralized rule by one coordinate power. Monetary signs enable this one center of rule to represent itself among the ruled in their mundane and vital processes of commerce. Taxation enforces territorial fealty and submission. Census marks who is of the house. All factors work within the sovereign God's designs of self-revelation. Such events and institutions do not simply make apprehension of the divine governor easier, but, following Eusebian logic, are themselves earthly echoes of divine economy.

Inherent in Eusebius's theory about the timing of the incarnation is a claim that God waited until the world was economically, politically, institutionally, and epistemologically prepared for this divine manifestation. Such preparation was of course also divinely orchestrated. Certain social realities influence consciousness and perception, enabling recognition of divine truths. Because of the unity brought under Roman imperial monarchy, which, as Eusebius writes in his *Oration in Praise of Constantine (Oration)*, "excels all other kinds of constitutions and governments" (3.6), and due to the presence of a money economy, humanity was better able to appreciate the reign of the one, true king of heaven and to accept and submit to the eternal administrator that was sent. Elements of the nature of God and of divine rule through the incarnation of the Son are thus best apprehended in light of imperial and economic expansion, integration, and consolidation.

Monarchy, monotheism, and money

Roman triumph not only demonstrates the power of the God who superintends such feats but also reveals that this God is a unity and is supreme over all other would-be deities. Monarchy and monotheism are, for Eusebius, mutually reinforcing. This becomes clear in his praise of Constantine, as he proclaims, "Monarchy excels all other kinds of constitutions and government. For rather do anarchy and civil war result from the alternative, a polyarchy based on equality. For which reason there is One God, not two or three or even more" (*Oration* 3.6). Eusebius moves from the political to the theological and back again. Noting the benefits of single rule for earthly realities, he subtly projects such patterns upon God as necessities, since God, being all-wise, surely manifests the ideal form of rule. That the supreme Lord of the universe is singular and rules as one in turn provides reciprocal justification for such earthly arrangements.

In correlating monotheism to monarchy, Eusebius invokes all that makes monarchic consolidation of power possible, including monetary economy. The influence of money may thus also be discerned in his exaltation of the one emperor and one Lord above. Ancient Greek anxieties about money and centralized power often appear in tandem, revealing potential correlations between the two. Greek critiques of tyranny and autocratic authority often go hand in hand with condemnations of abuse of monetary economy and of excessive wealth.[62] This signals awareness that where monarchical rule and centralized, autarchic state power are being considered, an evaluation of monetary economy should follow.

Money economies appear to require some form of centralized governance, where a single standard of account with enforced weights and measures provides the mediating, abstract, third category for exchange relations. While variations are conceivable theoretically, at least historically, money economies appear mainly in conjunction with empires, kingdoms, and other forms of state rule where a focal point of sovereignty is recognized. Money requires standardization, and tokens are sent out by a single center of power and reclaimed by that power through taxation, in an ebb and flow that would be disrupted with multiple, conflicting centers with different codifications of value. Indeed, new, competing currencies are very often issued in historical moments where a center of sovereignty is being contested. The fact that money, as coinage or notes, has always borne marks of its issuing power speaks to this requirement of a single grounding point to mobilize the circulation of tokens.[63] There are thus strong thematic correlations between money and monarchy—where the latter is taken as a cipher for a centralized point of sovereign decision.

If monarchy and monotheism are regarded as mutually reinforcing ideas, it follows that money's role in aiding monarchical power may reveal associations between money and monotheism as well.[64] Monarchy, monotheism, and money may thus be triangulated. In fact, scholars have linked the emergence of monotheistic ideas with the development of a money economy, given money's connections to centralized forms of rule. Money appears to be an influential factor in the ideological and conceptual frameworks operating under consolidated forms of political authority. To the degree that political monarchy serves as a screen upon which to project and construct ideas of singular divine rule, distinct attributes from monetary exchange may work their way into the assumptions and logic of monotheistic ideals.

Long before Eusebius exalted monarchy, the so-called Axial Age (ca. 800–200 BCE) saw the rise of large agrarian empires, social stratification and economic inequality, and hierarchical, centralized, and bureaucratized forms of rule. Theorists have noted the corresponding rise of monotheistic religions articulating transcendent deities during this period. Novel as well in this admittedly long time span are advances in abstract conceptual thinking, including the advent of money, first as abstract tabulations on clay in ancient Babylon (possibly as early as 3000 BCE) and then notably as coinage in Lydia and Greece (ca. 600 BCE). Further historical correlations thus become evident between the forms of abstraction and conceptual interchange that make possible (or are made possible by) money, on the one hand, and new religious and philosophical ideas, on the other. Scholarship exists on the influence of money on early Greek philosophy, for instance.[65] While initial links have been made, further investigation is needed on the potential influence of money on early religious thought.[66]

Richard Seaford argues that the new social and political formations brought about by monetary economy in ancient Greece find expression in philosophical and theological ideas of cosmic unity and centralizations of divine power.[67] He surveys a number of Presocratic thinkers whose novel understandings of the universe—as composed of one singular substance, subject to change and flux, or modulated from a single point or origin, for instance—appear to reflect, in part, the transition from the gift exchange practices of the Homeric world to city-states permeated by coinage. As Seaford claims, the novel assertions made by Xenophanes in the sixth century BCE about a stationary, singular deity who nevertheless controls all things imperceptibly with the power of his mind may correlate to money's role in monarchy (and tyranny) as a new political form in Greece: "[I]n the world of Xenophanes, co-existence of autonomous powers has in a sense been eliminated: were there two moneys, one would soon be absorbed by the other; political power, maintained and permeated by unitary money, is itself unitary—most strikingly in the figure of the tyrant. Deity is power, and so must be (at least on the model of money and political power) 'one'."[68] Increasingly pervasive money, used at the hands of political powers in the city-states, exerted a unifying effect that went beyond the territorial or social. There is ample evidence of ancient Greek unease around the new technology of money and its effects on social, political, and ethical practice. Philosophers regularly condemned its corrosive impact on traditional forms of communal reciprocity or ethical norms of pursuing the highest good, while noting its role in unseemly claims to power and usurpations of authority. Money's presence may also have influenced metaphysical speculations about cosmic or divine unity.

New political realities, facilitated in part by money, provided a mirror for new philosophical projections about the realm of the gods. As Seaford suggests, pointedly: "The invisible but ubiquitous power of money was in the sixth century a strange and radical novelty, which is reflected, I suggest, in numerous aspects of sixth-century philosophy, including Xenophanes' strange and radically new notion of a single nonanthropomorphic deity staying in the same place while nevertheless agitating all things by the thought of his mind and (probably) needing nothing."[69] Thus, the idea of a distant, impersonal, heavenly sovereign—something relatively novel in the time of Xenophanes—was most likely influenced by political realities. Such political developments were made possible in part by the consolidating power of money as well as its ability to allow control from a distance. Like a monetary sovereign who could manage an empire from the imperial seat through transactions mediated by money, the direct, personalized interventions by anthropomorphic deities could be supplemented by a vision of an unmoving and distant god influencing the world through unseen power mechanisms.[70] While some correlations remain speculative and invite further research, other conceptual links both between money and monarchy and between monarchy and monotheism are explicit. By the logic of transitive properties, the potential for thematic and conceptual connection between these first and third terms does indeed exist.

The link between monotheism and money is implicit in the associations Eusebius makes between God's manifestation as singular monarch and the unitary, monarchic power of Rome, a power that includes administration through money. In the discourse that correlates monotheism and monarchy, and in the coordination of incarnation to Roman power and unification, we find implicit association between God and money. God as the transcendent and sovereign center of authority, represented immanently and proximately through a governing sign of value in the incarnation, can be brought into analogous comparison with the centralized rule of Roman monarchy, represented by coins as circulating signs proclaiming imperial unity, power, and presence. As we will see, this implicit parallel between divine economy and imperial monetary economy, with the incarnate Christ being God's imperial coin, undergirds the capacity for early Christian thinkers continually to make analogies between imperial coinage and the stamp of God on human coins.

Before we consider such links between Christ and coinage, we must examine another analogue made possible by the correlation between money and theology: the idea of God as an economist or steward who oversees the management of creation and redemption. For the divine *oikonomia* presumes an *oikonomos*, one who regulates the accounts and manages exchanges. This model of God proves instrumental in new patterns of governance and imperial administration. Just as finance and the profit motive retain sway in models of *oikonomia*, emerging conceptions of the managerial God carry overtones of the very real governance of goods and resources, all aimed strategically toward cosmic goals of redemption and victory over spiritual opponents.

Government orders economy through money; indeed, this ordering is itself an economy. God orders creation through providence as well as through the Son and his incarnation. Money as a central aspect of sovereign rule and governance here begins to display its theopolitical resonances. Money imports a specific codification of value—sovereignty's accounting system—inserting itself into communal relations and consequently shaping patterns of life. This role of money—as incarnating and representing sovereign power—explains its resonances with Christology and suggests why monetary language proved attractive and useful in describing the identity and work of the Son in redemption.

The coincidence of incarnation with the height and centralization of Roman political and economic power reveals aspects of divine identity. Rome demonstrated a unified economic space, integrated (ideologically at least) by a single currency and method of account. Images of the single Roman emperor permeated and infiltrated this economy through coinage. Stability and infrastructure were the result of both military and political force as well as economic institutions. Political monarchy, law and legality, and the institutions and practices of monetary economy—including support structures like census—were all part of the Augustan moment as it revealed Christ. Thus, the coalescence of political sovereignty and the operations of money to forge a space of reign and governance and to discipline subjects under a particular pattern of value and exchange here becomes theologically meaningful in terms of incarnation.

As we will now consider, incarnation reveals the cooperative wisdom of the heavenly sovereign and the divine administrator: Father and Son oversee and strategically coordinate, by *oikonomia*, the allocation of resources in the relation between God and world as a function of creation's position under divine reign. Such an administrator and governor would become a model for bishops and emperors, leaders in ecclesial and political communities that came to shape Western patterns of rule and administration for centuries. This divine economist would also, through the narrative of redemptive *oikonomia*, become the chief coin and payment in this economy, modeling a pattern of self-sacrificial offering to be emulated by the faithful. Such an economic sacrifice would proffer itself as a strategy leading to spiritual—and sociopolitical—victory.

2

The Divine Economist

In what became a touchstone in modern constructive theology that engages the economy, M. Douglas Meeks describes God as an economist.[1] Reclaiming the valence of *oikonomia* as household management, Meeks portrays God as overseeing an *oikos* and as head of a family. A reorientation to household and familial relations under God, Meeks hopes, should provide an impetus for reshaping the economy in more life-giving ways that reflect the appropriate care, concern, and abundance that characterize an ideal family. Economic relations in God's household display concern for the vulnerable and needy, demonstrate justice, and embody sustainable practices to care for creation. Meeks retrieves the trope of God's household and laudably deploys it toward progressive ends of equality, justice, and economic redistribution. His *God the Economist* has inspired a tradition of reimagining the godhead in terms of economic relations and seeking social transformation accordingly.[2]

Yet the conceptual space of the *oikos* is ambivalent, and here Meeks is required to import a host of semantic content in order to decree what familial economic relations in a household must entail. Without such imposed stabilizations, the idea of God as head of a broad *oikos* can be and has been deployed in the interests of empire, as when Eusebius invoked "the well-worn political topos of the state as a properly governed household."[3] In such a scenario, communities can be forcibly inducted into God's household as territories are annexed by the imperial center. Just as a child does not choose the household into which he or she is born or adopted, such peoples must accept their fate. Ancient models of rule and command in the household, with fixed patriarchal order and slave economies, could easily sustain hierarchies and unjust apportionments of resources. Invoking the unity of the family of God within the *oikos* of God does not, therefore, necessitate just economic relations.

While posed as a constructive theological intervention and reimagining, *God the Economist* and other studies written in its wake actually take up a long tradition depicting God as an economist who manages an economy. As we have seen, the idea is not new, and the deep history of *oikonomia* reveals such concepts at Christianity's inception. What is more, this conceptual heritage is tied to an imaginary where monetary administration remains central and where financial and profit-oriented techniques inform management strategy even when depicted figuratively in the spiritual realm. Such governing valences must be reckoned with before the divine *oikonomia* is applied as a balm to assuage contemporary economic ills, many of which are tied to the ends of finance and uses of money. The idea of God the economist labors under the burden of a long and vexed history.

Furthermore, as Giorgio Agamben claims, *oikonomia* became central to the development of governmental power in the West. Even when the aims of Christian empire—God's *oikos*—receded, and Christendom gave way to the modern, managerial nation-state, the resonances of *oikonomia* were felt in the emergence of govermentality. Here techniques for managing bodies and populations combined with economic instruments used at the hands of political authorities. The space of the household proved central in the administration of such techniques, with the nuclear family as one key site of discipline in conformity to biopolitical ideals. It was pastoral power that proved a crucial predecessor to such strategies, and it was to God and God's economy that pastors turned for models of what such management would look like. Before it was converted into a new *raison d'état*, managing and stewarding the lives and resources of a governed flock was a central technique of pastoral *oikonomia*. In mobilizing the notion of a divine *oikos* to attempt to combat contemporary economic injustice, Meeks unearths more than he intends, for he retrieves a troubling legacy of pastoral power that is itself implicated in the dominance of economy in the modern West.

Following Eusebius's claims that God's purposes are aligned with Roman imperial consolidation and economic integration, and that the institutions and practices of monetary economy reveal attributes of God, this chapter considers the divine economic actor behind the *oikonomia*. What emerges in Eusebian theology is an understanding of the Logos, the Son, as the economic administrator of the Father, given the reins of governance by the ruler of all. The Logos manages the cosmos and arranges history much as a steward or money manager oversees and organizes accounts, apportioning resources and allocating blessings in the interests of a return. As a divine steward, the Logos conveys God's riches and rule to creation, justly apportioning blessings, ensuring their proliferation and return, and enforcing order and authority through resource management. This eternal steward and his kingdom in turn provide a model for earthly authority to execute political reign and economic governance according to the pattern of the heavenly economy.

Such a model is informed by the Roman imperial landscape, which serves as a parable for what God and God's kingdom are like. Eusebius reasons from political and economic realities back to the nature of the God who orchestrates them. The model of the divine economist is also deeply informed by Eusebius's role as a bishop and his inheritance and redeployment of a theology of pastoral power. The model he sets forth would come to influence imperial self-understanding, contributing to the theopolitical template of sovereignty and government in Western tradition. This chapter situates Eusebian theology of the divine economist within the material and institutional transitions of late antiquity, for such theology is meaningless without praxis and without the roles and institutions that rose up around such early Christian practices and were bequeathed to the West's political history.

From shepherd to economist

In his genealogy of Western techniques of government, Michel Foucault explores the pastorate as a critical progenitor of or what he terms a "prelude" to early modern state administration of lives and populations.[4] He claims that Christianity introduced an entirely new set of ideals and practices related to spiritual direction and oversight and to the institutional networks and official roles that rose up around them. We can better understand the modern administrative and governmental state, with its efforts at managing populations and stewarding the lives of citizens, when we consider the pastorate, its links to managing ecclesial communities, and its eventual relation to the political realm.

For Foucault, the pastor as shepherd, drawing upon ancient Near Eastern and particularly Hebraic models of God (and king) as shepherd, is portrayed as in charge of a flock and is called to be devoted to each and to the collective. Although it is certainly not his focus, Foucault admits the interrelation between pastoral practice and the ideas of God as shepherd that fund it. Already in his lectures, Foucault associated this work of shepherding with a type of economic activity that prefigures modern government, since "the essential issue of government will be the introduction of economy into political practice."[5] If the "Christian Church coagulated all these themes of pastoral power into precise mechanisms and definite institutions, [and] . . . implanted its apparatuses within the Roman Empire," a potent nexus of theology and pastoral practice that draws upon monetary economy and ever-attendant political institutions began to convey new paradigms of economic administration to late antique society.[6]

The shift in Foucault's lectures from pastor as shepherd to pastor as steward and manager of an economy is both sudden and subtle. He invokes Gregory of Nazianzus's claim that pastoral oversight is an "economy of souls" (*oikonomia psychôn*).[7] From here he moves on quickly to questions of conduct, drawing upon the ancient valence of economy as household governance. Conduct in fact becomes the central concern of his study, and pastoral economy signals broadly an idea of orderly management as the "conduct of conduct." Leaving the divine shepherd behind, Foucault does not consider what images of God superintend this economic practice, nor does he linger on the relation between *oikonomia* as governance of material goods—as economy proper—and the pastoral role.

While Agamben helps retrieve certain relevant understandings of God, he does not relate them to the pastorate. Furthermore, like Foucault, he does not tie themes of economic governance, whether earthly or divine, to an economy proper of goods and money. Neither does he explore the succession of vicarious representations from the divine economist, to the pastor as economic manager, to the emperor as ultimately inculcating pastoral economy in the state's administrative apparatus. Yet pastoral matters of managing conduct are everywhere traversed with concerns about uses of money and other resources, as well as with the types of spiritual exchanges made among the overseer, the flock, and God.

Agamben's incomplete archaeology is facilitated in part, Dotan Leshem argues, by his focus on Christianity's earliest deployments of *oikonomia*. Sidelined in importance are the councils of the fourth through sixth centuries that began to formalize orthodoxy's self-understanding, revealing a more thoroughgoing philosophy of *oikonomia* and reflecting the theopolitical integration of imperial sanction and enforcement.[8] A shift in focus would afford more attention to the development of pastoral economy as an immanent extension of God's managerial techniques aimed at salvation, and not merely attention to God's transcendent and providential orchestration of world history. It would also, I suggest, make space for the monetary and resource-specific orientation of economy to receive due consideration, given the ways Christianity would come to tie notions of transaction, surplus, and profit to salvation, spiritual growth, and ultimate redemption.

Furthermore, I claim that the potential for Agamben's recovery of *oikonomia* to shed light on the ongoing efficacy of the governmental paradigm falters near the conclusion of his study. Here he asserts: "What our investigation has shown is that the real problem, the central mystery of politics, is not sovereignty, but government; *it is not God, but the angel*; it is not the king, but ministry; it is not the law, but the police—that is to say the governmental machine that they form and support."[9] Rather, the novel Christian distinction, at the heart of which lurked *oikonomia*, was the insertion of duality and eventually trinity into the identity of God, implicating a fundamental fusion of kingdom and government within the godhead itself. It is this union, as Agamben's study reveals, that funds the increasing centrality of administration and management, bestowing divine sacrality upon governance. Despite Agamben's sudden concluding claim here, the productively unstable distinction is not between God and the angel, but between Father and Son. The Son marks the seat of government, unveiling, materializing, enacting, and, in a fundamental sense, legitimating the Father's kingdom on earth. The Father and Son each and together remain the one God, and this is the source of both the union and ongoing productive tension between the poles, as bequeathed in the "bi-polar" paradigm Agamben identifies.

Agamben blunts the force of his own exploration by suggesting that the heavenly analogue to the bifurcation of earthly regimes is the God-angel distinction. The angelic analogue relegates governance to a subsidiary rank, for angelic coidentification with God was never claimed. It thus undercuts Agamben's assertion that the governmental machine bears equal status with sovereignty as an object of inquiry. While it is true that ecclesial bureaucracies drew legitimation from celestial and angelic administrations, the figure of the bishop always performed the act of *christomimesis*, and the emissaries of pastoral power came not in the name of angels but in the name of the Son. The grounding of government in the deity of the Son means that government is invested with divine glory as well, just as the Father conveys such glory to the pole of sovereignty.[10] The weight given to such administration by the Christian legacy stems from government's identification with the godhead itself in the person of the Son. Thus, the acts of stewardship, management, and economic administration in the heart of government, drawing as they do from pastoral power, must be evaluated in light of the Son as the paradigmatic cosmic economist. The angels, like the bishops, are mere bureaucrats in the service of this christological administration.[11]

Pastoral oversight as economy

In addition to and for the purposes of stewarding souls, pastors and bishops in turn became instrumental stewards of financial resources. Churches served as clearinghouses for alms given by benefactors to support the congregation and to provide for the poor. Sensibilities of calculated strategy in the interests of gain, latent within understandings of *oikonomia*, are filtered into material practice in the context of emerging church polity and governance. Here language of redemptive, profitable governance influences roles, offices, and modes of praxis in the institutionalized Christian community.

Since divine economy "does not have as its goal the pure and simple seizure of power by all and any means," so too must ecclesial institutions employ "a fair and wise evaluation of the profits and losses pertaining to a certain office."[12] Governance must present itself as reasonable and measured and "should never be confused with the pure and simple appropriation of power."[13] John Chrysostom's *On the Priesthood*, for instance, contains many injunctions on the use of *oikonomia* in the priestly role, invoking it in the administration of souls and, in particular, the material allocation of goods and care for the needy and vulnerable. The calculative and profit-oriented valence of *oikonomia* is present and involves the proper distribution of resources. A good priest is an adept resource manager.

Reflecting on Chrysostom here, Marie-José Mondzain, in a telling passage, highlights the vivid convergence within pastoral *oikonomia* between a concrete sense of accounting and gain, on the one hand, and the stewardship of souls and the community, on the other:

> Because the economy implies both the notions of organization and expenditure, it justifies all the expenses entailed in maintaining its authority or in making a convincing case for its necessity. Thus alms, which are charitable economy (which will designate all the forms of social and hospital assistance), cover all expenses, the receipts for which are always anticipated by the church, spiritual though these may be. In this way, a meaning concerning accountancy enters into the notion of economy in a direct line from the Classical economy. The creation was an expenditure; Christ was an expenditure . . . But in this notion of expenditure, nothing is arbitrary or free. All the sacred expenditures, all the divine expenditures, are methodical, purposeful, justified, balanced by material profits as well as by spiritual benefits. This is a tidy piece of accountancy whose principle is the optimization of investments in view of a particular result.[14]

Here theology and organizational practice intertwine, as the nature and understanding of roles and responsibilities take their cue from divine economy. Not only does God manage creation and the plan of redemption, but all divine acts have a purpose and aim and are done with the outcome taken into consideration. God's acts may be gracious, in the sense of unmerited and superabundant, but they are not random, involuntary, or wasteful. *Calculation does not invalidate grace.* Mondzain thus claims that divine expenditures are "not free" in that they are not wanton, reckless, or done without consideration. They come at a cost and expect a return. They may still be free and gracious in the traditional theological sense of requiring nothing on the part of creation to initiate them. They may also be prodigal in the sense of supremely generous.

Although God's grace exceeds created capacities for comprehension and is marked by the infinite and expansive nature of divinity, the acts are ordered and strategic from the internal logic of divine *oikonomia* and from the perspective of God. God's salvific deeds have a purpose. Therefore priests—as representatives of God, stewards of the divine stewardship—are to mimic and reduplicate this non-wasteful, calculative, profit-oriented administration. They do so in their oversight of the church, both in the direction of the flock and in the prudent management of its resources, whether spiritual or material.

It is through the aim of caring for the poor, in particular, that priests and bishops emerged on the social and political scene and helped cata-lyze marked transformations in late antiquity. As Peter Brown recounts, the Christian practice of provision for the poor, which began to become widespread in the fourth century, was not the result of a new social demo-graphic situation or a gap in infrastructure into which Christian institu-tions step. The poor and vulnerable had always been present. What was new is the way in which they were construed, perceived, and consequently treated in Christian thought and practice. This was a symbolic and practi-cal revolution, a "change in the social imagination . . . the transition from one model of society, in which the poor were largely invisible, to another, in which they came to play a vivid imaginative role."[15]

In traditional Greco-Roman contexts, the civic benefactor or *euer-getes* was part of "a system of public giving and of a notion of social obliga-tion that anticipated in no way whatsoever the Christian notion of 'love of the poor.'"[16] Christianity brought transformations in the ways the poor were seen and in the public sense of responsibility for their plight, and it contributed to new sets of institutions and reallocations of resources based upon its novel ideals. One piece of the puzzle in discerning the effects of the conceptual nexus between God and money, as well as the impact of pastoral economy, is to be found here.

The ancient city-state relied on the gifts and support of its wealthier members, and forms of symbolic legitimation emerged to reinforce pat-terns of giving. Benefactors—the *euergetai*—gave for various reasons, including honor and praise, as well as a sense of esteem and satisfaction in providing for the *polis*. They gave for the fame and status of their name and legacy, and even for longer-term personal gain. Regardless of subjective motivations, these members of the elite class provided in the name of the city and for the sake of its citizens. Proof of citizenship, of territorial belonging to the city-state, was often required to partake of the dole. Benefactors thus demonstrated a marked lack of interest in the poor. They were not more "hard-hearted. They simply looked out on society and saw, above all, cities and citizens" not rich and poor.[17] The hungry masses at their gates or the displaced strangers in their midst were to a certain degree invisible to them as conceivable recipients of their largesse.

The new category of "the poor" stemmed, like the divine shepherd metaphor, from Hebraic and other ancient Near Eastern traditions. Conveyed through biblical idiom, the poor were the vulnerable and needy, not simply the materially destitute but also those suffering wrong at the hands of the more powerful. "What early Christians took for granted, as part of an inherited conglomerate of notions shared with Judaism, was that they were responsible for the care of the poor in their own community."[18] Dramatic social change took place when this private or local communal virtue was conveyed to the wider culture and its institutions.

The bishop proved to be a key fulcrum of change in this regard: "To put it bluntly: in a sense, it was the Christian bishops who invented the poor. They rose to leadership in late Roman society by bringing the poor into ever sharper focus. They presented their actions as a response to the needs of an entire category of persons (the poor) on whose behalf they claimed to speak."[19] Stemming from a "middling class" quite vulnerable to poverty, bishops and clergy, in symbolic parallel to the poor they championed, also relied on the support of their congregations. Bishops were stewards, managers of both their flock and donated resources, which they used to survive and from which they supported the needy: "in the name of the poor . . . they were to redistribute what remained from their own upkeep to the widows, orphans and destitute."[20]

A large portion of pastoral energy was taken up with raising, securing, and allocating funds and maintaining an attentive network of oversight that determined who was in need. As advocates for the poor, bishops also opened up new modes of relation with political elites, particularly as they conveyed appeals and arbitrated minor disputes, dispensing justice as eventual proxies for the state (*episcopalis audienta*).[21] Bishops also mediated funds from the state used to minister to the poor, tying their churches into the vast administrative networks of late imperial bureaucracy. In these ways, they conveyed the trope of the poor into public space through their rhetoric and practice, preaching on societal obligation to the needy, as well as forging and participating in structures that conformed to this ethic. As Andrea Giardina remarks, "The ecclesiastical economy essentially performed a 'democratic' function which the state economy could not provide (apart from the socially limited practice of distributions on behalf of the Roman plebs). The coexistence of and competition between these two economies were among the most significant aspects of the transition to late antiquity."[22]

Almsgiving and salvation

The poor became such central objects in the discourse of economy and pastoral power in part because of their role in sanctification and salvation. Ultimately, the poor were necessary for salvation, for not only was Christ present in the poor in unique ways (Matt 25:31–46), but mercy toward the poor in the form of material provision also retained pride of place as a spiritual discipline. Providing for the poor was interpreted as a way to provide offering to God, both in the sense that "he who is kind to the poor lends to the Lord" (Prov 19:17) directly, and that to sacrifice in such ways was to accrue "treasure in heaven" (Matt 19:21; Luke 12:33).[23]

This idea took on potency in part as a method of mimetic discipleship: to donate and provide for the poor and for the needs of churches in this way was an echo of Christ's condescension to humankind in the incarnation and sacrifice on the cross. As Brown rightly notes, almsgiving "was a formula heavy with echoes of the ransom of captives associated with the Redemption—of the ultimate ransom of all humanity by Christ himself."[24] Such an earthly and historical manifestation of Christ in turn divulged the eternal character of the Son as gracious administrator and heavenly economist. Hence the model for bishops and pastoral power was to encourage and reinforce this pattern of almsgiving, divestment, and sacrifice of material resources after the manner of the Son.

Much modern theology, in the wake of the Protestant critique of indulgences, has occluded the centrality of almsgiving in early church life and for its theological imaginary. Such theology has also downplayed the blatant claims of almsgiving as integral to the believer's path toward salvation. As L. Wm. Countryman notes in his survey of early church literature on almsgiving, "The principal reason urged by our authors for the giving of alms was that almsgiving would work for the salvation of the donor," and he finds it remarkable that "in all our literature, there is no clear attack on this calculus of good works."[25] Ideas of material and monetary divestment were bound up directly with a spiritual economy of placing treasure in heaven. We witness a direct merger and confluence of what one may be tempted to read as separate, or at best parallel, spheres: spirit and money. Inserting this dichotomy is akin to excluding *oikonomia*'s concrete, financial sense when assessing its lexical range and application. Actual practices of monetary economy and allotment had direct impact on the state of one's soul and one's eternal destiny. Giving and receiving real money influenced moral balances in the heavens. This is another way in which the economy proper of *oikonomia*—a focus on real goods, resources, and money—shaped ancient theology and church practice.

Such strong calls for monetary sacrifice were balanced with pragmatic needs. Most believers were not prepared to undertake these radical ascetic conversions of full divestment. Monasteries and convents were reserved for such elite and for certain adopted poor. Furthermore, many bishops encouraged ongoing, modest, and incremental giving by wealthy patrons as a way to sustain ecclesial communities, rather than large, one-time acts of total expenditure. The widespread, mundane, and popular acts of almsgiving may not have provided donors with the flare and glory of radical divestment, "[b]ut they retained the great images of the transfer of treasure from earth to heaven and of the preparation of heavenly mansions through regular almsgiving. These were much more to them than 'mere' metaphors . . . The constant use of the metaphor of 'treasure in heaven' charged the circulation of money, on all levels within the churches, with a touch of the glory of heaven."[26] In this way, monetary exchange was further sanctified and sacralized in its association with the salvific act of Christ and with its capacity to reenact such redemption for those who continued to give as he gave. Money was part of a very real circuit of exchange with the heavenly realm, and just as alms could be given on behalf of the dead to aid their journey to paradise, monetary tokens donated to the poor were transferred to a heavenly treasury of merits for the faithful giver.

We can discern here in this element of pastoral economy another seed or precursor of eventual governmentality. Not only does economic governance receive validation as divine praxis, as the form of power enacted by the Son as heavenly administrator, but, as we see now, such economic management is for the sake of salvation. All those who are needy are integrated into its circuits, and the economy is justified by its beneficence to all. Once imperial institutions become officially integrated into this almsgiving pattern under Constantine, the stage is set to construct state administrative channels for shepherding and managing lives and bodies in the purported interests of the governed. The benevolent ends of social, political, and economic salvation toward which this emerging governmental *oikonomia* is put may then justify whatever means are employed.

At both ends of the almsgiving economy, therefore, we find the divine economist. At one end, the heavenly manager is the one who is emulated, as donors give in the pattern of Christ and after the manner of the gracious cosmic benefactor. The example of the Son initiates the circuit of giving. At the other end, it is ultimately to Christ, to the heavenly steward, that these gifts are given, for donations to the poor pass on to God. God as the most faithful manager is entrusted to oversee and economize these heavenly treasuries for the sake of the faithful, ensuring the dividends and interest returned will profit to their salvation.

Stewarding the economy

Having retrieved the persistent financial and strategy-oriented valences in *oikonomia*, what further insights can be gained on the operator of such an economy? It was to such an agent that pastors and bishops appealed in their ministrations, and it was the generosity and philanthropy of this heavenly steward that the rich mimed in their quest for salvation. As Agamben draws attention to the political trope of a God who governs providentially, I want to access an economic trope and reconstruct a picture of the God who manages and arranges resources strategically and redemptively. Agamben does not explore the economic praxis of the Son as the Trinitarian person on whom government is modeled. Invoking the angels as bureaucratic ministers, he neglects the Son as governor and economist. Like Foucault, he does not dwell on the theological model—the divine person who undertakes this economic praxis—but focuses on *oikonomia* as a conceptual device in Trinitarian doctrine and governmental theory.

As we turn to the actual praxis of the divine administrator, Eusebius remains a key witness. He situates the Father and Son within his own clear conceptual distinction of reign and government in the deity, one that grounds Roman and Constantinian rule and administration. His depictions of the cosmic steward and economist will be important models for pastoral and imperial administration. Such ideas are integral to the wide-ranging, late antique transcript of pastoral power that is deployed ecclesially and imperially.

As is particularly emphasized in his *Oration*, Eusebius ascribes to the Father the role of supreme sovereign and highest God, while the Logos, albeit still divine, is called second in rank and designated as governor (1.2, 1.6). The Father is the origin of all and final seat of authority but has explicitly handed over the reins of governing and administering creation to the Son. For Eusebius, the Son of God, spoken of as a governor, is also a type of chief steward or administrator of the Father's kingdom. God's *oikonomia*, the divine management and steering of the world toward its good for divine glory, is overseen by that person of the godhead directly engaged with creation: the Son. The divine Son is set above and must deftly manage a vast cosmic economy.

Eusebius draws on a long-standing tradition of the role of the steward or administrator in classical and Christian thought. The terms used to designate stewardship and associated offices (*oikonomos* and *dioikêtês*) converge with financial and economic themes. The terms can be rendered "steward," "administrator," or even simply "businessman" and, in the Greco-Roman era, "more and more both *dioikein* ('to steward') and *dioikêsis* ('stewardship'), as well as other derived terms, came to be applied especially to financial administration, to the accounting of money, and to offices concerned with fiscal matters, as papyri and inscriptions particularly demonstrate."[27] The *oikonomos* was a common role, dispersed throughout Greece as well as later Hellenistic and Roman empires, so much so that the second-century Middle Platonic philosopher Numenius, who is cited by Eusebius, could speak off-handedly of "the proverbial *oikonomos* ('household manager' or 'economist')."[28]

In general, the responsibilities of an *oikonomos* or *dioikêtês* involved forms of delegated management of the resources or matters of a superior. The tasks assigned varied widely, but the role enjoyed at least a moderate amount of status that derived from the one represented. At times—especially with the term *dioikêtês*, which was sometimes ascribed to God to speak of divine administration—the sense of delegation or subordinate authority was muted. Indeed, while the Greco-Roman *oikonomos* came almost exclusively from the slave or freed classes, this managerial slave could achieve markedly high social status. When called to represent and manage the affairs of powerful masters or patrons, the steward or administrator partook of the master's prestige. Others wishing to do business with the master usually needed to deal with this steward, a fact lamented by upper class elites and possibly appreciated by slaves of lesser status.[29]

A particular arrangement of political power took place in Ptolemaic Egypt and persisted under Roman occupation, influencing Alexandria and its environs. Here the centralized and more autocratic rule of the Ptolemy gave rise to a single, supreme financial administrator (*dioikêtês*), subordinate only to the Ptolemy and given significant independence and rights of discretionary judgment. The *dioikêtês* reported infrequently to the emperor and may have on occasion been party to coups or other plots of overthrow. Arrivals of the *dioikêtês* into a local area were preceded by anxious preparation and ensconced in fanfare, outmatched only by visitations from the Ptolemy himself.[30] While in broader usage *dioikêtês* and *oikonomos* could be employed interchangeably, in this Ptolemaic schema *dioikêtês* designated the supreme financial administrator, while *oikonomoi* were stationed farther down the chain of command as more local-level administrators. "The whole system of administration with its many *oikonomoi* was thus familiar to all the people [in Ptolemaic Egypt], sometimes bitterly so. The *dioikêsis* or financial administration came directly into the lives of each of them . . ."[31]

The Ptolemy was ascribed divine status, as inscriptions of dedication by various *oikonomoi* reveal. His supreme administrator arguably shared at least a portion of the divine penumbra, as an intermediary or demigod carrying out this reign through the central tasks of (financial) governance. Considered in light of the eventual fusion of offices in Trinitarian economy, such that Father and Son represent imperial reign and bureaucratic administration, respectively, homologies between the *dioikêtês* and the Son are imaginable. At the very least, tropes of imperial, quasi-divine economic stewardship as an extension of kingly reign were certainly part of this Hellenistic context, particularly in Alexandria, which would become a determinative theological center. This set of conceptual tropes, so culturally pervasive, may have been a point of influence for later Christian theology. The category of steward or administrator (*oikonomos, dioikêtês*) invites consideration as potentially applicable to the Son.

As John Reumann asserts, "it was a pagan commonplace to speak of the οἰκονομία τοῦ θεοῦ, with Zeus, fate, nature, or reason as the administrator. Usually God was spoken of as διοικητής, not οἰκονόμος, because of the servile connotations which the latter term had come to have."[32] Philo and Epictetus use the term *oikodespotês* to describe God "as master of the world household."[33] In emerging Christian parlance, we find examples of *oikonomos* attributed to Christ from the Acts of Thomas, Peter, and Philip.[34] In terms of christological references, Irenaeus refers to the Son as a manager or dispenser (*dispensator*) of the Father's grace (*Against Heresies* 4.20.7). Clement appears to follow the pagan precedent of speaking of God as *dioikêtês* rather than *oikonomos*. Origen speaks of God as "the one, only, best administrator [of souls] (*eis monos oikonomos aristos*)" (*First Principles* 3.1.14), and Basil the Great was fond of calling God "the wise Manager (οἰκονόμος) of our life" (*Epistles* 263.1).[35]

Christian scriptural tradition is less explicit. While no direct application of the title of *oikonomos* is made to Christ, what one does find are tropes of stewardship. Moses and Jesus play the role of stewards performing service to God (Heb 3:1–6), and the apocalyptic image of Christ (Rev 3:7) holding keys and possessing authority has been taken as an antitype to the figure of Eliakim, the king's steward in Isaiah (Is 22:20–22).[36] Furthermore, the *oikodespotês*, or master of the house, in the so-called stewardship parables (e.g., Luke 12:39; Matt 13:27) is usually interpreted as a divine or messianic figure. Furthermore, Matthew (13:37) explicitly identifies the housemaster as the messianic Son of Man.[37]

The very common notion of pastoral leadership as stewardship of the flock also takes its cue from Christ as the chief steward. Here shepherd and economist converge. Ignatius of Antioch, in his letter to the Ephesians, provides a link between these themes and ecclesial leadership:

"Let a man respect an ἐπίσκοπος. For everyone whom the Master of the household (οἰκοδεσπότης) sends for his own household management (or administration, οἰκονομία), we ought thus receive as the Sender himself" (*Epistle to the Ephesians* 6.1).[38] Here a clear connection is made between the ideal of the supreme heavenly administrator and the pastor as the reduplicative representative and economist.

After his exhaustive survey of the presence of *oikonomia, oikonomos,* and related terms in early Christian literature, Reumann concludes:

> There is seemingly enough evidence to claim that we can speak of an overlooked, if minor, title in Christology, Jesus as οἰκονόμος θεοῦ. In sense the term relates to titles like δοῦλος [slave, servant], παῖς [child, servant], and υἱός [son], in that it emphasizes service and obedience. There are also connections to ἀπόστολος and to the idea of commissioning as an agent or representative of God, with his authority . . . Usage of οἰκοδεσπότης, ὁ οἰκονομῶν, and διοικητής for God the Father may have acted as a barrier on their application to the Son. However, enough such reflections survive in scattered passages to justify us in speaking of Christ as οἰκονόμος in the Father's οἰκονομία.[39]

This minority report in christological terminology helps to flesh out the conceptual picture of the Son as a divine administrator, dispensing and managing the riches and resources of the Father's kingdom. When considered in terms of the kenotic downward mobility of the Son in the incarnation, the humble or servile connotations align with this heavenly steward taking on the "form of a slave" (Phil 2:7). It is such a set of scattered images that Eusebius appears to activate in his coalescing picture of the Logos as God's economist.

The divine economist

According to Eusebius, the Son received from the Father the charge of superintending creation and specifically extending divine reign. The Son is thus a steward, administrator, or economist in the sense of purposeful and orderly management of resources. It is the Logos "who is in fact the Framer and Organizer of the universe, being Only-Begotten of God, whom the Maker of the universe, the One beyond and above all existence, Himself begetting of Himself, ordained Captain and Pilot of this universe" (*On Christ's Sepulcher* 11.11). In the position of the sovereign, the

Father stands outside and supports the governed sphere, indeed creating it by exclusion, for the world necessarily exists in a space that is not-God. The Logos-Son is a "kind of unbroken bond . . . bridging the chasms and not allowing them to fall too far apart" (*On Christ's Sepulcher* 12.7). The Logos provides the link between the Father and creation and instantiates the reign of the Father through delegated, representative governance in the immanent sphere. Because the Logos is divine, God is present in creation while, paradoxically, standing utterly outside it through radical, transcendent difference. The Logos is thus the present absence, the governance that makes distant sovereignty real. He undertakes "contact with this universe, and now directs and turns it by an incorporeal and divine power" (*On Christ's Sepulcher* 11.12).

In his ordered governance of creation, furthermore, the Logos possesses a "treasury" or "storehouse" (*thêsauron*) of goods, from which he provides for the cosmos. In his *Theophany*, Eusebius writes of the Logos as the source of structure and the all-pervading logic (as Logos) to the universe. The Logos sustains the realm with his resources:

So likewise the Word of God, the King of all, He who is extended throughout all, is in and pervades all that is both in the heavens and the earth; He is the governor of the things which are invisible and visible, and He directs by powers unspeakable the Sun, the Heavens, and the whole Universe. He is present to all things in His effectuating power; and He remains throughout all. He also makes to distil as rain, from His own resources, the never-failing light to the Sun, the Moon, and the Stars. He has established, and perpetually holds fast, the heavens as an image of his own greatness. He also fills from the treasury that is with Him, those hosts of Angels and Powers of intelligent and rational spirits, at once with life, light, wisdom, and all the abundance of every species of beauty and of goodness. And by one and the same effectuating art, He never fails to supply substance to the material elements, and to Bodies their commixture and concurrence; their forms, appearances, and characters. (*Theophany* 1.34)[40]

The Logos is thus seen as a generous administrator or manager, ensuring the steady functioning of creation by giving of his own goods. He is the source of a certain abundance, whether of resources to perpetuate a prescribed function (e.g., light for the sun), goods to fulfill purpose (e.g., wisdom for rational beings), or provision to enable existence (e.g., form and content to material bodies). To be sure, the Logos is depicted as gracious and generous, abundantly supplying to all what is needed for their proper function and flourishing. Yet such a gracious economy functions seamlessly with a structure of authority and regulation, for the Logos sustains the order over which he is supreme and shapes it according to his pattern, which he in turn has received from the sovereign God.

Eusebius ties together themes of governance, economic management, and resource provision with the idea of salvation in an early work, *Against Hierocles*. He invokes the order and limits established in the universe, a logic reflecting the good governance of the creator. One purpose of this divine economy is to convey and bestow blessing and support to creation and to the redeemed. The Logos is "lord of the entire economy (*tês oikonomias apasês kurios*) and of gifts of grace (*charitôn*)" who will "bestow plenteously an illumination as it were of the light which streams from him, and will dispatch the most intimate of his own messengers from time to time, for the salvation and succor of men here below" (*Against Hierocles* 6).[41]

Eusebius here ties *oikonomia*, as strategic and gracious management, to material blessing and exchange. Stewardship of a divine economy thus has as a central component the provision for those who look to God in hope. Not only does the Logos dispense economic goods upon creation in general, but it gives additional benefits to those who look to God for resources—the central one being God in Christ, afforded through the incarnation. Like coins circulating the imperial image while simultaneously benefiting their users, incarnation brings the image of God, the Logos, into the immanent sphere of creation for its blessing.

Constantine also finds a place in this economy of redemptive provision for creation as governed by the Logos. In introducing the *Life of Constantine*, Eusebius proclaims that "God the universal Saviour of all, who has stored up (*tamieusamenos*) benefits beyond mortal imagination for the lovers of true piety, gives even here as a first installment [or down payment] (*proarrabônizetai*) a foretaste of his rewards, somehow guaranteeing immortal hopes to mortal eyes" (1.3.3). Here the emperor can be seen in taking up the mantle of Christ, for Eusebius also uses such monetary language in reference to the Son's preincarnate theophanies to faithful Israelites. In appearing, the Son gives a "first installment (*proarrabônizomenos*) of the salvation that should come through him to all" (*Demonstration of the Gospel* 5.13). In language extolling Constantine as a first fruit of divine salvation, language that commentators note "is of money and banking," Eusebius depicts God as possessing and bestowing monetarily inflected spiritual goods upon the faithful.[42] Provision and blessing are passed on to the church and world through Constantine, a move made possible by the prior passing on of such goods from Father to Son. The Son as governor has been entrusted with the role of governance as well as with the divine resources to regulate the kingdom.

In his *Ecclesiastical Theology*, Eusebius describes the act of the Father handing over "all things" to the Son. He proclaims that "the Son, however, received them *like a faithful keeper of a deposit*, and accepted them, not as a word that is without being and non-subsistent, but as one who is truly a Son, only begotten and beloved of the Father" (1.20.v).[43] This assertion arises in the course of his defense of the Son as fully divine and yet as a distinct *hypostasis* not to be collapsed with the identity of the Father. Here Eusebius emphasizes that it makes little sense to speak of entrusting the goods of the cosmos to another if that other is either a nonentity or completely the same as the one entrusting. The Son has true and distinct identity and can therefore receive the task of governance. Remarkably, Eusebius ties the act of receiving a deposit to an argument about defined identity, allowing the role of the steward to stabilize and theologically authenticate the personhood of the Son. The economy of resource transfer provides a basis for asserting the Son's divine identity and the financially marked role of steward proves instrumental in making key theological claims in Trinitarian theology.

The Son fulfills the role of ideal steward and administrator as one who takes the reins of governance, yet does so in perfect conformity to the one who hands them over. By speaking of a "deposit," Eusebius at once signals the value and worth of what is handed over, describes the act of delegation as one of economic stewardship, and draws on images of economic administration, such as a royal treasury. The Son, as an administrator of the king's wealth, receives, safeguards, and multiplies the value of the goods contained in the Father's realm—in this case, creation. Eusebius here mobilizes the claims of the stewardship parables in the gospel narratives, where the "good and faithful servant" is the one who invests and multiplies the master's talents and so receives approval (Matt 25:14–30; Luke 19:12–27).

In these forgoing instances, Eusebius makes noteworthy connections between the divine governance and administration of the Logos and the language of wealth and resource provision. The governor is like one with a storehouse of material goods from which he gives generously to support the function and flourishing of his governed territory. Money, the chief good of any ancient royal treasury, here functions as a central implicit trope for that which is doled out to pervade, infuse, and empower the kingdom, circulating among subjects to the glory of the issuing center. Theological and political models coincide here with the claim that the ideal sovereign and exemplary administrator should provide for the ruled and seek to sustain subjects within a governed territory. The state administrative apparatus here receives divine legitimation for a program that uses economic channels and monetary exchange to benefit the populace.

Superseding *demiurgic* economy

Eusebius's marked distinction between the reign of the Father and the governance of the Son traded on a wider cultural imaginary that made clear distinctions between these roles. In particular, Christian doctrines of the Son of God were worked out in competition with, cooptation of, and contradistinction to ideas of the demiurge circulating in various Middle Platonic and gnostic traditions. The demiurge was typically ascribed a secondary status of divinity, having been charged with the work of creation and redemption, for "the First God is free from work of all kinds and is king."[44] This secondary figure was often maligned and viewed with suspicion for its interactions with the vulgar material world.

In considering the gnostic demiurge, Erik Peterson observes that "from the thesis that God reigns as king but does not actually rule may be drawn the Gnostic conclusion that the sovereignty of God is truly good, but the regime of the Demiurge (or demiurgic 'Powers,' usually seen as officials) is bad: in other words the regime is always wrong."[45] Since goodness resides with God alone, the identity and activities of the gnostic semi-divine administrator, as engaged with fallen matter and as charged with bringing order and submission in creation, fall into disfavor. According to Peterson, such gnostic reasoning means that government and administrative intervention in the lives of the governed are thus painted in a negative hue.

Christian realignment of such activities under the auspices of the Son effectively retrieves and redeems these associated theopolitical notions. In his description of the work of the Logos, Eusebius converts demiurgic activity to that of the Son, now construed as fully divine and as part of the unified, Trinitarian godhead (*On Christ's Sepulcher* 11.8, 11.10). Typically denigrated activities associated with the demiurge thus begin to acquire the prestige of divine sanction. Engagement with the matter of creation is no longer a cause for dishonor. Neither is it disparaging to function as a delegated governor, for God undertakes both activities directly. In Christ, God is both materially engaged and a delegated *oikonomos*.

The esteem brought to governmental administration through association with the Logos of God may thus contribute to a growing tradition of empowerment and proliferation of bureaucratic authority. In other words, not only is sovereignty of central importance as an object of honor and inquiry, but government administration also takes on newfound force and social significance since it, too, is associated with divine activity. This can certainly be seen in the development of ecclesial hierarchy and its concomitant bureaucratic channels, which come to serve as models for the state; indeed, such structures are in turn in continual interchange with state political institutions, with each informing the other as model. Agamben's relegation of such bureaucratic offices to the angelic realm rather than to the auspices of the Son misses the significance of this Christian political tradition of sacralization of government.

The economic implications of this transition from disparaged demiurge to honored Son are also important. Eusebius associates the "World-Creating Logos" with a long tradition of demiurge as master craftsman, critiquing pagans for worshiping creation and giving it "credit for the mastery of the craftsman" (*On Christ's Sepulcher* 11.8). Part of the gnostic denigration of the demiurge may stem from the ambivalent status of the artisan and craftsman in Platonic tradition.[46] *Dêmiourgos* may denote an artisan or handworker, while also indicating at times a magistrate or high official in the city. In the *Timaeus*, Plato's demiurge is a craftsman who fashions the world out of various materials, while in *Cratylus* the demiurge is also a lawgiver. Plato's well-known scorn for artists and exclusion of such craftsmen from the ideal republic is here counterbalanced with a salutary association with law and order. That the Middle Platonic demiurge occupies a space between honor and dishonor may partake of this ambivalent legacy. Such duality also foreshadows depictions of the Son both as the *origin*, architect, and firstborn of creation and as the Logos—the rational, ordering, and *legal* principle of the created order.[47]

From pastoral to imperial governance

In Eusebius's vision, the Logos governs the cosmos as an economic manager, leading it to the profits of salvation while also supplying it with all the necessary support from the heavenly treasury to function and flourish. With the blending of pastoral and economic themes, shepherd and steward coincide. Like the shepherd, this image of the divine steward and economic administrator offers a framework for bishops. It is a paradigm for pastoral power, as leaders oversee their flocks and manage very real church resources. Yet, for Eusebius, this trope also applies to the emperor who, now as a Christian leader of a territory devoted to God, assumes attributes of pastoral power. Eusebius merges themes of pastoral oversight with concrete resource management in the figure of the Logos, who is also, we must remember, thoroughly politicized as a heavenly governor delegated by the sovereign Father and ruler of all.

The shepherd theme, to which Foucault devoted attention, should thus be assessed alongside this image of steward or administrator, a role that Foucault recognizes in his turn to the language of economy but whose symbolic and theological systems he did not explore. God, bishop, and eventually emperor are seen as shepherds leading a flock, from which Foucault distills facets of governmentality such as individualized and totalized observation, relations of obedience, postures of vicarious sacrifice, and the management of both conscience and bodily life. Likewise, the economic coimplication of God and bishop, as overseers and managers of a strategic arrangement of goods that benefit the flock, can be applied in modulated fashion to the figure of the emperor. Governmentality as homologue to pastoral power, then, is also about economic stewardship and the management of goods and resources, as well as the extension of rule and discipline through monetized modes of representation. It is no wonder that governmentality emerges as the irruption of *economy* into politics.

The position of bishop as *oikonomos* is integral to his role as a representative of Christ. Called both to shepherd and to steward the flock and its resources, the bishop, like the heavenly administrator, oversees the valuable goods of human souls while also dealing with material resources. Pastoral stewardship of funds is one mode of protection for the flock and is integrated into one's duties as shepherd. It merges seamlessly with the overall work of an *oikonomia* of souls, managing spiritual and material goods in the interests of salvation. Such management of resources comes to a head in the early church around the fate of the poor and the spiritual and economic battles that emerge concerning the righteous use of resources. When this rhetorical topos enters the public sphere and becomes an imperial duty, pastoral economy collides with imperial governance.

The significance of imperial conformity to the pattern of "love of the poor" for late antique social transformation, in Brown's analysis, cannot be overstated. The conversion of Constantine "dramatically altered" the scope and orientation of this practice. "It was no longer a fiercely inward-looking matter, directed to the needs of the faithful alone. 'Love of the poor' became a public virtue, which bishops and clergymen were expected to demonstrate, in return for public privileges."[48] Through Constantine, with his (self-)designation as "bishop to those outside" (Eusebius of Caesarea, *Life of Constantine* 4.24), we witness beginnings of a transfer—with its attendant modifications—of the ideal of bishop as protector of the poor into the political realm. Constantine provided state funding for churches, connecting them to the infrastructure of imperial administration. As churches attempted to maintain ideological and theological independence while submitting to the emperor as God's vicegerent, money was one tie that bound both spheres together.

In giving from his imperial treasury, Constantine also participated in the dynamics of almsgiving as they structured late antique social practice. In a sense, he committed the state to the rhetorical logic and theological vision of donating money in exchange for blessings and salvation. Whereas it was initially wealthy private citizens who were invited to shed their monetary burdens and pass through the eye of the needle, the state under Christian rule subsequently assumed a new posture of *philanthropia*.

Just as all disciples with means were called to imitate divine philanthropy and be benefactors for Christian brethren and eventually for any poor and marginalized, here the state began to take on an institutional image of benefactor after the manner of God, bishops, and wealthy Christians.

The theology of the Logos as administrator and steward, while crucial in providing a model for pastoral duty, is thus also bound up with the person and role of the emperor and with wider political and administrative practices such as the management of resources and money. Although pastoral power "remains distinct from political power . . . the intertwining of pastoral and political power will in fact be an historical reality throughout the West."[49] In the case of giving and benefaction, both the old civic ideal of provision for the public good and the emerging Christian ideal of caring for the poor and marginalized operate together in complex fashion. We see a meshing of two principles, not the displacement of one by the other.

With regard to care of the poor and the experience of imperial graces, theological motifs are discernible from the perspective of the populace. The empire was perceived as close, with officials and representatives painfully present throughout its territories, and bureaucratic apparatuses permeating daily life.[50] Nevertheless, both God and emperor were regarded as transcendent, distant, and removed from daily realities yet ever willing to dispense benefits and grace.[51] Incarnation as a sign of divine condescension, mercy, and radical presence contributed to a sense of solidarity and belief that the emperor in his distant greatness nevertheless could and would deign to have mercy on those who appealed to him:

> It was a decisive change. Slowly, over the course of the fourth and fifth centuries, the relation between the emperor and his subjects, and between the different classes of society became tinged with a new *pathos* generated within the Christian church. The relations between the believer and God, between subject and emperor, and between the weak and the powerful came to be swallowed up by a single, elemental image—the image of the relation between the poor and the rich and powerful to whom the poor "cried out" not only for alms but for justice and protection.[52]

If Brown is right to give this theme such prominence, the economic and managerial senses of the steward, the *oikonomos*, should hold pride of place as a heuristic for assessing the emergence and transmission of pastoral power. To the theme of shepherd, then, we must add the economic steward and administrator. An effort to trace its sociopolitical potency must involve attention to the theological realm, to the sacred images and ideals that fueled and legitimated the practices of bishops and emperors.

What Eusebius gives us, therefore, in scattered glimpses and passing images is a sense of the divine Logos as an administrative governor over and type of currency within a providential economy. The Logos brings order to the cosmos, managing it according to divine purposes and administering the various resources and goods that enable creation's fulfillment of such purposes. The Logos resembles in part an administrator of an imperial treasury, using resources in the task of good governance of the ruled space. Just as the Logos brings and, in a sense, *is* law and order, this divine governor provides and, in a sense, *is* the sustaining material goods for creation and the kingdom. And while there can be many goods, the chief possession of an imperial treasury and the central element used both to supply and order an economy is money.

In Constantine, we see the transfer of the ideal of bishop as protector of the poor into the political realm. The model of the divine steward and benefactor informs this role theologically. Such a divine model is likewise shaped politically as theologians project earthly ideals onto the heavenly focal point. As we will see, Eusebius looks from Constantine to heaven, projecting imperial attributes onto the Logos. His gaze then returns to earth, transferring ideals from this glorious, heavenly governor and economist back to the emperor and his administration. In this double movement and ongoing dialectic, it is impossible to decide which comes first. Furthermore, no doubt Constantine, as a new "political bishop" to the poor, shapes ecclesial self-presentation even as he in turn seeks to emulate the bishops. Pastoral practice will thus come to modulate in imitation of, in competition with, and in distinction from the new Christian emperor's role of benefactor and *oikonomos*.

As the next chapter considers, Eusebius depicts Constantine, after the manner of both God the Father and the Logos-Son, as generously dispensing wealth and caring for the needs of all. Just as the Son, as governor and steward, mediates and conveys the Father's reign and resources to all of creation, so Constantine is charged with reigning over and managing Christian empire in the image of the reign and governance of the Father and Son. Sovereign authority, delegated governance, and material resource management thus combine in complex ways in the figure of the emperor and his administration.

Surpassing bishops, Constantine has the privilege of representing himself in the material realm with his image on coins, modeling the Father's own economic self-representation in the world through the Son. He also exerts sovereignty over a delegated arm of ministers and bureaucrats who apply his policies among the populace, effectively stewarding an economy of citizens. In this case, the ancient civic and the Christian ideals meet, for Constantine is presented as championing the public good and the flourishing of the entire empire even as he is understood as protector and chief benefactor of the church and poor. Constantine's beneficence is showered upon all who look to him for leadership and protection even as a special portion goes to the materially poor, particularly through church treasuries. The translocation of the bishop trope into the political sphere thus disperses the sense of obligation to the poor more broadly and complicates it through political institutional ties.

A significant transformation in late antiquity thus occurs when pastoral governance—inspired by the heavenly steward and manager—irrupts into the political. To be sure, this is not the governmentality that Foucault documents in early modernity, but we can observe that central tenets of pastoral power manifest themselves here and exert influence upon the political realm. Motivated by the Christian ideal of benefaction and care for the poor—an ideal funded theologically by God's concern for the world and for the poor in particular, by divine management of cosmic resources, and by Christ's outpouring and self-sacrifice as a form of payment on behalf of humanity—bishops and emperors follow suit. In this developing Christian society, protogovernmentality, as pastoral activity that mirrors the activity of the divine economist, continually interrupts the political sphere and shapes it in novel ways.

3

The Emperor's Righteous Money

As we saw in Eusebius's coordination of Roman empire with the incarnation, political and economic circumstances disclose divine realities. Eusebius offers a clear glimpse of the theopolitical zone, the conceptual and rhetorical blurring of theological and political spheres. In his writings about Emperor Constantine, the parallels and convergences between political and theological ideas of sovereign reign and governance are displayed clearly. Inasmuch as God is the authorizer of Constantine's reign, the emperor's earthly government provides clues as to what the divine kingdom is like and the manner in which the heavenly sovereign rules from above.[1]

Also evident, yet largely ignored, is Eusebius's attention to monetary and economic themes in Constantine's rule. Monetary economic practices inform his understanding of the emperor's government and in turn become influential in his theological project. According to Eusebius, Constantine's imperial management includes impartial financial dealings, righteous governance through monetary administration, and generosity to all. Because of the correspondences among Constantine, God, and the Logos, claims made about Constantine's financial administration reverberate back upon ideas of authority and governance of the Father and Son. An image of Constantine as ideal ruler, which includes monetization and resource management, in turn reflects the Son's cosmic administration of the Father's kingdom.

We considered how bishops enacted pastoral power in part after the model of the divine economist. Such *oikonomia* included generosity to the poor and focus on almsgiving, as well as the precise and just allotment of resources. Constantine takes up this charge and fulfills obligations of generosity and philanthropy through management of money and resources. Monetary economy also becomes an acceptable way for the emperor to exert influence and power, communicating to subjects via coin imagery, for instance, and demarcating the scope of acceptable exchanges within his realm. Just as the Father is represented in the world through the Son, Constantinian coinage represents aspects of the emperor's identity to his subjects, facilitating their very submission in the process. As the Son apportions the Father's resources generously, so the emperor and his administrative servants allocate imperial resources for the benefit of his people. As the Father and Son accomplish spiritual victory over demons through redemptive transactions and gracious philanthropy to needy humankind, so Constantine overcomes tyrannical, hoarding opponents through his generous use of wealth.

Eusebius as witness to and theologian of Constantine's reign thus provides a rhetorically crafted depiction of the emperor as enacting godly economy. The aim here is not (simply) to illustrate what happened historically or determine whether these scenes are accurate, but to reconstruct the image and template provided by Eusebius, which is informed by a theology of the divine governor and administrator. Eusebius offers an emerging theory not only of Christian kingship and empire but of its economic administration. As bishops and future emperors look to this model and perform their own mimetic praxis of economic governance, they in turn provide concrete examples and points of reflection for subsequent theological projections about God's management of heavenly affairs, contributing to a historical material dialectic between theological models and sociopolitical practice.

Eusebius was a great compiler and synthesizer who integrated a vast set of ideas and literary techniques from Greco-Roman tradition, which he preserved and adapted strategically for his apologetic purposes. He thus gives us a glimpse into how economic and monetary themes from prior intellectual tradition and social practice are conveyed into theological discourse. Furthermore, his adaptation of tradition to fit with his understanding of Scripture and coalescing Christian thought demonstrates the transformations of monetary themes as they are deployed in his Christology and political theology. His corpus provides us with a critical view into how theological and monetary economies interact and influence each other, contributing to the broader legacy of Christian theopolitics. This symbolic economy of money in Eusebian discourse reflects the milieu in which his foundational doctrine was undergoing formation, evincing the presence of monetary logic in his ideas that would in turn influence much Christian thought. Through Eusebius, Constantine functions as one crucial nexus for integrating monetary economy into emerging Christian doctrines of economic governance, both political and divine.

Constantine and correspondence

In the thought of Eusebius, many predicates of Constantine are applicable to God, and vice versa. Indeed, a certain *communicatio idiomatum* exists between assertions about Constantine's reign and the more originary sovereignty of the Father and Son.[2] Constantine mirrors both Father and Son, and so reflects elements of both sovereign reign and delegated governance, which remain conceptually distinct in Eusebius's developing Trinitarian discourse. His attention to Constantine's monetary economy offers clues about how his model of the Son as governor and administrator may be inflected with monetary themes.

Much has been made of Eusebius's apparently unswerving support for and legitimation of Constantine as the first Christian emperor. Erik Peterson famously made Eusebius the centerpiece of his argument about the failures of Christian political theology, citing the purported close correlation Eusebius makes between God and emperor.[3] It is in the context of Peterson's treatise that the distinction between reign and governance, imported from French political theory (*le roi règne, mais il ne gouverne pas*), comes to be applied to early Christian thought. It is Peterson's language that Giorgio Agamben takes up explicitly in exploring reign and governance in the Christian godhead. While there are notable flaws in Peterson's argumentation and dismissal of Eusebius, his observance of this dual dynamic in the bishop's thought and in other Hellenistic theopolitical literature appears quite accurate.[4]

Eusebius draws Constantine into relation with and correspondence to both the Father and the Son or Logos, differentiating the dynamics of reign and governance that are at work. There are ways in which Constantine manifests the sovereignty and authority of the Father, being christened "Autokrator" and "Victor," and having "modeled himself after the archetypal form of the Supreme Sovereign" (*Oration* 5.4). He also follows the delegation and administrative governance of the Logos. Constantine "pilots affairs below with an upward gaze, to steer by the archetypal form," for it is the Logos "who directs His Father's kingdom for all those under and beneath Him" (*Oration* 3.5–6). Constantine, furthermore, carries on the work of the Logos, bringing it into deeper material and historical fruition (*Oration* 5.1, 6.21). As such, he supports and fulfills a process begun with incarnation, and he is not merely an afterthought or extraneous agent but is critical in the extension of divine reign on earth. Due to his direct legitimation from the Father and complementary work as another "prefect" (*hyparchos*) in relation to the Logos-Son (*Oration* 3.6, 7.13), Constantine assumes a paradoxical position both subordinate to and equal with the Logos. An intimate "triadic relation" is effectively established.[5]

Because he is structurally integral to divine administration, attributes of Constantine's own reign and governance reflect back upon and reveal the nature of God's rule. Not only can we recount characteristics of the Father and the Logos and expect to see them in Constantine, but, starting with Constantine as a historical manifestation of divine rule, we can extrapolate his attributes back onto his heavenly King and Governor. This movement from emperor to God is also why, for Eusebius, God does not simply legitimate and prove Constantine, but Constantine's authority in turn proves and legitimates the truth of God.[6] Themes made prominent by Eusebius in the life and rule of the first Christian emperor thus offer windows onto what God is like and how divine reign and governance are performed on both cosmic and earthly stages.

Furthermore, the depictions of the emperor in the *Oration* and *Life of Constantine* offer idealized portraits and invoke a divine pattern.[7] The *Life of Constantine*, for instance, has been theorized as a *Fürstenspiegel*, or "mirror for princes," written as a leadership training manual for Constantine's sons.[8] Concerned to perpetuate Christian virtues in the transition of power, Eusebius understandably provides an idealized image of the standard to which these young rulers are called. If it departs from historical exactitude in reporting Constantine's acts, it does so to uphold a particular pattern as established, in Eusebius's view, by the Logos. Similarly, the oration praising the emperor quite possibly functions to remind Constantine of and hold him to the standard of the Logos, and thus presents a kind of ideal image of Christian imperial rule.

Because Eusebius offers a formal imperial portrait articulating theopolitical ideals, correlations can be drawn between Constantine—or any Christian emperor—and the Logos. Indeed, they are part of the textual logic and *must* be drawn. The Logos provides the pattern and image for such rule, and Eusebius openly acknowledges his selective rhetoric as he inserts stylized data from Constantine's life and rule to support the correlation. The very aims and structure of the *Life of Constantine* and the *Oration* set forth a conceptual system that mingles divine and political rule. Drawing correspondences between heavenly and earthly spheres is therefore not only appropriate but necessary. Failing to do so misses the point of the texts.

Constantine imitates both Father and Logos, so his rule in turn reflects their characteristics and techniques of governance. By extension, Constantine's entire state administrative apparatus, as a facet of his rule, receives divine legitimation and exhibits correspondence. Eusebius makes this clear in a telling passage, where Constantine addresses his governing administrators: "Testifying in plain words he announced to them that he would give an account to God of their activities; for the God over all had given him sovereignty over things on earth, and he in imitation of the Supreme had committed particular administrative regions of the Empire to them; all however would in due course be subject to scrutiny of their actions by the Great King" (*Life of Constantine* 4.29.4). Here Constantine is depicted as supreme sovereign after the pattern of the Father, while his administration assumes a structural parallel to the Logos. Just as the Father has delegated governance of the kingdom and creation to the Son, so Constantine delegates and empowers his governors and subordinates. In this way, the emperor and his entire administration receive divine sanction, and the practices and institutions inherent in bureaucratic administration bear the mark of the Logos. As we will see, monetary economy is a critical aspect of such governance, again bringing Christology and money into correlation.

Money, piety, and imperial representation

A central function of money in Eusebius's political theology is to provide a conceptual basis for Constantine's role as representative and image
of God. Like many church fathers, Eusebius employs the imperial image
as an aid in understanding the imaging of the Father by the Son: just as
honoring the image of the emperor passes on such honor to the emperor
himself, so to worship the Son is to worship the Father (*Ecclesiastical Theology* 2.7; see also 2.23).[9] The imperial image is more than a mere rhetorical device for presenting the relation of the Son to the Father. It evokes the
fundamental chain of authoritative representation between Father, Son,
and emperor, one that patristic thinkers argue is ontological. In employing it, Eusebius not only legitimates as commonsense the practice of honoring the imperial image, but he binds it integrally to an understanding of
the Son's representation of the Father. Just as we grasp something of the
reign and sovereignty of the Father through Constantine's rule, we can
discern aspects of the representational authority of the Son (and, by complex derivation, Constantine's own authority) through the prevalence of
imperial images throughout governed territory that function as they did
in the stead of the emperor.

Constantine's coinage serves for Eusebius as an entry point into
forging a political theology of rule. Eusebius demonstrates keen sensitivity
to the use of money in furthering the interests of imperial representation,
as well as how the power and worth of both money and image can be
mutually reinforcing. Eusebius is attuned to the use emperors make of
coinage to convey aspects of their identity and reign, effectively communicating with and shaping subjects in the process of governance. Eusebian
reflection on the monetary economy of God's chief political representative
is thus a crucial facet of the interconnections between divine governance
and monetary economy.

Seeking to make the case for Constantine's authentic piety, as he
does throughout the *Life of Constantine*, Eusebius speaks to the emperor's
minting practices: "The great strength of the divinely inspired faith fixed
in his soul might be deduced by considering also the fact that he had his
own portrait so depicted on the gold coinage that he appeared to look
upwards in the manner of one reaching out to God in prayer. Impressions

of this type were circulated throughout the entire Roman world" (*Life of Constantine* 4.15.1–2). This rich passage raises questions about the use of money as a communication mechanism and form of propaganda. It also signals directly the potent and complex relationship between money and the image, highlighting the significance of religious imagery on coinage in particular. Eusebius, both explicitly and also drawing on implied and inherited tradition, invokes the importance of coining practices for supporting sovereign reign and governance, highlighting money's capacity to shape belief and instantiate rule. He also uses these monetary dynamics to fashion theological principles validating the role of the emperor. What we glimpse in Constantine's coinage, claims Eusebius, is both the character of the emperor as pious and the nature of his rule as subjected to God and aimed at spreading belief. Eusebius also endorses the practice of using coinage by the imperial center to communicate and enforce a message. He affirms its propagandistic or empire-persuasive functions in the service of proclaiming a message of subjection to God and, crucially, God's emperor.[10]

Esteem, character, honor, and coin imagery converge as Eusebius recounts Constantine's honoring of his mother, Helena. Here Eusebius lauds the emperor's filial and hence religious piety. Constantine's fidelity is demonstrated by his promotion of Helena to the rank of *Augusta Imperatrix* and his stamping of her portrait on gold coinage (*Life of Constantine* 3.47.2). Yet it is noteworthy that these decisions are a culmination of a series of acts of and attributes seen in Helena that are marked, in Eusebian discourse, by monetary and economic language. Empowered by her son with imperial authority, which included, significantly, power (*exousian*) over and the right to manage (*dioikein*) the imperial treasuries, Helena's life is characterized by Eusebius as one of material generosity: "She showered countless gifts upon the citizen bodies of every city, and privately to each of those who approached her; and she made countless distributions also to the ranks of the soldiery with magnificent hand. She made innumerable gifts to the unclothed and unsupported poor, to some making gifts of money (*chrêmatôn doseis*), to others abundantly supplying what was needed to cover the body" (*Life of Constantine* 3.44). She lived her life in this way because "she made it her business to pay (*apodounai*) what piety owed (*chreos*) to the all-sovereign God" (*Life of Constantine* 3.42.1). In such acts she "shone brilliantly (*lamprunomenê*)," adorning churches with "shining treasures (*lamprois*)," while remaining true and humble in her devotion to God. Eusebius shows himself a veritable monetary wordsmith, exulting in the symbolic economy of coinage as he lauds the empress, all the while allowing the language of money and precious metals to inflect his prose.

Before departing this world, Helena "bequeath[ed] to each of her issue part of her estate, everything she possessed in the whole world" (*Life of Constantine* 3.45–46.1). Eusebius clearly depicts her as an ideal administrator or steward over both imperial funds and her own resources. Because of this *oikonomia*, she "reaped the due reward" in passing to the next life, having already received "a good reward from God even in this present life" (*Life of Constantine* 3.43.5). Her prudent management included generosity to the needy and financial support of the church, all done under the auspices of rendering debt to God and made possible by Constantine's delegated authority. Reflecting on the coinage of Constantine, Eusebius is led to a discourse on godly management of resources. He demonstrates the close interweaving of monetary and religious ideas of profit, as each serves to reinforce and further the other. Both contribute to an image of the ideal character of one in authority, called to steward material and spiritual resources in the civic space. For Eusebius, Constantine's coinage conveys Helena's attributes to the populace.

In singling out the imperial mother and her role as a just and generous steward, Eusebius may also be invoking an implicit theology of the matron. As Dotan Leshem recounts, this subtext in patristic thought deployed the gendering of household relations in *oikonomia* as a theological trope: the submission of the wife to the husband evoked human submission to God.[11] This model drew on a long history of Greek reflection on ideal household relations between husband and wife, and coincided with the Hebrew scriptural exaltation of the ideal wife (Prov 31:10–31), one who demonstrates fruitful management of household resources and contributes toward household gain. Implicated in this model for Christians, as well, and often explicitly gendered, is the Son's submission to the Father as *oikonomos*, steward, and governor. The matron, or mother of the house, thus emerges as an ideal trope of discipleship, as Christians arrange themselves in submission to God as *oikodespotês*, or master of the house, yet still in positions of responsible delegation and management. By dwelling on Constantine's mother, her exaltation on coinage, and her deft management of material economy for the blessings of others, Eusebius appears to be activating this ideal. Again, he deploys the logic of *oikonomia*, in this case within a framework of gendered power relations and models of authority, representation, and delegation. Coinage becomes significant in reinforcing this theological model, one that, in this case, is also bound up with political administration, for Helena is matron to the *oikos* of Christian *empire*.

Sacred and submissive money

One source of money's sacral aura in antiquity was its connotation as a transgressive medium, able to cross boundaries between sacred and profane. Money was used as a primary method of giving honor to deities and others set apart in authority through tithes and offerings. More significantly, ancient Greek thought saw a threat in money's deployment as a tool to challenge divine authority. For instance, the ancient tyrant's disdain for ritual and custom was enabled by access to money. Such unfettered power and influence through money combine as an affront to the community and its deities. The tyrant seeks to, in essence, violate the most holy realm of the gods when empowered by wealth.

As Richard Seaford notes: "In a famous fragment of Sophocles, money finds *philoi*, honors, and 'the seat of highest tyranny, nearest to the gods,' and is 'strangely clever (*deinos*) at getting to things not-to-be-trodden (*abata*) and things profane (*bebêla*).'"[12] A tyrant's pretensions to total power, redefining communal and sacral tradition and ignoring the gods or fashioning himself as coequal, are intimately tied in Greek thought to the uses and abuses of money. Money's apparent ability to be equated with all things and command unlimited power raises anxieties about its challenge to the gods. Money as sacred transfer mechanism enables one to attempt such access to the heavens—with disastrous consequences.

In the case of Constantine's self-depiction on coins, we can glimpse Eusebius's link between money and cultic or religious practice. Constantine's posture, appearing "to look upwards in the manner of one reaching out to God in prayer," confirms his submission to a superior and more transcendent economy. Unlike impious tyrants, implies Eusebius, Constantine knows his place in the cosmological schema, under the authority of God and the Logos. It is crucial that his coinage reveal this, since money is itself the potentially transgressive medium. The sacred image thus sanctifies his money, declaring its humble role in maintaining an earthly empire under the divine gaze. Constantine's pious money is emblematic of submission to a divine structure, which in turn is a pattern for his own governance, including his economic administration.

The sacral purpose of depicting a submissive emperor is confirmed by the interplay between this passage and one that is central to Eusebius's oration praising Constantine. Whereas we have seen that on his coins Constantine "looks upwards (*anô blepein*)" (*Life of Constantine* 4.15.1), in the oration Eusebius declares that Constantine "pilots affairs below with an upward gaze (*anô blepôn*)" (*Oration* 3.5). In its context, this latter passage establishes a definitive link between the heavenly governance of God through the Logos and Constantine's corresponding earthly charge. Constantine has been "outfitted in the likeness of the kingdom of heaven" (ibid.), a likeness or pattern of reign and governance that has been passed onto him as steward. The notion of piloting draws on a traditional trope of governance, used by Plato and applied in Middle Platonic contexts to the demiurge.[13] As is proper for a godly ruler, Constantine directs the gaze of his subjects above: while delivering addresses amidst shouts of acclamation, "he would indicate that they should look [upward] to heaven (*anô blepein eis ouranon*) and save the adulation and honour of their reverent praises for the King over all" (*Life of Constantine* 4.29.2).

Constantine's pious, humble governance, done in submission to the heavenly pattern, as attested to on his coins, legitimates his reign as God-given. Having been conveyed and entrusted with the divine model of governance, he refuses to use money to raise himself up to the realm of the gods and, as a result, is himself transported into heaven and entrusted into God's hands. This final movement is attested on a third set of coins considered by Eusebius, those of consecration issued at Constantine's funeral. After a description of the funeral ritual, Eusebius records that at "the same time coins were struck portraying the Blessed One on the obverse in the form of one with head veiled, on the reverse like a charioteer on a quadriga [i.e., four-horsed chariot], being taken up by a right hand stretched out to him from above" (*Life of Constantine* 4.73). These coins mark the moment of passage as the emperor enters God's presence, even as his legacy and symbolic presence are retained and transferred to the next ruler. The coinage recalls funerary rites that make use of the image, drawn into ambivalent relation to the emperor's body in order to symbolize both the loss and retention of imperial power during successions.[14] The coin's imagery confirms its use as a sacred transfer mechanism, here marking out a blessed passage. "Although he did not attribute this set of images to Constantine's directive, it formed part of Eusebius's evidence that Constantine 'shared in the imperial power after death, administering, as it were, the whole kingdom, and ruling the Roman empire in his own name, as Victor Maximus Augustus.'"[15] Constantinian aura and authority remain, ruling now from heaven alongside the Logos, as testified by his coinage.[16]

Eusebius's reflection on coinage under Constantine highlights his awareness of the role money plays in a system of rule and administration. Money is communicative and proclamatory, declaring the nature and values of the sovereign. It draws upon the imperial image, sharing in and augmenting its authority. Money is itself a critical image of the nature of sovereign character, a representation reaching out to the governed sphere. We can conclude that Eusebius was attuned to the significance of these dynamics even as he developed and articulated his broader understanding of Constantine's reign, which in turn reflected the rule of the Logos. The language of money and precious metals permeates his discourse. The linguistic proximity demonstrates the parallelism and interweaving by Eusebius of spiritual and monetary discourse on economy, value, and exchange. The character of coinage reveals truths about Constantine and, by implicit extension, the Logos. Furthermore, as we now consider, Constantine's relationship to money and wealth, in contrast with that of tyrants, displays the character of his—and his Lord's—rule and governance.

Money and tyranny

One prominent theme in Eusebius's work is a concern with tyranny in the political sphere. Indeed, the tyrant is a recurrent preoccupation in Greek political thought. Such concern also manifests in Greek poetry and drama, especially tragedy. Here the downfall of many a tyrannical leader is connected to inordinate desire for, among other things, money and wealth.[17] Studies consistently link condemnation of the tyrant to his abuse of resources.[18] What is more, the tyrant's rise to power and scope of influence are often portrayed as related to access to money and wealth. Eusebius was acquainted with the classics of Greek and Roman literature and philosophy. Not only does he preserve a number of fragments of such tradition explicitly, but he includes and reworks a variety of such ideas throughout his corpus.

Elaborating on the relations between money and tyranny in the classic Greek imaginary, Marc Shell provides a fascinating reading of one prominent myth, that of Gyges, as it appears in both Herodotus and Plato. Herodotus depicts Gyges as a (reluctant) usurper, whose success is due in part to his stealth, secrecy, and ability to remain unseen. As Shell argues, the trope of invisibility, as well as influencing outcomes at a distance without personal contact, reflects Greek concerns about a correlative power of money. An initial link between Gyges and money appears in the claim that Gyges was of Lydian origin, where coinage was purportedly first introduced.[19] In a variety of other contexts, he is spoken of proverbially as possessing great wealth and is also invoked in discussions about tyranny.[20] Indeed, "[m]any Greeks believed that Gyges was the first tyrant, and often associated him with tyranny; he was the archetypal tyrant as he was the archetypal minter."[21] His possession of wealth—and specifically coinage—links him to concerns about tyrannical power. Such dangers are understood variously as the ability to override communal bonds of ritual and tradition, seize power, command inordinate influence, and seek personal gain and enrichment at society's expense.

While Herodotus depicts Gyges as a reluctant usurper, Plato's account ascribes willful agency to Gyges in ways that provide further links to money. In this version, Gyges (or his ancestor) descends into a cave and finds a gold ring that enables him to become invisible. Whereas the Gyges of Herodotus is figuratively invisible, killing the king from the shadows, Plato's Gyges takes on the power more literally. He proceeds to abuse his invisibility by staging a coup, seizing political control, spying on subjects, taking goods from the market, and raping local women.[22] His ring grants him access to everything, without requiring direct or traditional interface with those he exploits. Shell notes both historical and lexical associations between rings and coins. Early coin types and inscriptions were quite possibly impressions made from a royal seal, which is normally worn on a ring.[23] Coins may have originated, like rings, as *symbola*, tokens given in pledge to repay an obligation or debt.[24] Furthermore, that the ring is gold also seems to invoke intentional resonances with wealth and money.

Gyges is free from accountability thanks to his invisibility, since his wealth allows him to come and go and take as he pleases. Indeed, the power of money appears to grant one a kind of hiddenness, in this case from the consequences of one's actions.[25] In the hands of a tyrant, not only does money promote lack of accountability, but it also spreads his influence as if multiplying his very presence. Gyges uses amassed wealth to gain power and to govern without consequences. Such wealth grants him ubiquitous access to his subjects as a kind of invisibility.

As Shell notes, for Aristotle, a tyrant comes to power through a dual play of visibility and invisibility. On one hand, he makes all citizens visible to him through spies and extensive channels of communication. On the other hand, he makes himself invisible in the sense of dissembling his true nature and motives. "The tyrant acts the part of a good king: he pretends that he is an honest businessman or economic steward of the state. To this end the tyrant renders accounts of receipts and expenditures, adorns the city as if he were a trustee and not a tyrant, and behaves 'as if he were the guardian of a public fund and not a private estate.'"[26] Money permits this sort of distance, since the tyrant is not bound by ritual reciprocity based on material need and can use wealth to accomplish his will from the shadows or confines of his seat of power.

Seaford sums up well the ancient Greek view on the convergence of money and invisibility in the trope of the tyrant:

The power of the tyrant is, to the extent that it is based on money, a mysterious combination of the personal with the impersonal. Whereas the [royal ring] seal embodies the identity of the ruler, the universal power of money is both impersonal (embodying nobody, and independent of all specific personal relations) and invisibly ubiquitous. And yet it may bind all men and all things to the will of a single person. The tyrant may seem, through the impersonal ubiquity of money, to control all things—without moving from the centre, without effort, without (reciprocal) personal relations.[27]

Recalling the convergence of monotheism, monarchy, and money, we see here that part of money's significance in centralized rule is the ability to maintain sovereign distance and hiddenness. Monarchy—or its extreme form as tyranny—can remain cloaked at a remove, transcendent to the space of rule, yet influential through the pervasive presence of its money. Because of its ability to cross all barriers and infiltrate all relations, and in light of its importation of a sovereign system of account, money brings the absent presence of sovereignty wherever it changes hands. The slippage between sovereign and tyrant is everywhere present in such discourse.[28] Indeed, tyranny in this case is an extreme form of sovereignty, where any perceived reciprocity between ruler and ruled is annulled.[29] The sovereign is described as tyrannical when his system too transparently manifests operations for his gain and undermines the communal order.

Constantine's godly mammon

The problematic relationship between tyranny and wealth is taken up by Eusebius and deployed in the interests of imperial validation and theological legitimation. The tyrant in Eusebian reflection is consistently depicted as greedy for gain, financially exploitative, and prone to take advantage of his affluence and power. Such tyrants are contrasted with Constantine who, bearing the marks of his Lord, the Logos—who certainly, for Eusebius, is no tyrant—demonstrates generosity and largesse. Constantine exhibits neither bondage to wealth nor the vices that come with it. Like his discourse on Constantine's coinage, discussion of tyranny demonstrates Eusebius's sensitivities to the operations of money in the political sphere and to both the perils and possibilities that come with money's links to sovereignty. It also raises parallels between Constantine's nontyrannical administration through money and the divine stewardship and governance of the world by the Logos.

Eusebius's antityrannical depiction of Constantine as just and generous is also situated in the patronal structure of the Greco-Roman world.[30] The Roman emperor assumed the role of supreme benefactor, as one called to support cities and citizens liberally.[31] As we saw, this value was heightened and transformed with the later introduction of Christian care for the poor and marginalized. Sharing wealth generously with citizens converged with a duty to protect and provide for the materially destitute. Constantine's role as the first Christian emperor evinces the complicated nexus of these two impulses, as the emperor was called to maintain status and dignity as *euergetes* or civic benefactor and to display piety as *philanthropos* to the poor and to churches. What becomes clear in Eusebius's discourse is that God is Constantine's benefactor as well, providing him with the resources and permission to rule, not to mention giving him the gift of salvation. Constantine's role as patron reduplicates the role of his divine provider. The appropriate response of the people as clients is fealty, adoration, and obedience. Money is one of several mechanisms of provision that ties the leader to the governed in these reciprocal relations of obligation.

As Eusebius recounts Constantine's rise to single *imperator*, he employs the theme of a tyrant's relationship to wealth to glorify the emperor and substantiate his rule theologically. As we saw in the case of Empress Helena, a link is made by Eusebius between the character of a ruler and his or her interaction with money. Constantine's pious coinage hints at his own submission to the divine order of the universe. In sharp contrast, Constantine's enemies are noted for their exploitation of their subjects, lust for wealth, and for the lack of accountability such wealth brings. In particular, Eusebius depicts the imperial rivals Maxentius and Licinius as tyrants who foolishly live as if invisible to God and divine judgment. In addressing the violent struggle for power that occurred between these emperors after the collapse of the second tetrarchy, Eusebius deftly weaves tropes of tyranny throughout the *Life of Constantine* in order to emphasize the distinctive and blessed reign of his one emperor.[32]

Constantine embarks on a campaign to liberate the oppressed Romans languishing under the reign of the tyrant Maxentius. The latter was known for his "murderous cruelty," committing wanton adultery and other moral outrages (*Life of Constantine* 1.34–35). He "imposed on his subjects unspeakable oppression, so that he brought them finally to the utmost scarcity and want of necessary food," revealing his rapacity and lust for wealth (1.36.2). Upon his victory over Maxentius, Constantine undertakes a litany of measures that demonstrate extreme financial generosity and which form the bulk and centerpiece of Eusebian description here: restoration of seized property, personal funding of church rehabilitation, distributions to the poor, land grants and titles to disgraced nobles, parents for orphans, and dowries for young brides (*Life of Constantine* 1.41–43).

Exalting the emperor's generosity, Eusebius proclaims: "Constantine shone forth with the rising sun from the imperial palace, as though ascending with the heavenly luminary, and shed upon all who came before his face the sunbeams of his own generous goodness. It was not possible to come near him without receiving some benefit, nor would the good hopes of those who looked to him for support ever be disappointed" (1.43.2). Like the sun, and hence like the Father as heavenly luminary, Constantine exhibits an effulgent dispersal of wealth, verging on spontaneous generation. Eusebius also speaks of Constantine's "general fatherly concern for all . . . bestowing everything on everyone with generosity of heart" (4.1.1). Unlike pagan emanationist conceptions, however, such a discharge of wealth and money is the result of free will, and Constantine's decision to be generous is a testimony to his piety. Recalling early Trinitarian analogies, as the sun sends out its rays, and as the Father sends the Son, so Constantine sends out money and material provision.[33]

In contrast, Licinius, the eastern rival, "had no regard in his mind for laws of friendship, oaths, kinship, or treaties," and thus like most tyrants was a bond breaker (1.50). Spurning the generosity and kindness of Constantine, he chose instead "to repay his benefactor with evil," indicating a propensity to pervert economy through improper exchanges. This is confirmed by his legislation that specifically overturns and disrupts acts of compassion and generosity by his subjects. Not content simply to take resources (as Gyges does), he outlaws charity itself: "He ordered that those suffering imprisonment should not be permitted charitable distributions of food, nor pity be shown to those in bonds perishing with hunger, nor any kindness be allowed at all, nor any kind deed be done by those drawn by natural feeling to compassion for their neighbours" (1.54.2).

Licinius's despotism is so pronounced, and his relation to wealth so inverted, that he extends his negation of generosity to his sphere of rule. Just as circulating coins impress the image of rule upon the populace, so policy and legislation—the conjunction of law and economy—work to enforce a particular sovereign exchange pattern. In this case, Licinian antigenerosity emanates. The trope of the invasive and omnipresent tyrant gives a clue to the permeating power of money to shape the most intimate exchanges: figuratively, in this case, a despot's character as ungenerous can be seen to corrode the capacity for generous relations among his subjects when linked via money.

Licinius's tyrannical legislation also subverts the use of money to alleviate social needs. He institutes the extreme punishment that "those exercising charity should suffer the same as those who received it, and that those who provided philanthropic ministrations (*diakonoumenous*) should undergo the same as those already in misery" (1.54.2). Those who help the poor are to be thrown into poverty, and providing food for the hungry incurs imposed starvation. The extreme perversity of this economy is highlighted in the inversion of justice. Rather than the punishment fitting the crime, as in talionic reciprocity, a good deed is repaid with the evil it sought to rectify. Licinius as perverse, tyrannical sovereign is depicted by Eusebius as drawing in and lapping up all resources within his realm, such that any acts of generosity violate the parameters of his sovereign space. Yet "his greed was insatiable. Hence when he had filled all his treasuries with an enormous quantity of gold and silver and money, he complained bitterly of poverty, his soul oppressed with Tantalus-like passion" (1.55.2).[34]

Redemptive oversight

Constantine is everywhere contrasted with this foe and thereby positioned as God's true ruler, a legitimacy validated in part by the proper use of money. In battle against the forces of Licinius, Constantine's compassion and generosity are so great that he bids his soldiers capture enemy combatants without killing them: "If sometimes he saw that the fury of the soldiers was out of control, he would restrain them with gold, ordering that the one who captured one of the enemy should be paid a fixed sum in gold. The Emperor's ingenuity invented this incentive to save human life, so that already countless numbers even of barbarians were saved because the Emperor purchased (*exônoumenou*; Lat: *redemisset*) their lives with gold" (*Life of Constantine* 2.13.2).

Constantine here demonstrates astounding mercy and compassion by sparing lives. He also exhibits that admirable craft of economy (*oikonomia*), devising an incentive program to promote mercy. Most significantly, he plays the role of *redeemer*, literally purchasing lives back from the brink of death. Eusebius here portrays Constantine as materializing christological economy, significantly in the context of battle and conquest. The figurative discourse of ransom from sin, death, and the devil in the Christian imaginary finds its theopolitical counterpart in Constantine's merciful use of money to spare the lives of enemies. Constantine, here in the military political sphere, is like Christ who buys back humanity from the enemy, saving them from condemnation and certain death. Just as Christ's victory over demons, as an extension of the Father's reign, is tied to his work of redemption, so Constantine in parallel fashion extends his earthly kingdom in part through redemptive acts in the midst of conquest.

A further type of redemptive victory linked with calculation and money is Constantine's practice of stripping pagan temples of material wealth to be recirculated in the economy (*Oration* 8.3). Commenting on this theme in the *Oration*, H. A. Drake notes that "Eusebius' description of the procedure of assaying and counting brings out the fiscal nature of the operation," that his wording "might indicate that there had been a prior calculation of the amount each temple would 'contribute,' as would be expected in an operation based on fiscal, rather than religious, motives."[35]

Drake notes further that Eusebius's lexical ambiguity at times may be aimed "to mask the fact that Constantine's demand was for precious metals, not religious images."[36] No doubt the emperor balanced needs for civic funding with some apparent focus on support of Christian churches.[37] Eusebius makes this perhaps largely pragmatic, economic, and fiscal act into a virtue by tying it to the ransacking of pagan temples and mockery of idols. Constantine is lauded not only for helping reveal that the statues index false gods, but also for his practicality in using wealth for better purposes—namely, to benefit his subjects and serve the church. Part of Constantine's just and virtuous relation to money is thus strategic reconquest of precious metals devoted to idols, reincorporating and stamping them afresh with his image so as to use the metal within his blessed economy.

Licinius's tyrannical predecessors experienced no such redemptive mercy, and their fate is significant both for themes of reciprocal economy and just reward and for striking optical language of sight and visibility. As we saw in the tale of Gyges, sight and vision are often linked to the power of money to cloak the giver or to dazzle the recipient. Money is seen as a tool of deception or manipulation in this regard, clouding one's vision or hiding one from the light of truth. Furthermore, vision matters in a money economy since it is a system of signs and representations of authority and quite literally makes use of images and symbols to enact its power. Tyrants do not see rightly, having lost a vision for the highest good, and also use money in manners of representation that deceive and dissimulate. Thus, Licinius persists in tyranny despite the precedent of condemnation of those before him, "those he had himself witnessed, when he saw with his own eyes" their downfall (*Life of Constantine* 1.56.2).

In this way, his predecessor Maximin, who was always devising novel and perverse punishments, "decreed that the organs of sight should be mutilated," and "great throngs not only of men, but of women and children, [had] the sight of their right eyes . . . maimed" (*Life of Constantine* 1.58.2). Yet, sensing that his demise was close at hand, Maximin shunned "imperial dress, for which he was not fit, timidly and cowardly slipped into the crowd, and planned to survive by flight; and then, going into hiding in one estate and village after another, he supposed he could escape detection dressed as a menial" (*Life of Constantine* 1.58.2). Having exhausted the invisibility that the distance of moneyed power brought him, enabling him to control and exploit his subjects from afar through economy, Maximin sought deeper invisibility by abdicating his role as sovereign. Perhaps he longed for the ring of Gyges, so that he might pass unnoticed among his subjects, or sought the fabled helmet of Hades, which makes one invisible to the gods.[38]

Regardless, Maximin could "not also elude the great eye which supervises everything" (ibid.). The measure of panopticism granted to the tyrant, or any monetary sovereign, to infiltrate and be "in, with, and under" the various transactions and accounts of his subjects, is here overridden by the greater panopticon of divine oversight. Monetized invisibility has run its course, and the sovereign of a higher economy enforces the terms of exchange. For his own accounting, however just or perverse, Maximin must render account and is found sorely lacking. He is struck by God, "so that his whole physical appearance (*eidos*) as he had been before became unrecognizable (*aphanisthênai*), dry skeletonized bones like mere phantoms being all that was left of him. As the chastisement of God became more severe, his eyes began to protrude and fell from their sockets leaving him blind" (*Life of Constantine* 1.58.2–59.1). Eusebius notes that such a verdict exhibited perfect justice for the ways it repaid his maiming of his subjects' sight. A tyrant's inverted economy is brought to an end with the proper, reciprocal justice of God, here remarkably framed, literally, as an eye for an eye.

The gracious dispensation

In nearly every mention of tyrants or tyranny in his *Life of Constantine*, Eusebius discusses misuse of resources, lust for wealth, and monetary exploitation. Whenever Constantine is contrasted with such tyrants, talk of his generosity and financial openhandedness abounds. Summing up this oppositional economy, Eusebius notes: "They were mastered by wealth, their souls enslaved to the passion of Tantalus; he [i.e., Constantine], with imperial magnificence opening wide all treasuries, made his distributions with rich and lavish hand" (*Life of Constantine* 3.1.7). Rather than being a slave to wealth, Constantine "has patterned (*chrêmatiseien*) regal virtues in his soul after the model of that distant kingdom" (*Oration* 5.2). In so doing, he has also patterned his acts after the divine administrator of this kingdom.

Rhetorically invoking the generosity of God, who pours out riches of grace from heaven through the Logos, Eusebius argues for the materialization of this economy in Constantine. As coordinate to the Logos, Constantine carries out in the material realm what the Son does spiritually. Yet these spheres continually interpenetrate and reciprocally inform one another. Just as Constantine demonstrates spiritual values of piety, humility, and generosity, the incarnate Logos effects material transformations in history, such as Roman imperial peace and its concomitant economic infrastructure. The blurring between christological and Constantinian economies perceived in the *Life of Constantine* is another instance of the interdependence of divine and worldly realms. Eusebius thus offers a vivid instance of the theopolitical zone, of the intermeshing and blurring of theological and political spheres. This Eusebian template of theopolitical reign and governance was passed on to emerging traditions of leadership in both the Byzantine East and Western Christendom.

Given what we saw of the theological significance of Augustan economy and governance, from revealing the unity of God to orchestrating the birth of Christ, it is understandable that Eusebius would emphasize Constantine's godly financial administration. Constantine is the fulfillment of everything prefigured in Augustus through which God worked for revelation and salvation. Just as tax census can be critically revelatory, so must Constantinian coinage and his nontyrannical disposition toward wealth speak truths about God. If even economic decisions by pagan Augustus convey divine administrative designs, how much more so must the entire life of pious Constantine, particularly his generous dispensing of resources and redemptive acts of purchasing lives from death, materialize divine truth?

Having considered *oikonomia* and its operators—whether divine Logos or earthly emperor—we must turn now to the material objects of its management—namely, money and other material resources. In light of the ends toward which Constantine put his wealth, we must examine the purposes of money in the divine economy. The first Christian emperor as *oikonomos* demonstrated pious uses of goods in the form of benevolence and mercy even as such resources were put toward extending and consolidating political reign. Such dynamics mirror the management of the divine economist, who directs goods toward both blessings and the extension of the heavenly kingdom. So committed is the steward to the ends of economy that he will enter its realm and become its very object. The heavenly Logos and administrator, associated with precious material resources, the image of God, and the redemption of the material world, will become the stuff of economy itself as its chief currency.

4

The Coin of God

While debates continue about the precise nature of money, most scholars recognize that money functions in part as a sign established by a sovereign authority in order to signify the center of power within its sphere of governance. Money circulates as a representation of the sovereign and is an extension and technique of governance as it regulates exchanges. That money can function as a facilitator of transactions speaks to its prior authorization by an overarching power and its mobilization through formal decree. While the market ultimately determines price, the parameters and available denotations of value in such a sphere occur under the terms of official money and its accompanying, authoritative accounting system. Money thus provides a disciplinary and shaping function, codifying the nature and scope of possible exchanges and demarcating ascriptions of value.[1]

As ancient reflection on the *oikos* blurred with that of the *polis*, *oikonomia* came to denote not merely domestic management but political governance and fiscal policy. The importance of money as a regulatory mechanism that allowed for ordering a governed space made itself felt as *oikonomia* commonly invoked managerial accounting practices. As governors employed whatever means necessary to regulate their territories, money was not only an accepted but often the primary means to do so. The operations of money as a sign of power, representing authority and disciplining subjects accordingly, coincide with the financial trace in *oikonomia*. As such, these key functions of money became useful for the theological doctrines that emerged as thinkers considered and articulated the *oikonomia* of God as both a father and a king, ruling an *oikos* as well as a *polis*.

Furthermore, as seen in Eusebius among many others, a continual slippage exists between the Logos as the steward and as the precious good that is itself stewarded within the *oikonomia*. For the Son is Lord and manager over a redemptive economy while also being its central payment and offering. Indeed, *oikonomia* at once signifies the art of administration and management and indexes the goods and resources being stewarded and the forms of exchange taking place. This chapter takes up this theme directly, examining the deployment of Christ as currency itself, and sets the stage to explore in the ensuing chapters the cosmic transaction that takes place as God acts to redeem humanity. Just as money is a tool of sovereignty and can be an agent of conquest, the monetized payment of the Son as currency serves as a linchpin—or as a key *dispositif*—for divine conquest and the reinforcement of God's reign over creation.

The language of money, currency, and coinage is employed in patristic thought both to depict human nature and salvation and to describe Christ and his work. Humans are portrayed as coins, impressed with the image of their creator. This image has been eroded by sin but is renewed by a fresh stamping or reminting by the savior. Christ is the paradigmatic image, the stamp used to make impressions of the *imago Dei* on humanity. He is thus incarnated as the chief coin, as the governing materialization of this ideal monetary image. Soteriological language of reminting and reissuing coins coincides with the widespread ancient practice of monarchs declaring their reign through new coin types. The fresh reminting of humanity thus proclaims the inbreaking kingdom of God. To be reminted and restamped in the divine image is as much a divine assertion of sovereignty as it is an act of redemption for lost humanity. The submerged idea of Christ as the currency of God, manifesting the redemptive economy of the Father, provides a structuring principle for explanations of Christ's work and the values of God's kingdom. Given that such a metaphor draws on concrete, material practices of minting and currency circulation, it meshes readily with governmental practices and channels of political administration, sacralizing and further authorizing the political economic power of money as a tool of government.

Words and images of power

In her study of the rhetoric of conversion in Late Antiquity, Susanna Elm explores the use of inscription language and tropes of imprinting to describe the process of transformation into a new way of life.[2] Examining fourth-century accounts of conversion, Elm focuses on Gregory of Nazianzus's sermons on baptism. She argues that his use of terms for inscription invokes a change in cosmological allegiance. To be baptized is to be written on by God inasmuch as it reflects being written on by Gregory's words of truth, which corroborate the gospel. The act and ensuing lifelong process signify conformity to a different cosmic pattern, after the image and word of God.

Terms such as "marking," "impressing," and "inscribing" partake of a broader ancient imaginary in which writing invokes power. Writing draws on the esteem of learning and pedagogy and signals their associated advantages. To learn to write is to be formed and disciplined into a particular trajectory of privilege and power. To be written upon marks one's social location and class status, laying out the parameters of possibility and advancement in ancient society. Writing invokes the role of representation in the public sphere, as of a son speaking and writing on behalf of his father's house. Inscriptions also occur on epitaphs, requiring the living to care for the memory of the dead, or on buildings, praising donors and instructing entrants. Indeed, in ritual context, "the act of writing itself was part of the ritual and its power."[3]

Noteworthy is the correlation of legal, imperial, and religious inscriptions with metalwork and the evocative power of bronze:

The inscription of official documents into bronze tablets (δέλτοι, στῆλαι, *in aes incisa*) and their display were of fundamental imperial and religious significance. Rather than providing the master copy of special laws, as scholars have long assumed, it is now clear that the primary function of bronze tablets was their visual-religious impact. Polished and gleaming, affixed to temple walls, bronze tablets suggested the eternity (*aes perennium*) both of the laws and the Roman Empire.[4]

Here the socially constructed esteem that inheres in writing combines with an economy of value and power signaled by precious metals. Each prestige economy lends its weight to the other. Official writings include royal decrees as well as census lists inscribing all inhabitants of the Roman Empire within a set hierarchy demarcating social status, tax levels, and legal privileges. In fact, the very same types of census recordings lauded by Orosius, those evocative of the divine Son's identification with humanity through taxation, might well have been inscribed in bronze. Furthermore, as Harry Maier notes, Augustus's own records of his conquest and establishment of empire, known as his *res gestae*, were to be "inscribed in bronze tablets and erected as part of the mausoleum" upon his death.[5] Here the accounts of his global dominion, reports that would resonate centuries later with Eusebius's celebration of the Roman Empire and divine monarchy, were fixed in writing upon precious metal.

The reception and reading of inscribed imperial decrees were solemn occasions and public events, approximating the arrival of the emperor himself. The emperor's written word embodied his presence. The reinscriptive power of such decrees could overwrite preexisting law, itself already steeped in the authority and permanence of writing and bronze: "A person's lifelong and hereditary inscription into one social place could be instantly modified, with consequences affecting himself, subsequent generations, and the entire hierarchical construct of later Roman society. Citizenship could be granted, obligations removed, infamy eradicated, and, of course, the reverse could also take place."[6] Inscription proclaimed and could reconfigure one's destiny. It is thus that Gregory of Nazianzus could draw on the evocative power of inscription to signal the realignment of a convert's identity and life trajectory with the kingdom of God. Given the cultural, aesthetic, and political power of inscription, to be written upon by God and God's servants was an event freighted with significance.

Notably absent from Elm's survey of inscription types is discussion of coin markings and the numismatic terminology that is also prevalent in early Christian discussions of conversion or salvation. This language and symbolism make use of the same status and power associated with writing and precious metals already identified by Elm. They also incorporate the decidedly political dimension of sovereign authority associated with coinage and the imperial image circulating on coins. Furthermore, coinage partakes of the discourse of prestige associated with precious metals, gaining much of its own efficacy in economic exchange from the symbolic power of the material itself. Just as laws written on bronze benefit from the visual impact of brilliant metals, the imperial image, inscriptions of value, and other ideological engravings benefit from their impression upon the gold, silver, or bronze coins circulating in the economy.

The possibility that an emperor would depict his visage upon coinage partakes of a much more ancient association between coin and image. The earliest numismatic evidence reveals that many of the first coins in ancient Greece portray simply an image or seal and lack any obvious markings of weight, value, or other verbal inscription.[7] While marks of specifically denominated value emerge later in history, centrally important at the inception of coinage is affirmation of a token's particular origin from a center of authority. The image indexes the entire sovereign exchange network and communicates power over and hence guarantee of the nature of the transactions in such space.

The image also conveys and evokes trust: because of the image, the coin is reliable as to both its content and the system it supports. The sovereign, imagistic guarantee of its content helps secure the ideological function of internal value to promote exchange. The internal value is monetarily irrelevant, for such content may not lawfully be accessed in a monetary economy. It has always been forbidden to clip or melt down coinage. What is important is belief in the value that such an image enables, belief which supports exchange.[8] Trust in the authority and in its coinage are thus correlated. Money is efficacious in part because of the marks it bears, marks that guarantee its authenticity. State interests in maintaining the correct proportions of precious metal content were often a prestige issue, marking the validity and vigor of sovereign power.[9] Appealing to the intrinsic value of the coin simply lends credence to the issuer.

Money's longstanding relation to the image means that it will eventually coincide powerfully with the imperial cult in the Greco-Roman context and remain a central element in cultic operations. Money both draws its efficacy from and helps legitimate and support the image of the emperor as sacred. Through the circulation of coins bearing imperial iconography, the populace is reminded daily of its position under imperial control as it engages in market and ritual activities. Coins participate ritually in imperial processionals, bestowed as donatives to onlookers, and are in return offerings to the emperor and the gods. In this way, images on coins ensure the presence of the imperial gaze in all corners and pockets of the empire.

Many of the same functions, honors, and beliefs attributed to the imperial image in statues and portraiture—superintending solemn ceremonies, overseeing the binding of contracts, or serving as sites of political asylum—are extended to coinage as well.[10] The union is so proximate that the sacred honor due to the imperial image protects imperial coinage. Clifford Ando notes that Romans

participated together in a system of beliefs and regulations that established direct and necessary correspondence between the legitimacy of an emperor and the sanctity and power of his image. In numismatic contexts these associations are expressed in the legislation that developed around the counterfeiting, altering, or melting of imperial coins. For instance, in 317 Constantine instituted the death penalty for anyone who cut off the edge of a coin because the imperial portrait on it was smaller than its surface: Our face is the same on all solidi, and the same degree of veneration is due to it, Constantine wrote, and therefore all solidi carry the same value, even if the size of the image on them may vary.[11]

Constantine's act provides a remarkable glimpse into the legitimating power of the image that substantiates a coin's circulating value despite variations in size and, presumably, purity.[12] The act is also evidence that fiat money—money decreed as such by state power and not by some intrinsic worth—is a longstanding and not merely modern practice. It is the presence of the emperor's face—the same emperor regardless of size of image size—that conveys value to the coin. What in turn occurs by association is an enhancement of the image, since it is coimplicated with the very tool by which subjects perpetuate life economically. Just as symbolically precious metals lend esteem to the imperial image on coins, money's very function to enable the sustaining of biological life in turn grants credit to the one who oversees the economy. In other words, as the image of the emperor on coins "looks upon" one's day-to-day efforts at seeking sustenance, security, and comfort through monetary exchange for goods and services, the sovereign is tacitly credited with making procurement possible. Regardless of the presence or lack of internal postures of submission or devotion among subjects, such exchange manifests trust in the sovereign and his exchange system, granting him symbolic authority over such commerce.

Imago Dei and Christlike *charaktêr*

The preponderance of images of the emperor in the Greco-Roman world provided an apt analogical resource for articulating ways God might be represented in creation. The imperial image appears time and again in patristic literature as a device used to make sense of and justify the Son's imaging of the Father. As honor and reverence shown to the imperial image pass on to the emperor, so worship is rightly devoted to the Son, for to worship the Son is to worship the Father he perfectly images—with the exactitude of ontological equivalence not available between the imperial image and the emperor himself.[13]

Imperial images permeated the empire in many forms, including statues, portraits, and figurines. While the many representations of the emperor could and did provide ways of thinking about divine manifestation, I suggest that the imperial image upon coins conveyed a unique subset of theopolitical attributes that warrant exploration. In other words, the characteristics of money and its economy offered up unique metaphors and dynamics useful for describing in theological terms what God is like and what God accomplishes in the world. Metaphorical ascription is pointless without the particular and concrete attributes of the symbolic economies brought into juxtaposition. Attention must therefore be paid to the discrete aspects of money when used theologically.

A link could be made between the imperial image impressed upon coins and seals and the divine image impressed upon the soul of humanity. Eusebius, in a section of his *Preparation for the Gospel* discussing the soul, includes a fragment from Philo as one authority on the soul's divine origins. Philo directly invokes numismatic imagery to describe the soul's identity as created by God:

> But whereas the others, who said that our mind is a part of the ethereal nature, connected man by kinship with the ether; the great Moses did not liken the form of the reasonable soul to any of the things created, but said that it was a genuine coinage (*nomisma*) of that divine and invisible Spirit, marked and stamped by the seal of God, the impress (*charaktêr*) of which is the eternal Word. (*Preparation for the Gospel* 7.18)[14]

For Philo, the soul, fashioned in the image of its creator, is like a coin that has been impressed with the image-seal of its issuing king. The metaphor invokes both the value and identity of the soul: it is precious, like a coin, and it is associated with a particular power. A coin reflects the character of its issuer. Just as any individual could look at a coin and determine its originating center, so should one, implies Philo, look to humankind and see the marks of God, the issuing emperor. Therefore, one way to understand the *imago Dei* is within the register of numismatic imprinting. In fact, a chief term used for the nature or character of a person—*charaktêr*—is derived from the practices of imprinting or stamping an image upon a coin, wax seal, or other object. As suggested by Eusebius's report of Philo's metaphor, this conceptual link between the imperial image stamped on a coin and the image of God impressed upon humankind would become an accepted and widely used trope in subsequent patristic theological reflection.

This coordination of the image of God in humanity and the image on a coin was made possible in part by a particular reception history of the famous "render unto Caesar" passage in the gospels (Matt 22:16–21; Luke 20:21–25). Here Jesus invokes image language in conjunction with discourse on money and ownership. The text's meaning has perplexed interpreters for centuries. Yet a common rendering of the meaning of Jesus's cryptic command to "render to God the things that are God's" appealed to the image of God in humankind, stamped as it was like Caesar's image on coins. Citing this passage, Tertullian raises the question and provides his answer:

Render unto Caesar the things which be Caesar's, and unto God the things which be God's. What will be "the things which are God's"? Such things as are like Caesar's *denarius*—that is to say, His image and similitude. That, therefore, which he commands to be rendered unto God, the Creator, is *man*, who has been stamped with His image, likeness, name, and substance . . . Christ bids the *denarius* of man's imprint to be rendered to His Caesar . . . (*Against Marcion* 4.38)[15]

The scriptural passage is thus taken to index consecration, obedience, and worship. The image-bearing human is devoted and wholly dedicated to God, as the coin bearing Caesar's image is properly rendered back to its issuing center through tax payments into the hands of the one who stamped and owns it. The passage signals the origins and ultimate destiny of humankind, created in the divine image and made to be returned to

God in devotion and, eventually, deification. Through reflection on this scriptural passage, Tertullian, among many early thinkers, contributes to a clear and enduring conceptual link between the imperial image stamped upon coins and the image of God impressed on humanity.

Just as colossal statues, miniature figurines, or portraits of the emperor each makes its unique subset of implicit points about imperial rule based on its materiality and discrete uses, so coins circulating the emperor's image communicate messages not necessarily apprehended in these other forms. These include the esteem and honor given to precious metals, whereby the association of such media with the image facilitates a transposition of value. The emperor becomes symbolically and affectively linked to the perceived worth of bronze, silver, and gold. Furthermore, the function of money to procure the necessities of life and to engage in need- and want-fulfilling transactions means that the sovereign of the economy is rendered implicit gratitude. The trust that is enacted by exchanging tokens for goods and services indexes a more overarching trust in this ruler and the system of value he represents. Finally, that the coins manifest a link to the governing center means they invoke structures and attitudes of obligation, such as taxes and tribute and the attendant postures of fealty or resentment. When coin terminology is subsequently related to God in theological metaphors, these various associations serve to validate divine identity, transposing implicit cultural, political, and economic approbations into a theological register.

Attention by Elm to the language of coining, numismatic markings, and coin impressions would have also connected to what she notes is a significant ancient link between writing, cosmology, and connotations of debt. Origen, for instance, reflected the popular view that the stars told the story of one's destiny. Stars were like "letters" in heaven, inscriptions in a heavenly book:

In Origen's case, the comparison [of the stars to heavenly letters] was all the more relevant for our subject, because of long-standing Jewish-Christian notions according to which good as well as evil deeds were recorded into a heavenly book of "deeds" or "works." Good deeds could, so Paul in Col. 2:12–15, erase bad ones as if a debt (χειρόγραφον) had been canceled. Those whose debts of bad deeds had been erased through good works would be inscribed into the roster of heavenly citizenship.[16]

Heavenly writing was like entries in an accounting ledger, a record of deeds as a gauge of moral or spiritual debts incurred or extinguished. Attention to numismatic terms employed to demarcate conversion and new allegiances would flesh out such economic language. Indeed, discourse from coining and minting, as well as broader dynamics of monetary economy, provides a crucial site of linkage between language of salvation and conversion (and the shifts in debt and value invoked), Christology, and the rule and power of God.

To the language of humans being written upon by the heavenly Word, the Logos of God, we thus can add the metaphor of being stamped and minted in God's image. Inscriptions marking the ownership of humanity by God, invoking the power of writing and legal code, are matched with the royal divine stamp—the *charaktêr*—impressed and sealed on the coins of humanity. Philo deftly wove both economies of word and image together when he called humankind "a genuine coinage (*nomisma*) . . . stamped by the seal of God, the impress (*charaktêr*) of which is the eternal Word." The coining metaphor invokes the esteem of precious metals while also signaling an exchange network overseen by the sovereign God and his heavenly administrator and regulated according to the values of God's kingdom. It signals an overarching *oikonomia* of divine redemptive management.

Propaganda and regime changes

Imperial imagery on coinage partook of the complex systems of command and obedience, persuasion and consent within the empire. Coins were a crucial feature of the ongoing dialog between ruler and subject as a ritual of power, whether fostered from above or emerging from below.[17] Words and images on money provide a venue for communication between an issuing center and a governed populace.[18] Coin type selection might be the product of imperially sanctioned efforts, emphasizing a more top-down form of proclamation. Other images might be chosen by mint officials and regional elites in an effort to demonstrate fealty to and appease the governing center.[19] Regardless of the design's specific origins, coinage was generally regarded by the populace as the product of authority and hence "from above."[20] Coin images represented official statements about the nature of present rule and were key dissemination vehicles for shaping public opinion.[21]

Coinage was so tied to notions of public opinion, as well as judgment about the character of rule, that Epictetus could make the following analogy:

human qualities, the stamp (*charaktêr*) with which a man comes imprinted on his disposition, [are] like the stamps we look for on coins too: if we find them, we accept their value, if we don't we chuck them out. 'Whose stamp does this sesterce bear? Trajan's? Take it. Nero's? Chuck it out.' The process is just the same. 'What stamp do his judgments bear? Is he kind, sociable . . . ? Accept him. Just make sure he hasn't the stamp of Nero . . .[22]

Epictetus moves fluidly from coin imagery to discussions of human nature and character. His speech signals a wider imaginary that made associations between the human soul and the nature of money, as we saw in Philo. For Epictetus, the nature of rule is summed up in the image, which signals a coin's ownership and reveals the nature of the ruler. It is not simply that analysis of coin imagery provides a useful analogue to ascertaining a person's worth, but that coins themselves convey the character of their ruler and the nature of his rule—hence Eusebius's intent focus on the depiction of Constantine on his coinage as one submitted to God.

Being portable and circulating widely, coinage was a means of propaganda to regulate the perceptions of power and responses made by imperial subjects. One central proclamation that coinage was regularly called to make was the accession of a new sovereign. Whether coming to power through legitimate means or coups, new emperors immediately issued coins proclaiming their reign. Since money was primarily disseminated to and through bureaucrats and soldiers, it was crucial that a leader assert his authority over both the state administration and the military, his primary arms of governance. These material declarations of rulership would then make their way out into the populace. This widespread practice shows recognition of the ideological and unifying character of money, as well as its uses in establishing and consolidating rule. Leaders vying for power might carry out part of their ideological battle through the issuance of competing currencies, hoping to convey legitimacy to the populace and so gain support. Not only would this simply disseminate the image of the new leader, but it would also lend its specific system of weights and measures to, and convey a sense of legitimation over, daily economic transactions by the people.

Ando recounts several such accessions and struggles for legitimacy, such as the moves by Procopius, cousin to Julian the Apostate, to claim power in 365 CE, revealing the importance of coins in his campaign. Attempting to sway the military loyal to a competing emperor, "he sent to them men bearing coins struck with his likeness. The gesture clearly attempted to elevate his crime from an illegal usurping of another's throne to the claiming of that same throne by its lawful occupant. In other words, Procopius presented himself as the legitimate emperor and provided as his only evidence these coins."[23] Procopius not only altered the images and markings on coins to reflect his claims to power, but he also made adjustments at the mint. Although more expensive, he issued new, heavier coins, no doubt attempting to convey the worth, esteem, and trustworthiness of his reign through the very materiality of his coinage. Both new markings and substantive changes in the coinage signaled the emergence of a new ruler. Accounts of usurpers such as Procopius, "like the actions of the usurpers themselves, draw their force from the assumption that the accession of a new Caesar or new Augustus was accompanied, indeed, to an extent validated, by the minting of appropriate coins."[24] Greco-Roman society was attuned to the cues intended by the issuance of new coins or alterations made in imperial iconography and inscribed messages. One critical and recognizable message was a change in sovereign rule and whatever attendant administrative and structural adjustments this entailed.[25]

Reminting and salvation

Given the prevalence and consistency of the practice of issuing new coins to signal regime changes, and in light of the association between numismatic imprinting and the image of God in humans, it is not surprising that numismatic language emerges in Christian theological discourse with regard to the reign of God and redemption. In light of the accepted notion of new coins announcing shifts in political power, the declaration of an inbreaking kingdom of a universal, sovereign God might also be marked in this manner numismatically. Following the tropes we glimpsed in Philo, it is humans who are the new coins, and it is God who oversees the mint. Such language draws upon a large corpus of literature describing the image of God in humanity as corrupted and in need of restoration.[26] Changes in the status of the image of God on the coins of humanity reflect cosmological realignments in power and authority.

Macarius of Egypt describes the fall of humanity in numismatic and imagistic terms:

Adam, on transgressing the commandment, suffered a twofold disaster. He lost the pure and lovely possession of his nature, which was after the image and likeness of God; and he lost also that very image in which was laid up for him according to promise all the heavenly inheritance. Suppose there were a coin, bearing the image of the king, and it were stamped afresh with a wrong stamp; the gold is lost, and the image is of no value. Such was the disaster which befell Adam. Great riches and a great inheritance had been prepared for him. (*Homilies* 12.1)[27]

Rather than precisely a destruction or erosion of the image of God in humanity, as it is often described in the literature, Macarius depicts the fall as a false numismatic restamping. Whether due to some error at the mint or, what is more likely, an attempted usurpation, the rightful currency of the king has been corrupted by a false mark upon it. As Macarius astutely notes, although the coin presumably continues to be made out of gold (he indicates no change in its content), the gold is described as "lost." Its intrinsic value is meaningless without the rightful stamp. The gold cannot operate as money without the proper imprint and image of the reigning authority overseeing the true economy. Its efficacy as token and sign of sovereignty is invalidated. Macarius's employment of the coin analogy is also useful for him in emphasizing the forfeiture of a heavenly inheritance. He can shift easily from the trope of minting to that of wealth. The valuable image of God in humanity is lost, and the blessed destiny of treasure in heaven is also negated as a result.

This text draws on the popular understanding of the importance of properly minted coins, coins bearing the rightful stamp of authority and used in authorized exchange. It incorporates and fuses the language of imperial image and coinage with theological language of the image of God in humanity, lost or obscured in the fall. Macarius takes the additional step of marshaling numismatic terminology in a discussion of eternal reward. In using language about coining, Macarius can transition to discussion of the goods of salvation. A semantic slippage

between material and spiritual goods results in productive metaphorical and conceptual possibilities. Macarius combines discourse about
the identity and origin of coinage with its value and usefulness in
procuring resources or reward, using both to describe the catastrophe
of the fall. In this way, the prevalent metaphors that link minting to
the image of God in humankind are deployed in descriptions of the
need for redemption, bringing numismatic terminology into the realm
of soteriology.

One way to restore fallen humanity, therefore, is through a fresh
minting or renewal of coin. Falsely stamped or deteriorated coins, circulating illegitimately, are reclaimed and impressed with the image of the
king yet again, marking out their true ownership and value. In the pivotal chapter of Gregory of Nyssa's *On Virginity*, he gestures precisely to
this renewal of the coin as a metaphor for salvation. He explores the fall
and redemption through numismatic imagery and themes of royal allegiance. Gregory begins by explaining the entrance of sin into the world:
the fall is a willful shutting of one's eyes to the light of God, obscuring
the capacity of the image of God in humankind to perceive the eternal
image. In his own rendition of Plato's allegory, Gregory emphasizes the
free decision to enter into darkness or, if you will, to descend into the
cave. Distortion has entered through free human will, obscuring perception of the eternal image and, by extension, humanity's capacity for
imaging. A type of imagistic renewal is therefore a necessary part of the
work of salvation.

Gregory turns to the parable of the lost coin (Luke 15:8–10) for aid
in explicating his point:

By that coin the parable doubtless hints at the image of our King, not yet hope-
lessly lost, but hidden beneath the dirt; and by this last we must understand the
impurities of the flesh, which, being swept and purged away by carefulness of
life, leave clear to the view the object of our search. Then it is meant that the soul
herself who finds this rejoices over it . . . all those powers which are the house-
mates of the soul, and which the parable names her neighbors for this occasion,
when the image of the mighty King is revealed in all its brightness at last (that
image which the Fashioner of each individual heart of us has stamped upon this
our Drachma), will then be converted to that divine delight and festivity, and
will gaze upon the ineffable beauty of the recovered one. Rejoice with me, she
says, because I have found the Drachma which I had lost. (*On Virginity* 12)[28]

Allegorizing the parable of the lost coin, Gregory identifies the coin (*drachma*) as the human soul, bearing the stamped image of God. In gleaming brightness, coins bear the image and impress of their authority and call subjects into relations of obligation to the issuing power. They also enable exchanges. Humanity's coin likewise bears "the image of our King," an image that must be recovered. Buried and befouled, the coin's impression and inscription need restoration so that "the image of the mighty King is revealed in all its brightness at last." Such numismatic imaging renewed, the soul will then be "converted," exchanged, transferred into its proper state.

In this passage, Gregory is echoing the words of one of his key theological predecessors, Origen of Alexandria. In his reflection on Genesis and the creation of humankind in the image of God, Origen, too, previously invoked this passage on the lost coin. As he encouraged believers:

> If you should devote your attention to the illumination of the Holy Spirit and see the light in his light, you will discover a drachma within you. For the image of the heavenly king has been placed within you . . . This image could not be seen in you as long as your house was dirty with filth and filled with rubbish . . . but now . . . having been cleansed from that whole earthly mass and weight by the Word of God, make the image of the heavenly shine brightly in you. (*Genesis Homily* XIII.4)[29]

Drawing on the logic we saw emerging in Philo, Origen invokes numismatic dynamics to explain humankind's creation in the divine image, an image that needs recovery. Part of the process of restoration includes a recollection and renewal of the imperial stamp led by the Holy Spirit, so that the coin of humanity might "shine brightly."

In this tradition, Gregory here incorporates monetary dynamics into his central discourse on imagistic renewal. He co-opts and redefines the terminology, reminting the language with a fresh theological stamp, circulating it within an alternative discourse about redemption. It is not simply that a precious coin has been found. Rather, its image—the image of its issuing king, which signals its origin, value, and destiny—has been restored. While not construed precisely as reminting, the point is that the divine, royal stamp, corroded and obscured through the "filth" of neglect and misuse, is renewed and allowed to shine clearly, enabling the coin to function rightly in its intended economy. It can now be put to use in a divine *oikonomia*, securing eternal reward and eschatological rejoicing. This is redemption. Gregory thus relies on numismatic imaging in a critical passage about the restoration of the image of God in humanity at salvation.

As a further subtext, Gregory appears here to activate an implicit theology of the matron, ensconced in his discourse on virginity.[30] The text sets forth virginity as an ideal to be embraced by all yet may be spiritualized and allegorized for the sake of married Christians. Already the language of virginity indexes questions of gender and of marital and sexual relations. In this pivotal chapter, Gregory invokes the parable of the lost coin, which places at its center the economic activities of the "woman of the house." Luke's parable exalts the matron by using her as a positive example of rightly prioritizing the values of God's kingdom. She is presented as one who deploys *oikonomia* with acumen: having lost one of her ten silver coins, she exhibits prudence and thrift in the interests of gain, literally setting her house (*oikos*) in order so that she might find it, rather than profligately dismissing it and consoling herself with her remaining nine.

Gregory invites the believer to adopt the position of the matron as he feminizes "the soul herself," who rejoices over receiving the renewed image of God. The ideal virgin soul is to be like the matron, wedded in submission to God as the master of the *oikos*, the lord of the economy, and is to act in the master's stead as a faithful steward and representative stamped with the master's seal and image. This feminine soul-coin, then, reflects the house to which it belongs and contributes to an economy of generosity that leads, as in the parable, to communal rejoicing. This slippage between the matron soul as steward and matron soul as coin is precisely what we observe in discourse about the Son. The Son is at once the heavenly economist and steward and becomes in Christ the very currency and coin of the redemptive economy.

Incarnating God's coin

Theological reflection on the image of God in humanity is directly related to Christology. Questions about the nature of the eternal image or pattern after which humanity has been stamped are resolved in patristic thought with language of the Son as eternal Image of the Father, as the originary and immutable paradigm for humankind. To be sure, the Logos is depicted as the rational structuring principle for the entire cosmos. Yet the image of God in humankind reflects humanity's particular and specific correspondence to the Son, since humans, as the pinnacle of creation, are patterned directly after this Logos. Humankind's existence as the image of God therefore indicates a more primary imaging undertaken by the Son as prototype. Both the Son and humans are described as images of God.[31]

As Michael Peppard notes, however, some tension and ambiguity emerge in patristic discourse as these early theologians work to distinguish these two types of imaging.[32] Many thinkers desire to maintain the uniqueness of the Son as the eternal and original Image of the Father, while pointing out the important but secondary imaging carried out by human beings. The natures of these two species of image must be kept distinct. Augustine, for instance, is content to employ the register of imperial coinage for humankind, speaking of humanity as "God's coin with intelligence and a kind of life" (*Sermon* 9.8.9).[33] Humans reflect their creator as coins impressed with the image of the emperor. They do so passively, as coins unaware of the prestigious mark they bear. Yet, concerned that the ubiquity of coins might undermine claims to the uniqueness of the one, true image, Augustine advocates sonship as the preferred paradigm for discussing the divine Son. While the emperor issued many coins, he had one son as heir. Humans might be likened to God's coinage, but the Son of God must be described as a son.

This is a marked example of the self-conscious use of metaphor in theological formulation and of the awareness that metaphors matter, for they both invoke and shape a conceptual system. This is not a throwaway comparison or an ornamental linguistic gesture. Augustine recognizes that the imperial coin metaphor has theological consequences. The depiction of humans as coins expresses their relation to God in a way distinctively captured by coinage, invoking positions of subordination to a sovereign, signaling a representational role, and indexing value. When the ascription of coinage resonates with the conception of humanity, Augustine finds nothing out of order—it does not clash with other principles of humanity that he wishes to uphold.

Yet Augustine sees that, while elements of coinage might be applicable in the case of the divine Son, coins conflict with the principle of uniqueness because a monetary system requires a preponderance of such tokens in order to function. While we can speak of a plenitude of human coins, we cannot do so in the case of God's Son. This tension reveals an actual and substantial conceptual interchange between a doctrine in formation and a monetary metaphor, such that Augustine must attempt to put a stop to such comparisons lest they alter the arrangement and implications of the theological system itself.

Augustine's deliberations here point to one of the central dynamics for which I am arguing: the integration of monetary economic language, whether through metaphor, analogy, or other conceptual comparison, has consequences for theology. He does not simply erect conceptual boundaries across the board between money and theology. Rather, Augustine demonstrates a selection process that—*through its very acts of judgment and discernment*—both assumes and further refines a synthesis between money and theology. Economy influences the theological system, and Augustine's attempts at regulation here reveal the relation at work.

Employing such discursive practices also reveals the importance of metaphor and metaphorical regulation in navigating the many diverse scriptural relations between God and money. On one hand, we find references that appear to insert a strong disjunction between the two: one cannot serve "God and mammon" (Matt 6:24), the rich must shed wealth to pass through the "eye of the needle" (Mark 10:25), and followers must divest themselves of wealth to find the true "treasure in heaven" (Matt 19:21). On the other, faithful discipleship is compared to profit-oriented economic investment, favorably described (Matt 25:14–30); shrewd and deceptive monetary methods are commended as a model for securing eternal reward (Luke 16:1–13); the generosity of the wealthy is praised without apparent call for divestment (Luke 19:1–10); and believers are positively described as having been purchased to freedom (1 Cor 6:20; 7:23). This ambivalent sourcebook has spurred a variety of theological claims and ethical models, many of which conflict given the diverse directions seen in these verses. The rules of metaphor are thus crucial in working out the nature of the transfers and the implications of such ascriptions.

Lingering with this particular coin metaphor, I claim that the logic of the numismatic image can cater to Augustine's concerns. In other words, we can remain within the register of coinage and continue to talk about the Son as unique. For the eternal Son corresponds not to another coin among many but to the standard mark used to strike coins. Scripture speaks of the Son as "the exact imprint of his [i.e. God's] being (*charaktêr tês hypostaseôs autou*)" (Heb 1:3). Likewise, he is the "image of the invisible God (*eikôn tou Theou tou aoratou*)" (Col 1:15). The language partakes of a broad set of terms for engraving and marking, associated with minting coins, impressing seals, or fashioning images more broadly (cf. Acts 17:29). As we saw in Philo, the human soul is patterned after and impressed with the stamp—the *charaktêr*—of the divine Logos. The Son is the eternal image of God that is impressed upon the coins of humanity.

As the official standard used, the Son can therefore be likened to the *type* and *die* employed at the mint. These terms refer to the specific set of images and markings as well as the actual mechanisms, such as hammer and anvil, used to impress a pattern upon the metal blank in order to make coins. Two different yet corresponding orders are therefore indicated, distinguishing the Son from ubiquitous coinage. The Son, as the eternal and invisible image of the Father, exhibits an ongoing representational role that sets him apart from creation. He is the royal mark and imperial seal, not the result of the seal when impressed upon created material. Augustine's worries about losing the Son among a hoard of coins need not be sustained, for the Son is not a coin but the mark used to forge all such coins.

In this scenario, then, the Father is the minter, while the Son is the unique, unchanging royal image existing on the minting apparatus. Both exist eternally and outside the sphere of creation. When God passes materiality through the minting device, hammering out impressions of the original type on precious metal, humanity is created. To the Genesis metaphor of God forming humankind out of the dust of the earth, patterning them after the image of the Son and breathing into them the Spirit of life, we can add the idea of God taking the precious material of creation—gold, silver, and bronze—and stamping it with the divine Image and Logos in order to create humanity. Humankind, like imperial coins, bears the image of its emperor, and the apparatus and image after which the impressions are made is the Son.[34]

Yet, according to the logic of incarnation, the Son as eternal image and divine stamp does become a coin. If humans are depicted as coins and the Son enters their sphere as a human, he, too, must be characterized by material, numismatic attributes. The problems that this introduces are problems of incarnation itself and cannot be avoided. In other words, that Christ is now one coin among many is precisely the challenge of the Son of God appearing as a human among humans, Augustine's concerns notwithstanding. This ambiguity and the threat of losing uniqueness are difficulties with which Christian theology has grappled throughout the ages. The challenge of perceiving the true identity of the Son of God as the paradigmatic coin, the one original, pure, and unadulterated currency of the king among so many coins, is the challenge of the mystery of God appearing hidden in the flesh.

Furthermore, just as the incarnation of the one legitimate Son enables all to become God's children through adoption, following Augustine's reflections on sonship, the materialization of the originary prototype of all coins reveals what their identity should be like and aids in their restoration. God's coin redeems human coins and corrects their obscured image, improper weight, impure content, or faulty uses toward which they have been put. It reintegrates them into the royal economy, managed under the auspices of the heavenly emperor whose image they bear. The implicit conceptual apparatus invoked by Macarius or Gregory of Nyssa is a theology of divine currency, of the eternal image and stamp taking material form, as the coin to renew all coins. The appearance of renewed and reminted human coins that mark the arrival of God's kingdom and declare God's reign is made possible, first and foremost, by the manifestation of this chief coin, through which all others are corrected.

Following Christian claims to his uniqueness, Christ is God's one true coin, the primary and originary fusion of the eternal image and stamp of God with perfect and pure materiality, setting the weight, value, and standard for all other coins issued by the divine emperor. If the Son is the eternal and perfect image of God the Father, and if, in the incarnation, the Son then also becomes the perfect human, the materialization of the type and die used to mark human coins makes the incarnate

Son the paradigmatic coin of the Father. Contrary to Augustine, if (as he admits) humans can be likened to imperial coins stamped with the image of their king, then when this eternal image itself takes on material form as a human, it enters the realm of coinage and emerges as the definitive and governing coin.

Christ as God's coin thus invokes an implicit structuring logic often at play within the patristic imagination. The trope trades on the various ascriptions of worth made about the Son in Scripture and tradition while activating the coining metaphor of the image of God in humans as well as the capacity of the imperial image truly to represent the emperor. It also makes possible and grounds discourse of Christ as a payment or redemptive offering. As an image represents an emperor in his territory and a son represents the father of the *oikos*, so the Son operates as a coin— the ideal and chief currency—in the divine economy, an administration that carries out God's reign over creation, achieves divine purposes for redemption, and forges a type of community to be governed. Just as we saw that incarnation coincided with imperial control and was a mode of governance by *oikonomia*, incarnation coincides with minting and the manifestation of the image of God on the precious metal of humanity as a similar method of sovereign reign and government.

The coin's theopolitical purchase

Alterations in coinage can reflect regime changes. New or modified coins proclaim a novel power at work or signal changes in systems of evaluation and exchange. Numismatic and monetary inscriptions and imagery evoke new sovereign centers of power. "Inscriptions and conversions" therefore mark allegiances that are theopolitically and economically freighted.[35] They indicate restorations of value to the tokens or subjects circulating within a particular economy. Whether in the form of new coins or a redeemed and refreshed human nature, the transition involves both a new authority structure and the reinstatement of its mode of self-representation.

The power of writing and images, together with the aesthetic value of precious metals, wedded to cosmological language, works with discourse about sovereignty and economic exchange. The result is a potent and rich web of conceptual tropes and impressions operating in the inter-stices between theological discourse and the sociopolitical imaginary. A widespread practice of reminting and restamping coins, marking changes in political power, lends itself to language about God's gracious power in salvation. Political and economic practices taken as commonsensical provide an orienting logic, as sociopolitical acts become theological meta-phors. These metaphors accomplish the work of providing conceptual content to describe divine activity and to argue doctrinal points of view.

Once wedded to transactions of cosmic significance, this theopo-litical nexus can *act back upon* and *legitimate* the political sphere. Just like emperors, God mints fresh coins to mark both the inbreaking of the divine kingdom in the face of demonic opposition and the slavery of sin, and to signal the good gift of a better life to human subjects. The trans-ference from the sociopolitical realm to the theological is forgotten, and God's spiritually numismatic acts take on their own self-sufficient potency within the context of Scripture and theological tradition. Embracing the sacral aura that money now possesses by rhetorical association with divine acts, emperors can undertake these practices with implicit and associative divine authorization, ruling according to a heavenly stamp.

This is precisely what is seen in Eusebius's paean to Constantine's righteous use of money. Occluding the fact that God has first been described as a cosmic economist through the subtle ascription of mon-etary tropes, Eusebius can declare that Constantine's acts simply mirror those of the divine, the latter taken as eternal and preexistent. We saw a similar dynamic in Eusebius's shrewd approval of monarchy: he claimed that monarchy was the form of divine government, so earthly government must follow the monarchic ideal as well. But he arrived at the fact that monarchy was the divine form by first observing that earthly monarchy was the best way to maintain power and peace. He could thus project this earthly political ideal upon God, suppress the dialectic, and act as if God were his conceptual starting point, moving in downward legitima-tion from heaven to earth.

The same dynamic takes place with the use of money as a form of economic administration by sovereign power. By ascribing monetary actions to God, these widespread imperial practices take on a divine patina and remain as a potent ideological reserve to be drawn upon by earthly powers when the need for theological legitimation arises. A material, political practice for asserting sovereign identity and governing territories can then be seen as implicitly beneficial to the lives of the governed, miming as it does God's salvific acts. By importing such political economic acts into theology, these early Christian thinkers render such baptized tropes back to the political imaginary and enrich its authorization of state activity through expanded vocabulary, new affective associations, and divine sanction.

Sensing the hidden presence of theological legitimation, lingering as it does centuries later, Walter Benjamin penned these enigmatic lines in his fragmentary reflections on capitalism as religion: "Compare the holy iconography of various religions on the one hand with the banknotes of various countries on the other: The spirit that speaks from the ornamentation of banknotes."[36] In this elliptical note for further study, Benjamin gestures to the connections between the use of authoritative and devotional imagery in icons and the images on money aimed to evoke trust in and dependence upon national currency.[37] While the resonances with paper banknotes and iconic images are noteworthy, stronger still is the interaction between metallic coinage and iconography. Considered from the point of view of the material artifact and the supporting system, the congruencies are noteworthy. Both coins and icons make use of imagery, appealing to the power of images and to images of power in order to declare their referents and invite response. Both make use of precious metal and the appeal of brilliant, reflective surfaces as emblematic of the value they signify. Both involve ritual, whether prostration and adoration or exchange and hoarding. Both travel far and wide within a territory, delineating boundaries, yet everywhere seeking new realms to inhabit. "Like the imperial coins that circulated throughout the economy of political power, [icons] circulated throughout the economy of belief."[38] Both coins and icons represent an economy, a broader system of management, administration, and representation of authority.[39]

Such gestural and allusive approximations between icons and money in fact materialized in dramatic and unprecedented manner around 692 CE: a popular image of Christ circulating on icons was merged with imperial coinage under Justinian II. In this famous Christ Coin, the image of the ascended Son as *Christos Pantokratôr*, displayed on icons used for worship, was impressed upon the precious metal of the emperor's coinage. The coin displayed the image of Christ on the obverse and the emperor's visage on the reverse, uniting the two imagistic economies in gleaming, precious metal. In this exceptional event, Benjamin's intuitions had already been substantiated over 1200 years prior.

The act applies and materializes the implicit logic that we have seen operative in patristic thought. Not only does such coining mime incarnation after the manner of the divine minter, but this theopolitical move literally coins the metaphor of the Son as the paradigmatic divine stamp. The patristic language of minting and coining applied to humankind, impressed and inscribed by the eternal image of God to function as earthly and material echoes of the heavenly representation, takes on form and gleaming substance in Justinian's coins. This act models the incarnation in the alternative register of coining and minting employed by thinkers centuries earlier. The implicit trope of the incarnate Son as the coin of the Father becomes explicit in this act of Justinian II, bringing into material and political reality this submerged theological idea.[40]

Such coins were material expressions of a doctrinal synthesis between the imperial image and theology about the image of God that had been taking place at least since the fourth century CE.[41] The Christ Coin of Justinian II materially united the already proximate and correspondent economies of ecclesial power and imperial, political economic rule, highlighting the ways economies of representation interpenetrate and support one another. As Marie-José Mondzain notes: "These choices of emblems, these novelties that appear on coins and seals, clearly show the connection between the iconography and the founding signs of both economic life and political institutions on objects whose essence is circulation itself. Thus the holy image circulates throughout the empire, yet is also limited by it, because the empire, in turn, determines the frontiers of its validity and its worth."[42] The conceptual proximity of the emperor's image and the divine stamp of God, used for centuries to structure theological reflection on the *imago Dei* as well as, as I argued above, Christology, is here put to concrete theopolitical use as monetary economy defines imperial territory and identity. The resonances that I claim exist between monetary and christological economies here erupt in vivid historical manner, further confirming suspicions of submerged, tectonic affinities between these systems.

Theopolitical links between coinage and Christology continue to surface during the ensuing iconoclastic period (730–843 CE), when questions about the validity and scope of the incarnation take center stage within church and empire. The idea of divine and representational economy remains a central part of debates about the depiction of God on earth and, consequently, about imperial and ecclesial representation. The iconoclastic emperor Constantine V demonstrates this melding of Christology and coinage. Having convened a council (ca. 754) to combat the adoration of icons, Constantine challenges the related honoring of Mary as *theotokos*, or bearer of God:

> Taking in his hand a purse full of gold and showing it to all, he asked, "What is this worth?" They replied that it had great value. He then emptied out the gold and asked, "What is it worth now?" They said, "Nothing." "So," said he "Mary" (for the atheist would not call her *theotokos*), "while she carried Christ within herself was to be honored, but after she was delivered she differed in no way from other women."[43]

In keeping with the apparent iconoclastic program of radically circumscribing the implications of the incarnation, Constantine V here draws a stark contrast between Christ as the incarnate Son of God and Mary as simply the one who bore him. In illustrating his argument, Constantine utilizes a common money purse to make his point.[44] Christ is compared to the precious gold and Mary to the leather pouch. It is noteworthy that this analogy comes around fifty years after Justinian II's material merger of the Christ icon and imperial coin. While the iconoclastic emperors removed the image of Christ from coins to replace it with further images of themselves or their sons, Constantine V reveals the persistence of the conceptual linkage between the two.[45] Just as Justinian II's coins materialized—incarnated—the preexisting conceptual bond between Christ and money, this vignette reveals their ongoing association, iconoclastic practice notwithstanding. Here Christ is conceptually likened to a gold coin in the service of iconoclastic argumentation. In this decidedly theopolitical act, the emperor uses money to make a theological point and enforce a political program while signaling the submerged theology of divine currency.

Imperial coins in the period after the iconoclastic controversy immediately reassert the Justinianic pattern of including the Christ icon, seen, for instance, in the coinage of Michael III (842).[46] Thus, a primary way for the empire to declare its allegiance to a particular theological vision—in this case, an embrace of the full scope of incarnation—is to proclaim the Christ icon upon its coinage. The incarnate Son as the materialized divine stamp from the Father's mint is again signaled and put to theopolitical use. In events recounted by the eighth ecumenical council at Constantinople in 869, "one of the stragglers of the defeated iconoclastic movement was confronted with an imperial coin of Basil I which may well have shown the image of Christ in addition to that of the emperor, and the iconoclast was admonished in vain to render to the 'theandric' image of Our Lord the same honor which he was willing to accord to that of the terrestrial Basileus."[47]

In this remarkable tale, an imperial coin presumably bearing an image of the incarnate Son is employed in the manner of an icon. The defeated iconoclast is called to show honor to the image, possibly to prostrate himself in *proskynêsis* before the coin. As we saw, the image of the emperor on coins rendered them sacrosanct in Roman law; ignoble use of coins, such as bringing them into toilets or brothels, could be taken as profanation of the imperial image. Here we see that a similar dynamic is extended to coinage through association with the iconic image of Christ. The presence of the Christ image on coins made them sacred. Ritual displays of honor to the Son of God normally carried out before icons could be extrapolated to coins. Of course, the merger of christological and imperial portraits on a single coin means that the honor rendered to the coin conflates the spheres so that prostration before the Christ icon on coins is also carried out before the image of the emperor on the reverse. Such conflation is theopolitically efficacious, as the sacrosanct images of Lord and emperor work to reinforce one another and as submission to both is ensured.

The implicit connotation of the Son as the type and die used to imprint the image of God on the coins of humanity—the Son who became incarnate as the chief coin of the Father—emerges in these various instances of material connection between coinage and Christ. Actual coins carry on the work of incarnation as material symbols making theological claims: they proclaim Justinian's imperial submission to Christ, they distinguish the hypostatic union from the body of the virgin mother, and they serve as ritual objects of iconophilic practice.[48] Significantly, this conceptual connection between Christ and coins emerges in political contexts during declarations of or struggles for sovereignty. The implicit idea of Christ as principal coin of the Father's kingdom proves itself repeatedly useful in imperial attempts at consolidation of power.

These historical sightings are exceptional moments that disclose the hidden norm, that of a substantive link between Christology and monetary economy in the Christian imaginary. Benjamin's intuitions about the religious nature of capitalism suggest this longstanding affinity, as capitalism emerged at the same moment that the new nation-state adopted pastoral power and economy as the method of governance. As God's *oikos* and the pastoral economy of Christendom were transmuted and transformed into modern, governmental reason, the market as one technique of regulation and discipline inherited the longstanding conceptual apparatus connecting God and money. Benjamin's move from imagery on banknotes to religious images and icons grasped momentarily at this deeper logic of Christ operating as currency. It was such conceptual scaffolding that made possible the link between coins and icons, among many other implications, and ultimately activated a powerful network of ideas and practices that would be redeployed in novel ways in capitalism.

Cosmic currency

The Son as Logos is a divine governor of God's kingdom as well as an administrator in charge of a treasury to dispense throughout creation. The Logos is also itself that very treasury and the treasure within. The coincidence of Christ and coinage reflects a broader economy in which the Son functions as currency deployed by God. For Eusebius, the Father "begot the Son before all the things that were going to be, like a ray of light and source of light and a treasury of goods (*thêsauron agathôn*) 'in which all the treasures (*thêsauroi*) of wisdom and knowledge are hidden' (Col 2:3), according to the godly apostle." Furthermore, the Logos "is extended throughout all, is in and pervades all that is both in the heavens and the earth." The Logos is ubiquitous, spreading throughout the governed sphere. The Logos is effectual, often in mysterious or unseen ways, as "He directs by powers unspeakable." The Logos "is present to all things in His effectuating power; and He remains throughout all" (*Ecclesiastical Theology* 1.8.3).[49] When associated with ideas of treasure and resource provision as in this passage, this language of ubiquitous, effectual power resonates with money.

While we might compare the infusing and efficacious power of the Logos with other metaphors such as light, fire, or wind, the specific context here is the distribution of resources and even material goods, highlighting an economy of exchange. Furthermore, money is rightly invoked as master trope because it is money—and not some commodity—that emerges and functions as the fundamental element and generative exchange power in economy. Moreover, it is money that serves as the central economic tool in sovereign governance of a territory and community, coinciding with the administrative and stewardly duties of the Logos.

Just as the stationary deity in Xenophanes invoked the "invisible but ubiquitous power of money" as it exerted influence throughout the cosmos, the Logos as omnipresent power that provides resources and goods, as from a "treasury," trades on an implicit pattern of monetary economy.[50] Money becomes all-pervasive and potent in society and yet operates in some sense mysteriously by bringing order to and allowing management of a territory through regulating exchanges, proportions, and accounts. Similarly, the Logos is the unseen yet pervasive medium of exchange, means of account, measure of value, and method of payment in God's redemptive rule over creation.

Monetary overtones emerge noticeably in Christian discourse about the Son as a type of currency in the divine exchange that takes place due to the incarnation, crucifixion, and resurrection of Christ. In other words, the potential connotations of the Logos as money come to a head in explicit discussion of Christ serving as some form of offering, sacrifice, payment, or compensation rendered either to God or, in some cases, the devil. It is because the Son is the originary numismatic stamp and cosmic currency that he can in turn become the incarnate coin and serve as the payment or ransom so central to Christian soteriology. Likening Christ to gold—as the iconoclast Constantine V did—while perhaps meant to indicate the precious nature of the savior, invokes the long tradition of discourse about Christ as a payment for sin. Christ is not merely valuable; Christ *is* value—the central, critical, determinative value in the economy of salvation. As the treasury administrator and lieutenant in the Father's minting process enters the economy as its essential treasure and currency, Christ as the coin of God comes to the fore as the crucial means of payment in a redemptive exchange.

5

Redemptive Commerce

Attention to early modern transformations in governmental reason, approached in studies by Michel Foucault and Giorgio Agamben, cannot neglect the concurrent and equally significant developments around models of the market at that time. As the role of the early modern state was being forged, particularly in relation to civil society, theorists worked out models of government in terms of the economy, now being theorized as a thing in itself.[1] Governmentality marked the insertion of economy into political reason, and thinkers took pains to examine in what sense economic exchange and calculation related to the project of modern statecraft and society.

One prominent innovation was the view that market transactions served a pacifying and stabilizing function in society.[2] In light of the wars of religion and troubling attempts by secular sovereigns to wield their now legitimated monopoly on violence, a solution was proffered via the new science of political economy. In other words, if both religion and politics proved unreliable founts of peace and social stability, perhaps the economy and humankind's supposedly natural propensity to truck, barter, and exchange might form the basis of a social ethic that fostered amity. A key result was an emerging consensus that economic exchange was the least of many possible social evils, that it provided a constructive diversion from and outlet for more aggressive impulses toward violence and domination, and that its selfish motives nevertheless accumulated to the net benefit of society.

Thus, Montesquieu could proclaim that "wherever manners are gentle there is commerce; and wherever there is commerce, manners are gentle," articulating the *doux commerce* thesis that commercial exchange was "sweet" or "blessed."[3] Such exchange reflected the highest refinements in human interaction, as baser passions had been "tamed" and self-interests cancelled each other out in mutual benefit. Commerce was the basis for a renewed civility, forming the bedrock of a social order that would be self-managing and internally calibrated, as it mobilized immanent (if still God-given) traits that would sustain the whole. Some theorists went so far as to claim that God had so ordained commerce as to arrange providentially for different resources to be distributed throughout the earth, in order to force different civilizations to cooperate through exchange.

These early modern theorists were plumbing the depths of received philosophical and theological tradition, and theologians were central contributors to emerging market ideals. Many were engaged in vigorous theo-political debates about the nature of divine government, given the regnant political concerns of the times. Adam Smith and Bernard Mandeville, among many others, were steeped in milieus where matters of divine government and cosmic management took center stage.[4] The specter of the divine economist was making itself felt. Because of this, most scholarly attention on the period has been paid to the ways such thinkers made use of a providential paradigm to argue for God's gracious redirection of selfish commercial motives for the greater good of the whole. It was such a notion of divine management that was famously secularized as the "invisible hand" and influenced models of market equilibrium and self-calibration.[5] Furthermore, following Max Weber's groundbreaking thesis, much attention has also been devoted to the religious ideas that forged an ethic of secular vocation, accumulation, and ascetically motivated capital reinvestment that were so central to capitalism's success. God's government of the cosmos and the ethical subjects of Christian virtue have thus been recognized as part and parcel of the new symbolic imaginary mobilized during the rise of market society.

In my view, however, equally if not more significant is the foundational basis in Christian thought that validates the graciousness of God as seen in providence or as manifest in the new Christian self: redemption. In other words, it is God's salvific mission that grounds Christian understandings of divine providence as benevolent or informs the ethical horizon toward which a new saved humanity moves. God's work of *redeeming humanity*, accomplished in divine *oikonomia,* therefore pertains directly to the sensibilities and conceptual systems that informed theologians and philosophers of the emerging market.

In our case, the notion that commercial exchange brings peace and unity drew in part upon and redeployed a major tenet in most strands of Christian tradition: a cosmic exchange, transaction, or payment, however variously portrayed, had brokered peace between God and humanity and had forged a society of believers at peace with one another. This ontology of peace stemmed from a prior ontology of pardon, one premised in patristic thought on a redemptive exchange that liberated humanity, cancelled its debt of sin, and drew it into renewed relationship with the living God. To grasp the traction of the invisible hand of providence or understand the force of anxiety in the lives of Calvinist believers, for instance, requires assessment of the redemption theology that gave such concepts their existential purchase and potency.

While Christian theories of salvation are diverse, and no consistent and monolithic soteriology has emerged in Christian tradition, arguably the dominant patristic explanations of Christ's saving work have been termed "ransom" theories of atonement. Reformers drew in part upon such traditions while articulating their new visions of Christ's penal substitution for humanity. Before the sacrificial offering of Christ's suffering and death was made doctrinally central in the medieval period, with its economy of penance and pain, patristic thinkers focused instead on a narrative of divine payment to and eventual deception of Satan, who had enslaved humanity. Release was secured through a form of compensatory and duplicitous exchange, one that ultimately set humanity free and overcame demonic opposition in the process. At the basis of an established cosmic peace, therefore, was a payment. This notion of transaction or exchange—whether of blood, suffering, honor, obedience, credit, or sinless innocence, for instance—remains constant in the various major strands of soteriology that develop in Christian tradition. As a complement to the reminting of coins as a metaphor for salvation explored in the last chapter, we must therefore consider the employment of this incarnated savior as cosmic currency in a redemptive exchange. For the coin of God was intended to be used in a saving transaction.

In this chapter, I turn to one of the earliest expositions of ransom theory in its robust form, that of Gregory of Nyssa. Gregory stands in a line of thought that includes Irenaeus, Origen, and Eusebius and takes up foregoing reflection on redemption in order to articulate a tale of humanity's debt slavery to the devil. The divine solution, as Gregory sets forth, is for God to mirror and match Satan, outdoing him on his own terms. As such, God offers Christ as a form of payment for humanity in a manner that, by the logic of just reciprocity, turns out itself to be a loan. Satan is brought into debt bondage to God, as the devil had first done to humanity. As I will suggest, while this exchange clearly valorizes payment as it celebrates divine kindness, it endorses the power dynamics of debt slavery and economic conquest, inserting them into soteriology.

Furthermore, Gregory's theory emerged in a late antique context well aware of the perils of moneylending and debt slavery and attuned to the tenuous borders of the empire as it conquered new lands, repelled invaders, and negotiated agreements with other outsiders. Themes of theopolitical struggle make themselves felt in Gregory's account, as his contemporary concerns emerge in coded form and as tactics of governance through economy are in turn conveyed in his account, however covertly and symbolically. This period and context was also awash in traditions of almsgiving as salvific. As we saw, Christians of means sought to imitate the self-donation of the savior through giving. A ransom payment made to save humanity could now be transmuted into an ethic of alms to save the poor, which in turn saved the soul of the wealthier giver. Gregory's account is thus as much a transcript for pastoral power and economy as it is an account of salvation, and it suggests models for economic stewardship, managing opposition, and engaging outsiders. These pastoral practices would offer themselves up to the state as governmental techniques as well.

As we will see, ransom theory displays a dual dynamic of a payment to make peace that simultaneously conquers an opponent. The ransom exchange as theologically depicted thus helps to reveal the agonistic mechanisms at work in monetary economy and belies presentations of the market as pacific. It is therefore unsurprising that many of the very discourses articulating the peaceful stability of economic exchange in early modernity also endorsed the market's global expansion in the new age of colonization and conquest. Pacification by economy works together with its forced imposition in the name of such peace. To be sure, I am not claiming a straight line of influence from the fourth-century ransom theorists to the eighteenth-century philosophers of the market. I do assert, however, that dynamics of economic conquest in the interests of salvation are central to *oikonomia* as it develops in this early Christian tradition, a tradition that is in turn passed on to emerging models of government in Christendom and in ensuing secular governmental reason. Such resources are embedded in the legacy of Christian thought, in this core piece of soteriological doctrine, making themselves available for creative application in the ensuing centuries.

Having argued that we must attend to the properly monetary and economic sense that lingers in *oikonomia*, I claim further that this intrinsic monetary economic specter to *oikonomia* is related to the emergence of economy as *the* field of government. Agamben does not appear to explain why *oikonomia* became "economy" or how such new governmental techniques chose economic exchange itself as a primary tactic to manage the bodies of the living. An answer to this essential connection is given in this chapter and the next. We see that the model of divine government emerged together with a core narrative of divine payment and commercial exchange for the sake of salvation and victory over evil. Inherent, then, to the ancient Christian *oikonomia* that foreshadows early modern governmentality is a core logic of economic exchange, payment, and debt obligation as a method of ameliorating evil and as a solution to opposition and power struggle. This provides one potential explanation, as a founding template, for the eventual focus on economic management and actual commercial exchange as modern tactics of governmental rule and for the centrality of money as a modern tool of sovereignty and conquest.

Bought with a price

Christian Scripture and patristic thought contain references to ransom as a mechanism of redemption.[6] The Pauline epistle to Timothy proclaims Christ a "ransom on behalf of all (*antilytron hyper pantôn*)" (1 Tim

2:6), and the apostle admonishes the Corinthians that they "were bought with a price (*êgorasthête timês*)" (1 Cor 6:20; 7:23). The gospels take up such language and speak of the Son of Man's life given as a "ransom for many (*lytron anti pollôn*)" (Matt 20:28; Mark 10:45). Such language appears to mobilize Hebraic notions of sacrifice and scapegoat, combined with Second Temple Judaic developments that introduced monetary and debt metaphors into scriptural idiom.[7] Spiritual culpability before the God of Israel could be construed as an insurmountable debt, one that resulted in debt peonage. Ransom by a kinsman redeemer or debt cancellation by a sovereign lord were two established means of release.

The inherited debt imaginary made itself present in Christian Scripture, structuring many gospel narratives.[8] Matthew likened receiving forgiveness from God to debt forgiveness by a lord (Matt 18:23–35), and disciples were entreated to ask God to "forgive us our debts" (Matt 6:12). Apostolic and patristic thinkers synthesized diverse discourses of ransom, sacrifice, and debt cancellation as they worked out their various and at times contradictory explanations of salvation. Although diversely construed, debt bondage was seen as an obligation to some tyrannous evil force, death, the devil, or at times to God or another divine figure. Such a power was portrayed as holding a binding loan obligation (*cheirographon*) over humankind, one acquired when humankind's first parents submitted or sold themselves to this controlling power, again for various motivations.

One typical exit from such a predicament, that of intractable debt obligation, required ransom or redemption: paying back or cancelling the debt. According to many emerging salvation accounts, Christ was a form of payment or other compensation for such debt, drawing on the scriptural assertion that Christ had "cancelled out the certificate of debt (*cheirographon*)" decreed against humanity (Col 2:14).[9] Arguably, this notion of Christ as ransom, payment, or other atoning recompense remains a central tenet in most Christian reflection on the mechanisms of redemption.

Diverse gnostic traditions provide some of the earliest articulations of the ransom motif, and emerging orthodoxy constructed many of its salvation theories in the context of polemics against gnosticism. Irenaeus of Lyon operates as a key transition figure who co-opts and transforms certain gnostic terminology about the economies of God such that "the term *oikonomia* becomes technical in the language and thought of the Fathers of the Church in relation to the use the Gnostics make of it."[10] Irenaeus claims that, by denying the incarnation, the Gnostics "overturn . . . the entire economy of God," failing to grasp the true profundity of God being identified as both Father and Son, and of the Son's material appearance in the flesh (*Against Heresies* 5.13.1).[11] *Oikonomia* thus emerges as an operative term in describing the identity of God and God's work in redemption in heated theopolitical debates about the scope of ecclesial authority and institutional identity vis-à-vis competitive traditions.

Neil Forsyth's magisterial study on the history of Satan and the combat myth helps to situate emerging ransom theory in this agonistic context of debates about *oikonomia* and church authority.[12] As Forsyth clarifies, Irenaeus leveled his attack on heresies against both gnostic Valentinians and the Marcionites. Both viewed matter as a hindrance to true spirituality, and their tales of redemption consequently included an antagonistic construal of creation. The demiurge, as that divine figure responsible for creation, was portrayed negatively as a jailer of sorts, imprisoning humanity in flesh out of jealousy or other malicious intent. In a remarkable reversal of the Genesis myth, certain gnostic tales posit the serpent as a redemptive—even christological—figure, helping to set humanity free from the material tyranny of the demiurge through eating of the tree of knowledge.[13]

Marcion's insistence that the true God was not involved in creation prompted Tertullian, Irenaeus's contemporary across the Mediterranean, to provide his own monetary jibe at Marcion: "Let Marcion's god look after his own mint . . . The truth, however, must be confessed, this god has not a *denarius* to call his own!" (*Against Marcion* 4.38). We have seen how the discourse of numismatic stamping was extended to humanity. Tertullian uses it here to discredit Marcion's god as being devoid of authentic followers, since this deity, per Marcionite doctrine, did not participate in their minting—namely, their creation. Here money as authenticating sovereignty, with coins revealing the mark of true and respectable authority, is used in a theological battle to discredit rivals. In launching this attack, Tertullian implicitly endorses the view that powers should make use of money to declare their reign and signal their control as legitimate. Without coins bearing their images, rulers are taken to be illegitimate, just as Marcion's god cannot have true followers without directly coining, or creating, them.

In response to gnostic denigration of the material world and belief in a liberative gnosis, Irenaeus asserts an alternative scenario of redemption. He begins by emphasizing the crucial aspect of material incarnation: "For in no other way could we have learned (*discere*) the things of God, unless our Master, existing as the Word, had become man. For . . . we could have learned in no other way than by seeing our Teacher, and hearing His voice with our own ears, . . . having become imitators of His works as well as doers of His words" (*Against Heresies* 5.1.1.).[14] If there is to be any salvific knowledge, Irenaeus claims, God must reveal it, and such revelation must be historical and material. Taking up the language of 1 John, Irenaeus appeals to the significance of the embodied presence of Christ. Assurance of accurate reception and the authority of proclamation stem from "what we have heard, what we have seen with our eyes, what we have looked at and touched with our hands" (1 John 1:1). Irenaeus here asserts the centrality of incarnation while deftly claiming ecclesial authority through direct apostolic succession. The institution of the church derives from direct "imitators" of Christ who provide the scope for "communion with Him."

It is this enfleshed Savior who, by means of an embodied, material transaction, redeemed humankind: "We . . . have received, in the times known beforehand, [the blessings of salvation] according to the ministration of the Word, who is perfect in all things, as the mighty Word, and very man, who, redeeming us by His own blood in a manner consonant to reason (*rationabiliter redimens*), gave Himself as a ransom (*redemptionem*) for those who had been led into captivity" (*Against Heresies* 5.1.1.). The mention of blood was no doubt scandalous to gnostic sensibilities. Here it is the operative element in a redemptive exchange.[15] The transaction, moreover, is perfectly reasonable and rational: it reflects a deeper order and logic to the cosmos, one predicated upon the identity of the Word itself. Irenaeus here also introduces a theme of captivity. He proceeds to explain the nature and origin of the bondage:

And since the apostasy tyrannized over us unjustly, and, though we were by nature the property of the omnipotent God, alienated us contrary to nature, rendering us its own disciples, the Word of God, powerful in all things, and not defective with regard to His own justice, did righteously turn against that apostasy, and redeem from it His own property, not by violent means, as the [apostasy] had obtained dominion over us at the beginning, when it insatiably snatched away what was not its own, but by means of persuasion. (*Against Heresies* 5.1.1.)

Using language of ownership, property, and exchange, Irenaeus separates out discourse on evil and fallenness from a creator God, attributing it to a separate (satanic) figure. He uses language of capture and conquest—a common path toward enslavement in the ancient world—while later depicting humanity as "death's debtors (*debitores mortis*)" (*Against Heresies* 5.23.2). Irenaeus weaves together ideas of slavery through conquest as well as debt obligation to depict the situation to which God responds.

Additionally, "by his stress on justice, Irenaeus is trying to turn the idea of a Just God back against Marcion, its proponent. So he insists that it was the Good God who acted justly and that the apostasy had gained power unjustly."[16] As Forsyth explains, for Marcion, "mankind is entirely the creation and property of the demiurge." The distinct "Good God" revealed in Christ enters into creation out of goodness in order to help set humanity free from the demiurgic creator god. For Marcion, "Christ's role is that of a purchase fee. He buys mankind with his blood and thus cancels the creator's claim to his property. That claim is 'just' but not 'good.'"[17] Goodness and justice form distinct polarities in Marcion's system, with the wrathful Old Testament God signifying the juridical order of the demiurge that is ultimately repugnant to the gnostics.

For Marcion, the redemptive exchange is "a simple purchase—the offering of Christ by the Good God to the demiurge in payment for his rights over mankind . . ."[18] In such a scenario, the claims over humankind by the demiurge are just. Payment is in order. Irenaeus challenges the Marcionite opposition of goodness and justice by uniting them in a single deity, attempting to vindicate both attributes in an account of redemption. Humanity, being the creation of the Good God, rather than that of a secondary demiurge, is consequently divine property and is thus possessed in unjust fashion by some power of evil. Redemption follows a pattern at once merciful and fair. For Irenaeus, then, redemption is "a ransom paid to the 'apostasy' . . . [and] Marcion's straightforward purchase becomes a redemption, a buying back, of what had been unjustly 'carried into captivity.'"[19] A transfer takes place in which further justice is served, with the rightful belongings of God returned and the power of injustice deposed.

Importantly, therefore, Irenaeus adds captivity, slavery, and liberation to the exchange situation, introducing new power dynamics into
what may have initially been taken as a simple monetary transaction. By
invoking the specter of tyranny, Irenaeus also signals political dimensions
and concerns of unjust lordship. "Tyranny" is a loaded term, drawing on
a long history of reflection and anxiety in Greco-Roman thought about
illegitimate political sovereignty. A variety of innovations made by Irenaeus will remain central to ensuing ransom accounts as they develop in
Christian thought: attempts to reconcile goodness and justice in God's
payment, themes of slavery and redemption, and matters of tyranny and
unjust lordship. More than a simple spot payment and market exchange,
Irenaeus and later patristic thinkers will inflect ransom with theopolitical dynamics, signaling the struggle over institutional identity and the
church's relation not only to rival sects but to imperial power.

Pastoral economy and exception

As noted, one shortcoming of Agamben's theological genealogy of
economy is its failure to highlight the explicitly financial and properly economic trace that remains in much discourse about *oikonomia* in ancient
and patristic contexts. While *oikonomia* does indeed signal themes of governance and administration—the focal point of his inquiry—its object is
frequently one of resources, various goods, and even money, with a horizon of profit kept in sight. We can see the significance of this oversight
when we consider that ransom theories develop in the same discursive
space as the orthodox view on *oikonomia*. In other words, a model of
divine economy emerges concurrently with a defense of a view of salvation
in which *tropes of payment and economic exchange* are centrally operative.
At the heart of redemptive *oikonomia* is God's management and administration of an exchange of valuable goods: Christ as payment for humanity. Attention to the properly economic valences in *oikonomia* might have
highlighted the link to ransom theory, itself thoroughly economic, and
allowed Agamben to formulate a more robust theory of the relationship
between theological understandings of *oikonomia* and actual, governmental administration of the economy.

This notable omission of ransom theories is transferred to Dotan Leshem's overall insightful corrective to Agamben. Leshem demonstrates that Agamben neglects the soteriological paradigm as manifest in incarnation and cross, and as administered and stewarded by pastors and bishops. It is the latter ensemble that, as Leshem rightly notes, provides much of the basis for eventual governmentality. What Leshem brings to light, furthermore, is that the state of exception, related as it is in modern politics to elements of governmentality, has its ancient analogue in pastoral exception to applications of canon law.[20] In tying governmentality to themes of exception that become important for his project, drawing as it does on Carl Schmitt, Agamben invokes the ban, claiming *homo sacer*'s exclusion in Roman law as the originary form of exception.[21] As such, for Agamben, exception is characterized by an *inclusive exclusion*: driven out from the political, *homo sacer* exists on the outside, defining the boundaries in a way that grounds and informs the logic of the whole. Inverting this, Leshem claims that ecclesiastical exception is marked by an *exclusive inclusion*: those otherwise outside the ecclesial fold may be brought in and welcomed by virtue of strategic exceptions to canon law made at the discretion of pastors in the interests of redemptive economy. Forgiveness and embrace of ecclesial outsiders can be accomplished through exceptions to church law. Leshem persuasively offers a better template to foreshadow modern governmentality, centered as the latter is on growth and on the exceptional co-optation and colonization of all bodies into its expanding purview in the name of economy.

Within this important corrective, however, Leshem does not emphasize that it is ransom and redemption, the heart and purpose of divine *oikonomia*, that make pastoral exception possible in the first place. The end of incarnational *oikonomia* is the salvation of humanity accomplished in the redemptive exchange. As we saw, pastoral government is modeled after the divine economist and predicated upon the philanthropic condescension of the Son to humanity in service and sacrifice. The only factor that allows pastoral governance to make exceptions to canon law is *the prior and founding exception* made by God to liberate and embrace humanity in redemption. As Scripture and pastoral tradition claim, "while we still were sinners, Christ died for us" (Rom 5:8). This enables the fundamental Christian pastoral conviction that forgiveness and embrace offered toward sinners is based on the prior and originary forgiveness of God in Christ (Eph 4:32; Col 3:13). If pastoral economy prefigures the exception in governmentality, it is based on the founding exception of redemption in Christian thought, accomplished when the divine economist becomes currency and is used to purchase back a captive humanity.

This transactional pattern and foundation signal a more basic inability in Christian thought to successfully integrate a notion of unconditional debt forgiveness as the ultimate divine exception. Despite resources available in preceding Second Temple Judaic tradition, and despite strands of such thinking in early Christian communities, coalescing orthodox thought resisted construing salvation as simple debt forgiveness or cancellation. Instead, orthodoxy insisted on the necessity of some mechanism—whether ransom, sacrifice, or atonement—to make possible and justify the cancellation of humanity's debt and consequent liberation. In other words, the pure state of exception wherein God accepts sinners without condition was deemed unacceptable. A price had to be paid. In this sense, for Christianity, *economy is victorious even over the exception.* Moments of exception in ensuing tradition—such as pastoral exceptions to canon law—will always have this prior and undergirding theological and economic ground, one that I claim is articulated most clearly in ransom theories. Exception is made possible by the founding exchange. Attending to this structural principle would allow the inquiries of Leshem, Agamben, and Foucault to reckon with governmentality's thoroughgoing permeation by economy proper—and even, I would add, by the explicit logic of money and debt.

From the outset, these early patristic attempts at defining divine *oikonomia* and articulating ransom theory are tied to concerns over ecclesial identity and authority. Through incarnation and by displacing the demiurge, the divine Son reverses gnostic denigration of institutions of law and governance.[22] The material realm and institutional structures of rule and administration are sanctified. For Irenaeus, those who understand divine economy rightly are those who hold to the fully incarnate Word, who founded a historical church, with which communion is required for salvation.[23] Those who have institutional communion are thus also the ones who benefit from a monetarily and politically inflected cosmic exchange in which blood is given as a payment to liberate from tyranny.

Ransom, as the internal mechanism rendering *oikonomia* efficacious, is also the central means for institutional belonging, enabling, as we saw, subsequent exceptional methods for including outsiders within the fold. Accepting the sacrament of Eucharist thus remains the pivotal practice for ecclesial identification. After all, Eucharist is the memorialization or reenactment of ransom: "this is my body *given for you*; this is my blood, poured out *for you*." Exchange and transaction with God coincide with exchange and transaction with the church. In denying Christ's materiality, gnostic "heretics" refuse to acknowledge the central ransom exchange at the heart of economy and shirk institutional belonging and governance, and in so doing take themselves out of exchange relations with salvific power, both ecclesial and divine.

Rather than by violence or fiat, God carries out divine ends through persuasion, claims Irenaeus. The institutional implication is that the church, in dealing with opposition, should also resort to persuasion rather than violent imposition—hence Irenaeus's impassioned *discursive* appeal and attempts at victory through argumentation and rhetorical *oikonomia*. Significantly, however, *persuasion involves payment*. In Irenaeus, God appears to purchase cooperation, paying to have the divine will accomplished. Marion Grau astutely recounts this conflation of discourse and money in her own engagement with Irenaeus: "Semiotic and material economies become curiously interrelated in a divine 'deal' where true money and true words buy out false currencies and heretical teachings. The Word—the true and single narrative of divine economy—becomes the genuine currency that replaces the counterfeit strategy of the many apostate narratives."[24] The idea of payment or economic transaction in the struggle between God and the devil will retain pride of place in many ensuing patristic reflections on salvation.

It remains to be considered to what extent paying for cooperation, broadly construed, emerges as an additional facet of the divine model that church and empire sought to imitate. In keeping with God's example, perhaps the best way to deal with political and legal opposition is not through violent assertions of power but through monetary economy. There arises a subtle valorization of payment exchanges depicted as a means of interaction when differing authorities conflict. In the earlier authors of the ransom tradition that I consider here, this exchange is ultimately duplicitous and involves subterfuge. In its development in later medieval context, however, with a thinker like Anselm, ransom or satisfaction have become fully legitimated forms of exchange, ones that are rightfully due the offended Lord if justice is to be served.[25] This raises questions about the types of practices being commended for imperial and ecclesial power as they seek to emulate the divine standard. It also signals the possible early fusion of theological tropes with ideas of economy as pacifying and of commercial exchange as a route to stave off social and political violence, themes that we saw come into full bloom among early theorists of capitalism.[26]

Primordial exchanges

Irenaeus's description of a redemptive exchange is taken up and amplified in ensuing tradition. In Origen, we find further speculation on the nature of the ransom exchange. Reflecting on the giving of Christ's life, Origen asks:

But to whom did He give His soul as a ransom for many? Surely not to God. Could it, then, be to the evil one? For he had us in his power, until the ransom for us should be given to him, even the life [or soul] of Jesus, since he (the evil one) had been deceived, and led to suppose that he was capable of mastering that soul, and he did not see that to hold Him involved a trial of strength greater than he was equal to. (*Commentary on Matthew* 16.8)[27]

Here Origen probes some of the ambiguities present in Irenaeus's account. Talk of blood has been replaced with the soul of Christ, reflecting perhaps Origen's own Platonic tendencies. The soul, not the blood, is the prime locus of value. The satanic specter to apostasy in Irenaeus is here made more explicit. Origen posits the receiver of the payment as the evil one. Note the incredulity expressed by Origen that God could somehow be the recipient of Christ's life. This same spirit will be repeated in later thinkers in the opposite direction, when they find it impossible and offensive that the devil could actually be the legitimate payee and instead turn the payment toward God.[28]

Although speaking in terms of ransom, Origen does not here invoke a notion of monetary exchange or a cancellation of debt per se. On his reading, the mechanism is instead a trial of strength, and divine power overcomes the hold of the devil and sets humanity free. He brings the account into a context of struggle and conquest. Origen also introduces a notion of deception, complicating the image of persuasion in Irenaeus. Was the opponent deceived or simply persuaded, such that the transaction can be understood as free and fair, reflecting the desire of both parties? In what sense can a fair exchange be made if a struggle for authority and power is what is at stake and one party ends up defeated?

Origen provides more monetary detail on this theology of redemption in his reflections on Exodus. Exploring the sources of humanity's bondage in the wilderness of sin and drawing on the Israelite experience as allegory, Origen turns to the dynamics of debt slavery invoked in Scripture. He first recounts the views of his opposition, the "heretics" who "say of the Savior that he 'acquired' those who were not his; for with the price which was paid he purchased men whom the creator had made. And it is certain, they say, that everyone buys that which is not his own" (*Exodus Homily* VI.9).[29] Here we see the views that Irenaeus had combatted: there were those who saw a sharp distinction between the creator God and the redeemer Christ. Clearly, if Christ had purchased humanity for salvation, this implies that humans came from elsewhere, for what sense would it make for Christ as God to buy what he had also created? Humans must have stemmed from a different God who made them and repressed them in flesh and law, and from whom Christ had purchased them to freedom.

The gnostic market logic makes good sense. Yet, in response, Origen recalls the words of Isaiah: "You have been sold for your sins and for your iniquities I sent your mother away" (Isa 50:1). Amplifying this process, he continues: "You see, therefore, that we are all creatures of God. But each one is sold for his own sins and, for his iniquities, parts from his own creator. We, therefore, belong to God insofar as we have been created by him. But we have become slaves of the devil in so far as we have been sold for our sins" (*Exodus Homily* VI.9). Origen appeals to an even earlier transaction that helps make sense of the purchase by Christ. Humanity had been created by God but through sin had been sold to Satan. Christ's offering facilitated not a new acquisition but a buying back of humanity from the devil. Rather than eschewing monetary economic logic, Origen builds on it to depict a more primordial exchange that set the stage for the eventual redemptive purchase. He draws on money and the economy both to help defend the Trinitarian unity of

Father and Son—for the same God is both creator and redeemer—and to make sense of the process of redemption.

What does it mean to say that the devil had first purchased or acquired humanity? Origen provides a remarkable description of the "wages of sin" (Rom 6:23) that brought bondage:

Murder is the money of the devil; for "he is a murderer from the beginning" (John 8:44). You have committed murder; you have received the devil's money. Adultery is the money of the devil for "the image and superscription" (Matt 22:20) of the devil is on it. You have committed adultery; you have received a coin from the devil. Theft, false testimony, greediness, violence, all these are the devil's property and treasure for such money proceeds from his mint. With this money, therefore, he buys those whom he buys and makes all of those his slaves who have received however insignificant a coin from his property of this kind. (*Exodus Homily* VI.9)

For Origen, humanity's decision to sin was the equivalent of entering into an exchange with the devil and accepting his currency. In exchange for performing demonic deeds, they received compensation. This led to humankind's enslavement, for humans became dependent upon this satanic salary. Yet, it remains unclear how such an exchange might lead to debt slavery, as Origen will elsewhere acknowledge: "For each of us in these things which he commits is made a debtor and writes the [bond] documents of his sins" (*Genesis Homily* XIII.4).[30] Attempting to negotiate the various images and metaphors in Scripture, Origen maintains that humans had somehow transacted with the devil, receiving a death-dealing compensation for their iniquity that also amounted to their enslavement and debt servitude. The purchase by Christ the redeemer made sense and was justified, and it freed humans from this debt bondage to the devil and returned them to God, their creator and rightful owner. Subsequent reflection would help to clarify these multiple dynamics and amplify the role of debt slavery in this monetized exchange.

Gregory of Nyssa's ransom theory

Gregory of Nyssa offers an important window into themes of ransom, debt slavery, and redemption for a number of reasons. He formulates one of the earliest, more developed ransom accounts, establishing the terms to which many subsequent thinkers respond, whether to defend, modify, expand upon, or refute.[31] He also synthesizes much of the foregoing received tradition into a fairly coherent narrative. As one of the first robust accounts, it had not yet benefited from the modification of ensuing commentary and tradition. It is therefore worthwhile to grapple with the presentation at its most direct and perhaps troubling, before the theory has been apologetically nuanced and its starker features suppressed and transmitted more implicitly into Christian soteriology.

An ancillary benefit of taking up Gregory of Nyssa is that his thought provides some continuity with our engagement with Eusebius. Eusebius, inheriting Origen's library at Caesarea as well as much of his philosophical and theological perspective, functions as a bridge figure, conveying aspects of the Alexandrian's theology to later thinkers like Basil the Great, Gregory of Nyssa, and Gregory of Nazianzus.[32] Although the three Cappadocian theologians in no way represent a monolithic and unified body of thought—on certain topics, including ransom theory, they are at odds—we can assume some commonality of influence by inherited theological tradition. Indeed, all three became pivotal thinkers in the development of discourse around *oikonomia*. Gregory of Nyssa, in particular, would articulate *oikonomia* as a different mode of discourse than *theologia*, one addressing God as revealed in redemptive acts rather than as conceived of in God's self.[33] He would also depict such an economy as centered on growth.[34] There is a discernible line of thought from Origen through Eusebius to these three diverse thinkers. Nyssen reflects this Origenist tradition in the ways he relates Platonic thought to Christianity. Indeed, one crucial link back to Origen is evinced in Nyssen's ransom theory, which takes up and extends Origen's reflections. Given Eusebius's own prominent place in this tradition, we can assume Gregory of Nyssa is familiar with the work of this vaunted former bishop of Caesarea and witness to Constantine's ascension.

Furthermore, regarding political power and authority generally, the Cappadocians' "attitude to the Emperor was Eusebian."[35] They tended to uphold and respect Eusebius's established model of the emperor as the divinely chosen representative of God in the political sphere. As we saw in Irenaeus and Origen, ransom theory includes claims about representations of power, struggles for authority, and resistance to tyranny which raise theopolitical questions. The Eusebian vision of imperial authority as legitimated by and in turn legitimating the rule of God remains a crucial backdrop in considerations of Nyssen's ransom narrative. Divine actors and actions in these tales have as potential analogues various figures and structures in the political sphere. Thus, in championing the Origenist tradition, Eusebius includes additional political layers, the traces of which will also be discerned in Nyssen's ransom theory.

In particular, we should recall that Eusebius took up and developed Origen's celebration of the peace and stability brought by the Roman Empire. Such secure infrastructure enabled easier proclamation of the gospel of peace, at the center of which was the message of Christ's ransom of humanity. As we saw, Eusebius articulated a full-fledged metaphysic of empire in which the unifying power of Rome reflected the unity of the monarchical God. A significant correlate to such imperial unity, seen both as cause and result, was proclaimed in popular encomia or speeches of praise to Rome, "according to which the Roman Empire had made free commerce possible," and which in turn aided in peace and stability across the empire.[36]

Couched, then, in Eusebius's claim that the incarnation was timed to this historical moment and even reflects characteristics of this period is the importance of unity, stability, and peace brought through economic exchange. Not only does such economic exchange reflect the heavenly governance of the divine economist, but Eusebius's historical hermeneutical logic suggests that something about incarnation itself relates to economic peace. Keeping in mind the Christian claim that incarnation's primary purpose was soteriological, that Christ came to save, we glimpse further potential correlation between Roman economic peace and ransom as the *telos* of incarnation. As we explore ideas of cosmic peace accomplished by a ransom exchange, this political theological background contributed by Eusebius must be kept in view.

More to the point, Eusebius provides an important political twist to ransom and redemption tropes by including Constantine in such acts. Not simply fulfilling the unification initiated by Augustus, Constantine is depicted as a "friend" and supplement to Christ by carrying on his redemptive work. As we saw, Constantine serves as a concrete model of theopolitical redeemer by *literally purchasing the lives* of captured enemy combatants (*Life of Constantine* 2.13.12). As in the case of Rome's unity, earthly events have their heavenly and cosmic parallels, even in the case of salvation. Here is one Eusebian answer to the question raised previously of how the church and the empire might carry out redemptive acts in the service of peace, imitating the divine model of payment for cooperation. Of course, just as the imperial church did not necessarily follow Irenaeus's model of peaceful persuasion over violent imposition, neither are these Constantinian acts of redemptive purchase necessarily historically accurate.[37] The point, however, is that Eusebius *discursively and ideologically construes* the state as replicating materially and in literal form the use of a redemptive payment in the service of peace and the saving of lives. A theopolitical template emerges where monetary exchange appears useful to extensions of Christian rule.

We see glimpses here, in inchoate form, of economic administration in the theologically legitimated management of the living. Payment and economic exchange have purportedly been used by God to broker cosmic peace and facilitate the flourishing of life. How much more should empires, states, and other authorities be involved in these transactions in furthering their own interests, interests that allegedly serve the flourishing of the populace? Given that *oikonomia* can include a sense of monetary management, it makes sense that monetized payments emerge as part of the ensemble of techniques of governance. Furthermore, if *oikonomia* permits the use of even suspect means in light of the salvific ends they serve, the door is thrown wide open to a variety of techniques of governance that may gain approval on account their purported goal: the welfare of the governed.

Bound by unbounded desire

Gregory of Nyssa's ransom account occurs within a section of his *Address on Religious Instruction* that expounds the doctrine of incarnation and its redemptive impact. Like Irenaeus, Gregory defends the centrality of incarnation before its detractors, insisting that such material incarnation is salvific in a way that will involve redemptive exchange. In answer to apparent charges from Greek and Jewish critics that the glory of divinity is attenuated in the incarnation and death of Christ, Gregory is concerned to show how these events best exhibit divine attributes.

Beginning in chapter twenty, he announces a theme that governs the ensuing exposition of ransom exchange: "Everyone agrees that we must confess the divine to be not only powerful, but also just, good and wise, and whatever leads the mind upwards to some noble idea. It follows, therefore, that in the case of the present dispensation (*hê parousa oikonomia*), it is not reasonable that one or another of the divine attributes should tend to be manifested in history, while another is absent" (*Address* 20).[38] As we saw in the Marcionite ideas combatted by Irenaeus, certainly not everyone agreed that goodness and justice needed to be united in the same God. Yet Gregory assumes as a *fait accompli* the necessity of the coinherence of goodness, justice, and wisdom in an all-powerful godhead. Gregory's conviction is that there is a proper order and logical sequence to divine *oikonomia*, with goodness here being the governing concern to which the other attributes will be added in appropriate fashion.[39] To such goodness is allied wisdom, here manifest as technical skill. Wisdom involves an appropriate and fitting response to the need, a remedy that matches the ailment. The dictates of wisdom also proclaim that the remedy or solution to the plight of humanity must be just, which is the next theme of his exposition.

Strikingly, the divine solution must be just not simply because God is just but because humanity's fall into bondage was itself just. How can this be, given that it is described as a kind of tyranny? Gregory claims that we first need to recall the mutable nature of humanity (*Address* 21). While created in the image of God, humankind is not identical to God, having come from nonbeing into being and thus evincing capacity for change. As a changeable and dynamic form, humanity is always on the move, so to speak. Such processual nature heads towards perfection and the good, or toward its opposite, which is a type of nonexistence, a loss of being. The engine of movement is desire, the goal toward which it strives is beauty, and the mechanism of action is the will, which, Gregory maintains, is free. Second, claims Gregory, we must note the nature of this beauty toward which humanity strives. Beauty can either be true, indicating a correlation between surface appearance and depth, or deceptive, in which case the appearance misleads to a false and destructive core. It is the gift of the rational mind to be able to discern between the two. Because of free will, one is responsible for the consequences of whatever notion of beauty one strives after, whether true or deceptive.[40]

To illustrate his point, Gregory recalls Aesop's fable of the dog that, looking at its own reflection in a pool, drops the true food out of its mouth to seize that which is reflected. The dog can justly be faulted both for being misled by the false appearance and for foolishly chasing after phantoms, as well as for the desire which impelled it to act. While already possessing food, inordinate craving drove it in pursuit of more, causing it to lose even that which it had. Resonances exist between Gregory's employment of this tale and Eusebius's invocation of the myth of Tantalus in his critique of tyrants (Eusebius of Caesarea, *Life of Constantine* 1.55.2; 3.1.7). As we saw, Tantalus represents desire never satisfied, always longing for fulfillment. This is the condemnation of tyrants in their lust for wealth and power. The hunger can never be sated, claims Eusebius, and they are led into deeper ruin.

In light of Gregory's familiarity with and prominent use of Greek tradition, we should recall that, for Plato, money is not simply another vice among others but is "the chief instrument for the gratification of such desires" (Plato, *Republic* IX.580e).[41] Thus the question of limits and boundlessness with regard to desire in Greek thought often relates to the anxieties around money. Developing Plato, Aristotle claims that the principle threat of money is precisely its capacity to fuel unlimited desire (Aristotle, *Politics* I:1256–58). Use of money to procure goods to satisfy finite needs is legitimate and, as such, permitted within *oikonomia*, but unlimited accumulation (*chrêmatistikê*) of money is illegitimate or unnatural. Partaking of the order not of need but of desire, which knows no bounds, money directly indexes desire, for "in this art of wealth-getting there is no limit of the end" (Aristotle, *Politics* I:1257). What is more, as Aristotle observes, money is unique in its capacity as universal equivalent to define the values of all other goods and pursuits. Money is of a different order and functions as a potential governing framework, both in the register of desire and rational capacity to assess what is good. These monetarily inflected concerns about desire that stem from philosophical critiques of money lurk in the background and make themselves felt in Gregory's ensuing description of satanic entrapment and liberation.

Having recounted both the changeable nature of humankind as well as the potential for deceptive appearances, Gregory proceeds to build a case for the presence of justice in humanity's plight:

In a similar fashion [i.e., to the fabled dog], the mind, being cheated of its desire for that which is really good, was carried away to what is unreal through the deception of the counsellor and inventor of evil, by having been persuaded that that truly is beautiful, which is the opposite of beautiful. For his guile would have been quite ineffectual, had not the semblance of the good been spread upon the hook of evil (*tôi tês kakias agkistrôi*) like a bait (*deleatos*). (*Address* 21)

The devil made use of the potential both for malleable human nature to be "carried away" and for appearances to deceive. Gregory here introduces his famous "fishhook" (*to agkistron*) and "bait" (*to delear*) metaphor to describe the process. Humanity was lured into a snare just as a fish is led to bite a hook: because the trap was made to appear appealing.

Despite this deceit, Gregory holds humanity to account: "Man then was freely involved in this disaster; he had yoked himself to the enemy of life through pleasure" (*Address* 21). Driven by desire, humankind opted for bondage and slavery. Humanity is responsible for choosing, just as a fish is responsible for biting the bait. It does not matter that the bait is a deceit. To bite is a free choice, an act without coercion. Mutable humankind followed its own inordinate desires and, failing to discern properly between surface appeal and the true depth of beauty, chased an empty reflection. In so doing, it lost what it already had as gifts of divine grace. The consequences are therefore just. As there is a logic and order to redemption, there is a logic and order to the initial process of enslavement. God's fair measures to counteract this tyranny will match in inverse fashion the steps taken to bind humanity.

Balanced justice and fair dealings

Gregory of Nyssa's sense of justice here is not primarily a conformity to some legal requirement or code. Rather, justice entails what is fitting or fair as intrinsic to the process under consideration. Although the result is anything but desirable, the process by which it was reached followed the course of desire and free decision. The fish were not wrested from the water by nets, fully against their will. They ensnared themselves through pursuing the appealing bait and attached themselves to the hook.

Even though Satan used deceit, humanity followed its desire for the pleasurable lure and so rightly incurred the consequent slavery. While the end result is not good, what is just for Gregory is the *process* of enslavement. God's justice, in turn, is to respect the process and to follow an appropriate counterprocess. Although God is powerful, choosing to manifest a power devoid of the wisdom, goodness, and justice that are also divine attributes would be tyrannical. God does not force the release of enslaved humanity, for this would give Satan a right to cry foul, since his ownership of humanity was fitting, given their initial folly.

Gregory helps the reader understand this dynamic of just slavery and redemption by turning to the world of loans and debt bondage:

> Even as those who have sold their own liberty for a price are justly slaves of those that bought them, [so] it is not right for them or for anybody else to claim liberty on their behalf. This is, indeed, even the case with well-born persons who have so surrendered themselves. If anyone in his concern for such persons should use force against those who purchased them, he will seem (*doxei*) to be unjust in tyrannically (*tyrannikôs*) wresting such lawfully possessed captives from the grip of their just captors. (*Address* 22)

By their free decision, the debtors' desire for the bait of money has led them to swallow the hook of indebtedness. Following desire, they have received some good—the money they have borrowed. This is overshadowed by the loss of their freedom and by the new obligation to the lender. Savoring the pleasure of the bait, having access to funds, is mitigated by the piercing reality of the hook of debt slavery until repayment. Like the foolish dog chasing the reflection of food, they pursue the semblance of agency and freedom in having money but lose what freedom they have in greater levels of bondage. Debt slavery is a condition that Gregory condemns as undesirable.[42] Yet those who enter it when they follow the conventions of monetary economy do so "justly" and are rightfully and fairly in bondage. The process is logical, coherent, and respects free will, and the end result, however distasteful, follows properly.

The appeal to justice and lawful possession here for Gregory speaks first and foremost to the internal consistency and proportionality of the monetary transaction. While he may be signaling actual legal codes that enforce these types of relations, his appeal, in keeping with the sense of justice in the wider context, is primarily to balance, coherence, and process. There is a justice to monetary exchange that does not need law codes, for it is clear or conventionally accepted that an exchange includes agreements about both the nature and consequences of the transaction. This is economy's archaic connection to talionic reciprocity, to evidence of a possible co-origin of money and law in culturally embedded notions of fairness and balance.[43] Before we even need to speak of codified legal statutes, we can identify a supposedly more originary law of economic rationality seen in claims to proportion, which are conventionally accepted.

Therefore, a person can freely, although foolishly, sell himself into debt slavery for the sake of the immediate gratification of having money on hand to use. While Gregory will elsewhere have harsh words for those who practice such lending and in so doing tempt the destitute, his claim here is that the process is nevertheless just in the sense of logical, proportionate, consequential, and respectful of free will. Any steps taken to remedy the situation must follow a similarly conventional and proportionate order. Those in bondage may be purchased to freedom if the creditor who has enslaved them agrees to a price in exchange.

Applying these monetary dynamics to the spiritual register, Gregory claims: "In the same way, once we had sold ourselves freely, the one who was out of his goodness to lead us back again into freedom must think up a method of recall which was not tyrannical (*mê ton tyrannikon*) but just, and therefore must be one which allowed the captor to select any ransom (*lytron*) he might choose in return for his captive" (*Address* 22). Here goodness remains the governing principle, for God desires to release enslaved humanity. Wisdom dictates conceiving of an appropriate method of liberation. Justice here means a method that matches the method of enslavement. Humankind's first parents accepted an advance on certain goods, received a transaction they found appealing, and in so doing willfully chose a state of debt bondage to one who opposed God. Proportionately, humanity cannot be wrested from the grip of the devil, plucked out of the realm of death by fiat. A countervailing enticement is needed, something that will induce the devil as debt lord to release humanity of his own accord.

The gleaming coin

Gregory of Nyssa explains what type of price would be appropriate and tempting enough to entice the devil to release humanity. As a tyrant, the devil desired greater resources for his territory and found a more productive or rich potential source for power. The virtues and miracles of Christ tantalized the devil for the power he in turn would acquire in claiming Christ as his own. "The enemy, then, perceived this power in him, realized that by the exchange he would acquire more possessing him than he already had. Therefore, he selected him (i.e., Christ), to become the ransom (*lytron*) for those who were constrained in the prison of death" (*Address* 22). Deity needed to be veiled in flesh, lest the devil be frightened by the overwhelming force of the approaching power. Just as the gleam of the metallic hook might alarm a fish and so requires the overlay of a worm or other tempting bait, so the divine nature needed to be veiled in a supreme example of humanity to tempt Satan to bite.

In light of the incarnation, the merger of deity with full humanity, the ruse was effective. The power and identity of God were hidden in the flesh: "in order that the exchange might be more easily effected, the divine was concealed by the covering of our nature in order that, after the manner of a greedy fish, the hook of the deity (*to agkistron tês theotêtos*) might be swallowed down along with the bait of humanity (*tôi deleati tês sarkos*)." In this way, light and divine power were brought into direct contact with darkness and the power of death. The result was an immediate reversal, one that we can also call just in the sense of being logical and consequential: "in the presence of light darkness has not the power to remain, nor has death any power where life is active" (*Address* 24).

Gregory acknowledges that such an exchange might appear unfair upon first blush, yet contemplation of the nature of justice and its coordination with wisdom and goodness dismisses such concerns. First, "it is in the character of justice to render to each his due." This is the principle of balance and proportionality. Wisdom, on the other hand, coordinates the principle with the good end toward which it works. "By justice due recompense is given; by goodness the end of the love of man is not excluded" (*Address* 26). Wise justice renders proportionate retribution with an eye toward redemption.

Gregory then applies these principles to the ransom exchange itself. The criterion of justice is met by the deceiver being deceived. Basic talionic reciprocity is at work. Goodness and wisdom are both vindicated when the aims of the just deceit are considered. For it was for the good of humanity and, we will learn, for the devil himself that this duplicitous exchange took place.[44] Gregory then invokes a principle of *oikonomia*:

The conspirator and the one who cures the victim both mix a drug with the man's food. In the one case it is poison; in the other it is an antidote for poison. But the mode of healing in no way vitiates the kindly intention. In both instances a drug is mixed with the food; but when we catch sight of the aim, we applaud the one and are incensed at the other. (*Address* 26)

Here seemingly identical acts are distinguished based on the intention and aims inherent in the procedure, enabling a value judgment to be made. The case of healing is illuminative because the antidote is often of the same material as the poison. In other words, all the steps are apparently identical, even down to the type of drug mixed with the food. Only with the end result—or if the intentions of the heart are disclosed—can assessment be made. Satan engaged in deceit to enslave humanity and corrupt its nature; God practiced deceit to liberate humanity and redeem it and the devil from all evil and darkness. God's act was just because it repaid the devil in near-identical fashion for what he had done. Yet it was good and wise, and in this sense even more just than simple recompense in that it accomplished good rather than evil, fully ameliorating the situation.

While the metal of the hook—the power of deity—was cloaked by humanity, Christ's uniqueness shone through, for Satan clearly perceived his greater worth. Arriving as ransom payment, the Son as God's coin, now manifest among the coins of humanity, gleams brightly as the chief coin and standard bearer. While Augustine was concerned that Christ as coin would lose the Son's uniqueness, Satan is still able to discern that this coin is more valuable than human coinage. Resonating with the perplexing gospel tale of the fish caught with a coin in its mouth to enable payment of the temple tax (Matt 17:27), Satan swallows the Christ coin as payment for enslaved humanity.

A hidden excess

At first blush, it may appear unfair that the liberation of humanity required the exchange of an object of higher perceived value. Does not the law of reciprocity and proportion, the intrinsic demand of justice, call for an equal exchange? Are not aesthetic categories of balance here violated? How can Christ be fair payment in exchange for humanity?

The implicit logic at work in the exchange, which renders this trans-action in fact just, is the *law of interest*. The reason why debt slavery was so pernicious, and why its timeframe could easily be extended, is that the lender required more than simple repayment of the initial loan. Laws of interest had long since emerged in the ancient Near East and Greco-Roman world, and it was culturally accepted and expected that loans were repaid with value added. This, of course, is one primary reason for the critique of moneylending: the practice bears unnatural fruit, increas-ing improperly, without the toil of the lender and at the expense of the debtor.[45] In the case of debt slavery, the debtor needs to work and toil until the principal and interest are compensated for, or unless a redeemer can offer a price equal to the initial loan plus interest.

God's offer of Christ to Satan as value added meets the require-ments, according to Gregory, since "by the exchange he [i.e., Satan] would acquire more possessing him than he already had" (*Address* 23). Thus, it is not merely an exchange or barter swap but a redemptive payment fol-lowing the "just" structure of a loan, revealing monetary themes at work. Apparently, God not only respects the justice of the debt situation but follows expected conventions of rendering added value by paying interest to set the debt slaves free.

Attributes of balance, proportionality, and justice are discernible in this exchange even when considered beyond the detail that Gregory provides. Satan tempted Adam and Eve with the knowledge of good and evil, assuring them that they would not die (Gen 3:1–7). Accepting the offer, they received what was advertised. Their eyes were opened to such knowledge, and they indeed did not immediately die. There was nevertheless an unrecognized surplus, for they also acquired much more than they bargained for or understood that they were acquiring. Christian tradition posits a type of spiritual death that took place, as well as, we learn from Gregory and other church fathers, a bondage to the devil.

Satan thus offers a perverse and nefarious generosity, providing what was promised (knowledge of good and evil) plus an excess that placed humanity in Satan's debt. Understood in terms of the "wages of sin" set forth by Origen, Satan did not merely pay humanity with satanic currency for their individual evil deeds. Rather, in providing humans with an entirely new orientation and capacity for independent judgment apart from God, Satan bestowed upon them a nefarious excess. This surplus turns out to be a loan that indebts them to the devil inasmuch as it also converts their allegiance and identity to align with a new, usurping lord. Humans get more than they bargained for, yet are held to account according to the supposedly fair terms of loan contracts. When one signs to accept a loan, the logic goes, even if one does not fully understand the terms or the consequences, one is rightly held accountable for repayment.

The divine response matches these dealings, with the exception of aiming to undo these bitter consequences. God offers Christ to the devil. The devil accepts and indeed receives Christ, getting what he bargained for: the price of humanity plus interest. Christ is killed and thus brought into possession of the devil in the realm of death. Yet Satan also receives so much more. Christ's value exceeds the terms, and Satan has received far more than he deserved. Christ's divinity enters the devil's realm and works its effects, reversing death and toppling the devil's power. From the satanic perspective, God is also demonstrating a perverse generosity, an excessive giving that undoes the devil's authority. Told theologically as Gregory does, however, and from the perspective of redeemed humanity, it is a good and wise justice. Satan receives what he gives, for he acquires a payment plus a vast surplus, just as he had provided to the first humans when he gave them knowledge of good and evil plus the excess of debt subordination to himself.

The language of excessive giving and surplus may bring to mind discourse on the gift. At a surface level, gift dynamics may be at work in this scenario. If so, they follow a classic Greek trope of subversive gifts much like the Trojan horse (*timeo Danaos et dona ferentes*). These are trickster gifts that provide value and yet mask ulterior motive made manifest in unforeseen excess.[46] Yet Gregory's narrative is not primarily about a gift transaction. In the tale of Troy, the horse is a unilateral and unsolicited offer, a feigned symbol of honor and obeisance. Beyond this, gift dynamics do not typically involve price negotiation or immediate reciprocal exchanges but eschew quantified value and introduce delays of return.[47] Gregory's tale of God's dealings with the devil, on the other hand, operates in a more properly economic sense of an exchange of goods based upon an agreed upon set of terms. Clear value calculation comes into play and an immediate swap takes place. Yet, even more than this, it operates within the explicit language and dynamics of moneylending, debt slavery, and repayment.

The effects of excess and surplus are in fact the very notions that characterize debt and render the lending economy so pernicious, according to Gregory. According to the law of interest, a loan generates more of itself, such that money and consequent obligation multiply. When one signs a bond of indebtedness, one in a sense knows what one is accepting, but one gets more than one bargains for as interest compounds. In this regard, the interest generated operates as the *unforeseen excess*, the surplus that traps the borrowers and catches them by surprise. Gregory depicts this sense of excess well: "So it is with persons who receive a large amount of loaned money; for a short time they have it in abundance and are later deprived of their paternal home" (*Against Those Who Practice Usury*).[48] Thus, while the language of excess in this cosmic exchange is reminiscent of the gratuity and superabundance often associated with gift economies, Gregory's direct illustration drawn from moneylending and the language of transaction, value calculation, and immediate exchange between God and Satan accentuate that a loan in monetary terms is taking place.[49]

Predatory lending

Attention to Gregory of Nyssa's use of fishhook (*to agkistron*) and bait (*to delear*) imagery drives home the fact that his tale is thoroughly permeated with the logic of moneylending and debt slavery. Much discussion has occurred over these terms, which, coupled with an idea of divine deception, have prompted criticism from modern authors, who have labeled the accounts "immoral," "childish," or "grotesque."[50] Yet, as Nicholas Constas notes in his perceptive study of the theme:

Far from being a grotesque idiosyncrasy limited to the writings of Gregory of Nyssa, the image of a divine fishhook baited with the flesh of Christ was used by dozens of writers from the mid-fourth through the seventh centuries and beyond, including such notables as Athanasius, John Chrysostom, John of Damascus, and Maximus the Confessor, to mention only a few. Among Latin writers, Augustine introduced a variation on this theme in the form of a mouse-trap baited with Christ's blood.[51]

The category of deceit was flexible and could be construed as a virtue given proper goals and intentions. In keeping with a patristic understanding of *oikonomia*, certain means were permissible based on their benevolent ends, such as parents deceiving children for the sake of discipline, teachers tricking students as a pedagogical tool, and doctors duping patients in the interests of healing. God, too, could employ strategy and calculation in the service of redemption. No ancient authors appear to have had difficulty with Gregory's employment of these images or with the notion of God's deceit of the devil.

Reflecting on the origins of the fishhook imagery, Constas explains: "this seemingly peculiar metaphor was not invented *ex nihilo* and subsequently imposed upon Scripture. Rather, it was derived from a theologically consistent conflation of several biblical passages, including Job 40–41; Ps 104:26 (LXX 103:26); and Isa 27:1, all of which are concerned with mocking the cosmic dragon and dragging him up from the depths of the sea on a fishhook."[52] Some scriptural precedent appears to exist for the imagery. To be sure, the metaphor was widespread and employed in a variety of ways in patristic texts. As such, it could conceivably invoke a broad set of notions of victorious trickery and strategic deception for the sake of divine purposes.

By using these terms, Gregory might be drawing upon a general sense of deception. Yet his usage, I suggest, is much more specific and revealing. The immediate context provides the best clues as to the sense of these terms, a range of usage to which surprisingly little attention has been paid. As we have seen, the primary illustration Gregory employs to explain ransom and redemption here is drawn from the world of moneylending and debt servitude. In keeping with the economic sense behind the idea of ransom, and in light of a precedent invoking spiritual debt and repayment in Scripture and in thinkers like Irenaeus and Origen, Gregory makes use of a cultural practice to articulate what has taken place on a cosmic scale according to such traditions. Moneylending and usury are social conventions that he and his fellow bishop-theologians repeatedly condemn. They are practices fraught with confrontation, power struggles, concerns about value, short- and long-term strategy, open calculation, and veiled intent. As such, they make apt analogy for the clash between God and the powers of darkness.

In his sermon against usury, Gregory describes loans in this way: "Money lending carries a purse and dangles bait (*delear*) as a wild beast to those in distress in order to ensnare them in their need (*sunkatapiôsi tou tokou to agkistron*)."[53] Here the illustration of bait and hook describes moneylenders using the offer of immediate funds as a lure to obtain greater gain through debt servitude. Concerned both about the harm to the impoverished debtor as well as to the sinful lender, Gregory warns further that "those who are quick to loan and pierce themselves with hooks of moneylending (*tois agkistrois tôn tokôn*) recklessly harm their own lives." To speak of bait and hooks, for Gregory, is to invoke the world of money-lending and destructive financial dealings.

The use toward which Gregory's older brother Basil put the imagery is also instructive. Gregory claims to have learned theology from Basil and we can be sure that Basil's thoughts and rhetoric exerted a formative influence upon Gregory.[54] Indeed, Gregory apparently defers to his brother on the description and condemnation of usury specifically, claiming that the "holy father Basil's advice [in such matters] is sufficient" (*Against Those Who Practice Usury*).[55] In his own homily on the topic, Basil describes the seductive way in which a moneylender speaks to a destitute loan seeker. He feigns friendship and amity and speaks of the reduced interest rate he can negotiate: "With pretenses of this kind and talk like this he fawns on the wretched victim, and induces him to swallow the bait (*to delear*). Then he binds him with written security, adds loss of liberty to the trouble of his pressing poverty, and is off. The man who has made himself responsible for interest which he cannot pay has accepted voluntary slavery for life" (*Second Homily on Psalm XIV*).[56]

Basil thus employs the same expressions Gregory uses to describe both Satan's original temptation and ensnaring of humankind and God's responsive luring and entrapment of the devil. Enjoining his poorer congregants to remain wary of borrowing money, Basil warns: "Let us not wait for those hopes [of the means of repayment] and let us not go like fish after bait (*hôsper hoi ichthues epi to delear*). As they swallow down the hook (*to agkistron*) with food so we also through money are entangled in the interest (*dia ta chrêmata tois tokois peripeirometha*)" (*Homily 12*).[57] Here a direct linguistic and conceptual parallel is provided to Gregory's description both of the fall as well as of Satan's demise. The bait and the hook clearly signify lent money and the entrapments of compound interest.

Based on the uses of both Gregory and Basil, we can infer that when Gregory employs the fishhook and baiting imagery to describe the interaction between God and Satan, *he has the world of moneylending and debt slavery primarily in mind*. Rather than general images of trickery and deceit, bait and fishhook language reinforces the conceptual connection with moneylending, debt, and obligation.[58] Elsewhere, Gregory and Basil may employ such imagery in other figurative applications for simple deceit and entrapment. But given the contextual discussion of moneylending, loans, and the snare of interest, it is reasonable to claim that the metaphor, when used here for the acts of God and Satan, underpins—or provides a conceptual hook for—the analogical relationship to these widespread and problematic monetary practices.

It is also noteworthy that Gregory takes an image often used to explain *oikonomia*—that of a physician attending to the sick who provides a strategic cure that matches the ailment and works toward healing— and applies it negatively in the case of moneylenders: "Do not live with feigned charity nor be a murderous physician with the pretence to heal for profit; if you do this, a person trusting in your skill can suffer great harm" (Gregory of Nyssa, *Against Those Who Practice Usury*).[59] Basil, too, speaks of the plight of the poor loan seeker, using tropes of poison and antidote that we have seen Gregory employ: "Coming for assistance, he found hostility. When searching around for antidotes, he came upon poisons" (Basil, *Homily 12*).[60] Moneylending is a negative or destructive *oikonomia*. It pretends to heal or address the need but in reality multiplies suffering. As such, it is precisely satanic in the ways invoked in our passage from

Gregory's *Address*. Satan demonstrated such a negative economy when he hooked humanity with that first, fateful loan. This is also reminiscent of the inverted—indeed perverted—economy of tyrants explored in Eusebius. There, all acts of generosity are forbidden and punished, for they do not fit within the structure of a satanic economy of insidious gain at the expense of others.

In this key section of his *Address* exploring ransom and redemption, therefore, Gregory employs fishhook and bait imagery from the world of loans and debt obligation beyond the specific illustration about moneylending in the passage. This serves to extend the economic sense of the moneylending illustration into the passage as a whole. In other words, it is not as if Gregory is describing redemption and then merely using a discrete analogy about moneylending to make his point. The apparent aside about moneylending in his narrative is the central *exemplum* and *reveals the logic of the whole*. He employs fishhook and bait imagery throughout the entire account, sprinkling hints of the economic rationale at work, and then inserts at a pivotal point a summary of debt relations to drive home the structural relationship.

The entire scenario of ransom and redemption as Gregory depicts it here is inflected with, permeated, and indeed conceptually structured by moneylending, debt slavery, and the ties of obligation and servitude that result. Critics who see in this passage a strange and childish dramatic narrative with random tropes of fishing and deception have utterly missed the point of Gregory's use of such images. He is working out the logic of a debt-based monetary exchange, applying the dynamics to their fullest in depicting what has taken place spiritually and morally. Literalizing the financial sense that we found to be lingering in ideas of *oikonomia*, God is depicted as carrying out an economic transaction at the cosmic level. Calculative exchange enters into the heart of the redemptive narrative.

Some of Gregory's ancient critics were attuned to these economic dynamics, raising protest about such depictions of God. They were not concerned that God engaged in deception or even that God snared Satan; indeed, God's involvement in predatory lending seems to have escaped their evaluation. Their protests stemmed rather from the sense that God and the devil appear to be depicted as economic peers engaging in a neutral market exchange. How could God transact in this way with the devil?

Why would God respect satanic rights of possession? Why would God offer what is most precious to the prince of darkness? As I will claim, Gregory's narrative withstands most of these critiques. The operations of monetary payment and debt obligation provide a solution to the very problems they appear to raise. They also highlight the residual traces of economic conquest at the heart of redemption narratives, raising further questions about the possibilities for application of such patterns in social and political realms.

6

Of Payment, Debt, and Conquest

It is a truism that the early modern colonizing project worked part and parcel with a missionizing impulse, as the expansion of European empires coincided with efforts to spread the gospel to the ends of the earth.[1] While this allegiance was certainly agonistic, and while examples can be multiplied of both missionary support for and opposition to certain forms of colonial conquest, rarely was there much question about their overall compatibility. Nor was there a question that the very sites and populations receiving religious instruction would also benefit from the political and economic impact of such annexation by the imperial center. From the graciously civilizing processes of education, to the benefits of market exchange and infrastructural improvement, to the glories of imposed Western forms of governance, colonial presence brought its own purported blessings to the benighted races, those who were simultaneously receiving the good news of the savior.

Whether or not accompanied by overt proselytization, the global extension of markets bears a salvific patina, even in its more secular contemporary manifestations. Globalization as the spread of capitalism is hailed as the "rising tide to lift all boats." It is touted as a necessary handmaiden to the expansion of democratic impulses around the world. Political freedom and free markets must coincide. Authentic liberation must include the liberation to produce, trade, and consume.

In incipient globalization, we hear transmuted echoes of the ancient Christian celebration of the unitary Roman Empire that brought enforced peace and stability across diverse lands, enabling the effective transmission of the gospel. As capitalism was hailed in Europe as the saving means to bring stable and "gentle" relations among new nation-states, it was extended globally as that method by which to bring salvation to those further behind on the path of human progress. The underside of the gospel proclamation that markets bring benefits like civilization and democracy, of course, is that imposing markets requires force—whether the force of law, the constraints of structural adjustment programs, or even military and police presence, for instance.

The last chapter highlighted the redemptive and pacifying nature of economy as it was lauded as a source of amity in society. This chapter considers the other side of the coin, the uses of economy in conquest and victory over opponents as a mode of extending reign and control. The two dimensions work together, for aggressive insertion of economy into foreign territory is justified by the peace and salvation it is said to bring. In revealing how Gregory of Nyssa's ransom account does not succumb to ancient critiques that it constrains God or puts God and Satan on equal footing, I draw out the implicit claim, required by the logic of the narrative, that God in Christ has imposed a counterloan upon the devil. What is more, attending to the political language in Gregory's account, I show how his ransom narrative emerges as a theopolitical tale of competing sovereigns engaging in economic struggle. God can be seen as annexing and colonizing satanic territory through a commercial transaction that employs Christ as the coin of God, the chief currency of the kingdom. Such a narrative provides one possible glimpse of colonizing economic rationality embedded in Christian thought that will come to fruition a thousand years later as Christendom initiates its formal project of colonizing religious and economic others.

There exists, then, an inherent if implicit allegiance between the expansion of economy, even in the face of opposition, and basic Christian narratives of redemption as glimpsed in ransom theory. From the persuasive payment in Irenaeus, to Constantine's merciful purchase of enemy combatants in Eusebius, to the binding loan against Satan in Gregory of Nyssa, formative Christian soteriological tradition correlates redemptive economy with conquest. The centrality of economy for governmental reason in the West thus operates together with the apparent necessity for the

West to engage in colonizing movements, endlessly expanding economic territory into foreign lands in the name of peace, security, growth, and sociopolitical salvation. Such colonial expansions derive an initial motivating impulse from missionizing concerns to incorporate the unsaved into the redemptive economy of Christian empire, a dynamic that suggests longstanding affiliation between such theology and monetary economic growth. This chapter considers one ancient manifestation of this fusion of redemptive conquest through economy.

Divine embargo

Gregory of Nazianzus's ransom account is worth considering both for the concerns it raises and for its contextual proximity to Gregory of Nyssa's. As a longtime colleague of Nyssen, Nazianzen is acquainted with a similar theological and philosophical heritage and would be familiar with many of the cultural tropes and practices Nyssen invokes. Their theological systems and emphases are distinct, however, and they certainly had their interpersonal differences. Nazianzen takes a different direction on the idea of ransom payment in redemption:

It is worth our while to examine a point of doctrine which is overlooked by many but seems to me deserving examination. For whom, and with what object, was the blood shed for us, the great and famous blood of God, our high-priest and sacrifice, outpoured? Admittedly we were held in captivity by the devil, having been sold under sin and having abdicated our happiness in exchange for wickedness. But if the ransom belongs exclusively to him who holds the prisoner, I ask to whom it was paid, and why. If to the devil, how shameful that that robber should receive not only a ransom from God, but a ransom consisting of God himself, and that so extravagant a price should be paid to his tyranny before he could justly spare us! (*Oration* 45.22)[2]

According to Nazianzen, the devil had no just claim over humanity. Humanity's bondage to the devil was more akin to a robber or usurper stealing God's rightful possession than a just economic transaction leading to debt slavery. What an outrage it would be for God to pay the robber to reclaim what already belongs to God. That God might give Christ, the most valuable possession and indeed "God himself," as a payment is too much to bear and adds insult to injury.

Turning in the other direction, however, Nazianzen encounters a similar impasse: "But if [ransom was paid] to the Father, I ask first, how? For it was not by Him that we were being oppressed; and next, On what principle did the blood of His only begotten Son delight the Father, who would not receive even Isaac, when he was being offered by his father?" (*Oration* 45.22). Here he finds it equally inconceivable that God the Father should be the recipient of payment, echoing Origen, who asked: "But to whom did He give His soul as a ransom for many? Surely not to God" (*Commentary on Matthew* 16.8).[3] Despite such concerns, some ensuing patristic thinkers and medieval theologians would indeed develop the idea of God as the legitimate payee. Of course, the position of God as recipient of the ransom raises its own forms of scandal.[4]

Despite his protests, however, Nazianzen holds to similar tenets as Nyssen: humanity had indeed been "sold" into bondage to the devil; human agency appears involved in a willful "abdication" and "exchange." Whether the devil is seen as a robber or not, some transaction did indeed occur. He admits that the nature of the situation seems to permit a notion of ransom being paid to the devil. He responds with offense and repugnance, but he does not challenge its soundness. Rather, it is "shameful" to think that God would cooperate with such a thing. Desiring to uphold the narrative of redemption and to glorify God as the savior of humankind, Nazianzen is left to conclude that "the greater part of what we might say shall be reverenced with silence" (*Oration* 45.22).[5] Avoiding the theme of ransom, Nazianzen seems content to speak more often in the language of sacrifice because it arguably circumvents the offensive notion of a payment to the devil.[6]

For Nazianzen, God's payment to Satan appears as a violation of justice given the devil's role as a usurper. Nevertheless, whether missed by Nazianzen or simply rejected, the concept of the just bondage of humanity in a narrative like Nyssen's is coherent and consistent with the latter's overall presentation. Again, if we construe justice not as conformity to some fixed set of statutes or framework of legality or morality, but understand it as Nyssen presents it, as the appropriate consequences of a logical and freely chosen set of steps, then satanic bondage can be deemed just. The fish desire the bait; the fish bite and are hooked. This is proper fishing, and the fisherman has appropriately caught his quarry. Similarly, the poor desire money to address their needs: they accept the offer of a loan from a predatory moneylender; they freely ensnare themselves and have been appropriately even if repugnantly caught. God's wisdom and aesthetic appreciation for balance and proportion mean that retrieval of the stolen fish or freeing of bonded humanity will follow a pattern of similar logic, demonstrating superior sportsmanship.

This justice claim need not conflict with a notion of Satan as a thief or usurper. Satan was not fishing in his own pond, so to speak, but infiltrated waters belonging to God. Within this larger perspective, his actions are unjust. While it may be well within God's rights to pull rank, asserting ownership of the pond and taking back by force the stolen fish, God's response is to play along with Satan and outdo him at his own game. For Nyssen, it is a far more glorious response. God demonstrates *oikonomia*, using deceit as an acceptable means based on its redemptive and ameliorative results. God even uses practices that Nyssen and all other fathers and church tradition condemn—namely, moneylending and loaning at interest—but does so with redemptive ends in mind, justifying the means. God's use of the baited fishhook to unseat the devil is thus portrayed with approval in patristic contexts. Nyssen's is a precise and nuanced account, the technicality of which is seemingly lost on subsequent readers because of the distracting offense of an apparent validation of the devil's rights.

What can be glimpsed in Nazianzen's response, however, and what comes through more clearly in other critiques of portrayals such as Nyssen's, are concerns that such a transaction puts God and Satan on equal footing. As Adamantius complained, God and the devil appear as "two friends" doing business as usual (*Dialogues* I.27).[7] By appearing to respect the nature of commercial exchange, God seems to stoop so low so as to confer neutrally with the divine archenemy. Deceit and entrapment of the devil were fine, but simple exchange between God and Satan appears unseemly. Part of Nazianzen's outrage, and part of what constitutes the apparent "shamefulness" of ransom accounts, is that, by participating in such commerce, God seems constrained by the devil's (economic) desires, for the devil can appeal to the "just" dynamics of monetary economy to ensure fair dealings. Indeed, Nyssen expressed this as a potential concern of onlookers, as he worried that Satan might accuse God of being unjust if God forcibly retrieved humanity from his demonic control. Does God's condescension to an exchange of payment for property under market terms constitute some necessary equalization and neutrality? Is Satan able, by the internal laws of commercial exchange, to force God's hand?

Such concerns may stem from a commonsense and naïve view of monetary economy as a sphere of objective and neutral reciprocity. God and the devil may appear as dispassionate market actors, hawking and purchasing wares in a cosmic bazaar. Yet, as Nyssen maintains throughout his narrative and as we have seen in his diatribe against usury, these economies are anything but neutral, innocent, or devoid of power relations. Such exchanges do not nullify conflict and struggle. Money's longstanding links to sovereignty also give clues to the potential dynamics of power at work. Indeed, Nyssen's entire account can function within a narrative of divine conquest.

Christus Victor Economicus

Gustaf Aulén famously attempted to group and codify many ancient depictions of salvation under what he termed the "classical" view of soteriology.[8] Concerned with an incipient or at times explicit legalism in modern models of salvation as well as an overemphasis on human agency, Aulén asserted these patristic views as evocative of the sovereignty and unilateral activity of God in redemption. In his view, salvation is a process initiated and completed by God and centrally involves divine defeat of sin, death, and all powers construed in opposition to God and to human flourishing. He explores ransom accounts, highlighting their presence in many of the early theologies he champions, and he renders a mixed judgment on their relevance and appeal.

Aulén notes the language of justice used in ransom theory by Nyssen and other Greek theologians, claiming that "the essential idea which the legal language is intended to express is that God's dealings even with the powers of evil have the character of 'fair play.'"[9] As part of his polemic against so-called Latin legalist accounts of atonement, Aulén here asserts justice as simple fairness. As object of his critique, he has in mind primarily Anselm, who depicts sin as a violation and offense against the laws and honor of the sovereign. Aulén seeks to distinguish earlier tradition from the excessive focus on a violation of divine legal codes seen in later accounts. His reading of justice as fairness and balance coincides with our analysis of Nyssen. As we saw, Nyssen appeals in his invocation of justice not to legal codes or frameworks but to the rational process by which enslavement and redemption take place. Justice is about balance, proportion, and a commonsense view of fairness.[10]

For Aulén, ransom theory also helps preserve a sense of "the responsibility of man for his sin, and that the judgment which rests on mankind is a righteous judgment."[11] Here he upholds the view maintained by Nyssen that humankind has drawn just condemnation and incurred bondage for its actions. Even if the tyranny of Satan is unjust, and even if debt slavery is a deplorable condition from which God seeks to redeem humankind, humanity's predicament is in the first instance "just" or fair because it was made possible by human desire and free decision. Ransom theory shows that humankind had some agency in entering into the bind in which it finds itself, and it emphasizes that real costs are incurred by these decisions. It reveals, figuratively, the consequences of acts of rebellion against God and points to the steps God takes to make the situation right.

Overall, however, Aulén misses much of the logic and force of ransom accounts. Appearing to uphold the consensus view that the depictions are "grotesque" and "absurd," at least when followed too closely, he maintains that the import of such accounts is to demonstrate God's presence in, commitment to, and sovereignty over redemption. Serving his broader argument about the unilateral activity of God to save humanity, ransom stories, he claims, show that: "God does not stand, as it were, outside the drama that is being played out, but Himself takes part in it, and attains His purpose by internal, not external, means; He overcomes evil, not by an almighty fiat, but by putting in something of His own, through Divine self-oblation."[12] Aulén here appears to elide senses of ransom and sacrifice and asserts that ransom shows divine self-giving and involvement. Ransom is a figurative assertion that God contributes what is of most value to God so as to redeem humanity from its plight. Thus, for Aulén, ransom tales are fundamentally about God's grace, love, and consequent self-involvement, the "childish" details of a duplicitous monetary exchange notwithstanding.

Given what we have observed about the nature of monetary economy and the logic of debt, however, I submit that ransom theory harmonizes more closely with the themes of victorious conquest and divine sovereignty that Aulén wishes to recuperate. The presence of ransom motifs in many of the patristic accounts he summarizes is not happenstance, and these narratives do not merely tell an ancillary tale of divine concern in the midst of victory over the devil. Rather, they fit completely within and function as *a central conceptual mechanism* for such a story of God's triumph over opposing powers.

This dynamic of conquest is crucial to recognize because tales of ransom, redemption, and sacrifice are often told simply as gestures of divine love and compassion. From humanity's perspective, they certainly are this, but they also serve as so much more. An interpretive framework informed by monetary economy helps to reveal that ransom tales fit into and substantiate claims of divine reign and government. Ransom theory shows the inner workings of the divine *oikonomia* as it overcomes opposition and moves forward in its governance of creation and management of redemption. Given theology's legacy in Western political economic practice, this raises questions about how churches, states, and other authoritative institutions might make use of or indirectly benefit from these concepts in their own mechanisms of rule. If ransom is simply told as a tale of divine benevolence without attending to the details of economic struggle at its center, this is analogous, for instance, to endorsing governmental programs in the name of the benefit they purportedly offer the governed without considering the forms of institutionalized, economic violence they might contain.

For Gregory of Nyssa, lending money is a predatory gesture, an act of aggression. It is like fishing, going in search of prey, for victims who are then caught unawares based on their needs and desires. As he chides the wealthy in his congregation, exploitation of a poor person in this manner "turns him into an adversary" (*Against Those Who Practice Usury*).[13] Lending makes an initial apparent "gift," a sum of money which, like the worm on the hook, can be seen as good in itself. The loaned money takes care of pressing needs, just as the worm on its own provides sustenance. Yet the initial money, like the bait, cloaks a hook, an offensive weapon intended to trap the recipient. The debtor is drawn into a situation of subservience, being obligated to repay the sum plus interest or to enter into debt slavery to work off what is owed. God's ransom payment, more accurately seen as a counterloan, is an aggressive act toward the devil. While couched in terms of eventual good, for it redeems humanity and even Satan, this act within divine *oikonomia* is one that captures and topples God's enemy. Although gracious from the perspective of liberated humanity, seen within the microcosm of the world of debt slavery and moneylending, God's monetary act toward the devil is hostile.[14]

Phishing Satan

In his recent engagement with market dynamics in light of biblical tradition, Harvey Cox notes the long-standing prohibition against predatory lending in the ancient Near East as conveyed in Scripture.[15] He likens such practices to contemporary phishing scams, in which unwitting borrowers are lured into entrapping loan situations. The term "phishing" is of modern coinage, but it harks back to the ancient employment of an actual fishing metaphor to describe such lending practices. Although Cox does not mention the connection between the term for this modern scam and this ancient metaphor, it seems clear that contemporary phishing is an echo of a long-standing practice that was once likened to fishing itself. In the context of Gregory of Nyssa's narrative, Satan has phished humanity. God, in turn, has phished Satan. In raising the biblical condemnation of phishing, Cox signals a key offense presented by Gregory's account: God engages in a type of transaction that looks a lot like predatory moneylending, or at least appears to cooperate with its intrinsic "justice." Although Cox invokes the biblical censure of moneylending, in our scenario God appears to abide by the terms of such practices.[16]

In Gregory's logic, the moves of the devil and God are structurally mirrored, meaning that God does not simply make a redemptive payment to nullify the satanic loan. God is not merely a kinsman redeemer here, buying debt-enslaved humanity from the devil's grasp. If God simply gave the devil the appropriate amount required, in this case Christ—who, for the devil, would be equal to the value of humanity plus interest— the terms would be satisfied, humanity would be released, and the devil would go on his way with Christ, his fair payment. This would be a bare market transaction. The devil would presumably be free to enter into new relations of debt obligation with unwitting victims. That the devil receives an unforeseen excess, however, and finds himself now in a bind as subjected to God, indicates the dynamics of moneylending and debt slavery.

Whether or not the devil fully realizes the implications, *he has received a counterloan from God.* Satan transacts with God, receiving the lent sum of value (Christ), but suddenly finds himself in bonds of obligation with God, snared on a christological financial fishhook. In offering Christ as God's currency, God provided compensation for enslaved humanity, paid the interest due, and also gave an infinite excess that tips the scales in God's favor and obligates the devil. In the language of binding gifts, this was a perverse and excessive giving intended to obligate the recipient. God offered something of so much worth to the devil that the devil was eternally obligated to God. The devil received so much more than the worth of humanity, or the interest due, that he was in turn bound by repayment. Christ was unable to remain as property in the devil's possession but ultimately had to return to God, indicating the irresistible movement toward repayment of the loan. The hidden surplus of God's payment to the devil reveals itself to be a loan that must be repaid.

Just as moneylenders trap borrowers with loan contracts, both the devil, initially, and then God, in response, use loans and broader monetary economic dynamics in a struggle for domination. Moneylending is an aggressive and predatory act, seeking gain and aiming for profit at the expense of the victim. Being enslaved to Satan, humans were subjects in a satanic economy under the devil's lordship and participated in destructive exchange relations. Through ransom, which works out to be a type of counterloan and insertion of divine currency, humanity's release is secured and the devil is entrapped. This move is justified through *oikonomia* because of its redemptive ends. Since God's actions are intended with a glorious, just, and compassionate end in sight and work for the salvation of humankind and Satan, they are permitted even though they mirror the devil's. They are allowed by exception.

The logic of a requisite loan repayment explains the irresistible return of Christ to God. Without the idea of repayment, the tale of Christ's resurrection makes little sense in the context of the monetized ransom account. If ransom is a simple payment, there is no reason why the devil should not be able to retain it. There is no sense in which the devil should be described as snared or hooked, as this term was imported from the world of moneylending and debt slavery. Furthermore, without such logic, the exchange cannot remain fair and cannot prevent the devil from crying foul. Gregory's concern to see that God engage in culturally acceptable economic play here would collapse if at the end of the exchange God simply pulled rank and through fiat retrieved the Christ coin from the devil's grasp. This would obviate the entire foregoing subtlety of the phishing endeavor. Rather, the payment ruptures Satan's hold and returns to the issuer in a manner deemed appropriate and fitting for *oikonomia*, proving that it was initially a loan. Satan is entrapped and obligated to God as an unwitting borrower finds himself or herself indebted to the bondholder. The devil is brought into a permanent and fixed relation of subservience to God, just as a debt slave is to the lender. That the devil is never off the hook reveals the inability for Satan to adequately repay God for the worth of Christ, even as Christ is recognized as cosmically always originating from and returning to God.

The politics of debts and contracts

In discussing Gregory of Nyssa's narrative of redemption by a ransom exchange, Adam Kotsko suggests that it anticipates modern social contract theory, particularly in its Hobbesian form. Adam and Eve are depicted as freely electing to enter into an agreement to submit to the devil in a mythical "state of nature," empowering Satan as their Leviathan lord. As Kotsko rightly notes, here the tale is inverted, because Eden was not a state of "war of all against all" to which the satanic sovereign might bring enforced peace. Rather, in opting for their new lord, their situation declined as conflict and death were introduced into the world.[17]

Missing from Kotsko's rendition of freely contracting agents is the logic of debt that figures centrally in the account and in the nature of the devil's lordship. If anything, the tale is posed in the first place as economic. The encounter involves an exchange between unequal powers that results in imposed debt slavery and its attendant connotations of domination. Satan already appears to be an authority figure who, rather than being elected or empowered by humans, comes to them with an offer of switching allegiances. Humanity is already marked as belonging to God the originary sovereign. That Satan is posited in ransom accounts as a tyrant and usurper signals the dynamics of political struggle among preestablished sovereign centers. If ransom accounts do prefigure social contract, they do so in a way that exposes the myth of such political theory. They show its naïve assumption of two equal, self-contained, rational individuals freely choosing to contract with each other and support an overlord, rather than an actual encounter of agonistic imbalances of power where forms of constraint are always operative. Ransom may give the lie to social contract theory and signal the always already existing debt that operates in relations with Leviathan.[18]

Furthermore, rather than a neutral contract between God and the devil, the exchange is rich with themes of combat and competition. Even attending to the warlike imagery, however, it is not enough to regard the ransom encounter as one between an average moneylender and unwitting borrower. God and Satan are not two anonymous transactors within a single economic space. Theopolitical dynamics are at work here. In the first place, God is described as "sovereign of the universe" and "sovereign of all" (Gregory of Nyssa, *Address* 30, 35). The devil, on the other hand, is referred to as "our overlord," and Gregory speaks of the "tyranny of the adversary" (*Address* 23, 25). Gregory tells us that the devil has set himself up against God since the beginning of time. The devil has committed an initial act of aggression against God by leading away humankind, who, although "justly caught" based on their desire and free will, are rightfully God's. God is the king and final authority, and Satan emerges as a challenger of sorts, intent on undermining divine rule and establishing a region of rebellion to such sovereignty. The encounter is politically inflected, with a depiction of Satan as *tyrannos* drawing on the long history of reflection on political tyranny in Greek thought.

Indeed, Gregory in this text demonstrates familiarity with Eusebius's invocation of tyranny to describe political opponents of divine purpose, as well as Eusebius's appeal to progress in the ecclesial political realm as evidence of divine victory. In a passage that could have been pulled directly from the pages of Eusebius, Gregory speaks of "those who were forced by tyrants to renounce their faith," recalling the "deceit of demons" and "madness of idolatry" of previous times. After the incarnation, however, "altars, temple porches, and precincts and shrines have entirely disappeared, along with the ceremonies practiced by the devotees of demons for their own deceit . . . The result is that . . . [t]hroughout the world, churches and altars have been erected instead in the name of Christ" (*Address* 18). Eusebius had claimed previously that "by the confusion of evils of unnatural idolatry they [i.e., tyrants] enslaved first themselves and then all their subjects to the deceits of evil demons," noting, significantly, that such tyrants also "held the threat of very heavy taxation over all men" (*Life of Constantine* 1.13.3). Constantine served as the primary divine agent responsible for replacing pagan altars with churches as a sign of vanquishing demons. As a testimony to his victory over the "tyranny of the godless," inspired as such tyranny was by the "dragon" and "crooked serpent," Constantine erected a painting of "the dragon under his own feet and those of his sons, pierced through the middle of the body" (*Life of Constantine* 3.3.1–2). Remarkably, here also Satan is depicted as pierced in a tale of political conquest, in a way that prefigures piercing by the fishhook.

Because of the supreme authority of God and the theopolitically construed challenge of Satan, this economic exchange is not just one among many that might occur within a sovereign economic territory. Even moneylenders are beholden to the final political economic authority, whose money they lend and attempt to multiply and to whom they, too, must render due in the form of taxes and tributes. Neither are God and Satan simply two prepolitical free agents in a mythical "state of nature" engaging in mutual, contractual exchange. In our scenario, God *is* a sovereign center of authority conducting an exchange with a political rival, one who has set up an alternative economy, who regulates exchanges by another set of weights and measures, and who has taken political economic prisoners from divine territory.

We considered how tyranny is often tied in Greek thought to economic rapacity and the misuse of resources, and the devil has been portrayed as an ever-desirous lord who made use of finances to enslave humanity. The debt slavery that humanity thus experiences is slavery to an alternate political power. Satan is not a simple moneylender operating inside the economic territory of God. Just as political leaders in the ancient world issue new coins and proclaim new weights and measures in an effort to distinguish themselves from rivals, the devil asserts an alternative economy and lays claim to God's subjects. As Origen recounted, in agreeing to sin and follow Satan, humanity "received a coin from the devil . . . the devil's property and treasure . . . money [that] proceeds from his mint. With this money, therefore, he buys those whom he buys and makes all of those his slaves who have received however insignificant a coin from his property of this kind" (*Exodus Homily* VI.9).[19]

Satan is thus seen more accurately as an insurgent prince or vassal power who establishes his own currency in challenge to God and who, in bringing humanity into debt bondage, draws God's subjects into a different political economic circuit. This is why God's dealings with Satan here are inflected not merely economically but also politically. Even as economics is always properly political, in such an encounter it remains explicitly so. Satan is a competing political authority aiming at tyranny, one who is toppled in the course of a monetary economic and debt-based transaction. Satan is not depicted as another subject of God simply enslaving fellow subjects through neutral, market-based debt transactions but as a challenger to divine lordship over humanity and consequently as a political rival. This is why the tale of spiritual debt slavery and ransom is not just about an economic exchange but is a *theopolitical parable*.

Simple exchange relations with a tyrant seem unjust, as Gregory of Nazianzus rightly protests. One should not do business with such types; they deserve *economic embargo*. An alternative approach, which Gregory of Nyssa offers, is *economic conquest*. Rather than eschewing exchange relations, God uses the agonistic power differentials in monetary economy and in debt relations to topple a political foe. Such takeover entails bringing the devil into an exchange relationship with God as sovereign and revolves centrally around the devil accepting the divine loan and royal currency.

The devil, like Nyssen's critics, has a naïve and commonsense view of monetary interaction or perhaps, just as naively, thinks a barter swap is taking place. Satan appears to imagine that monetary exchange can occur and leave power relations unaffected. He does not sense the approaching sovereign economic threat, cloaked as it is in the surface appeal of Christ as the brilliant and shining token. This advancing power offers to do business with the devil, giving him the Christ coin in exchange for enslaved humanity. The devil finds God's coin to be of more worth and value than his debt-bound subjects, an appropriate compensation plus interest to revoke the bond of indebtedness. Yet, by accepting the payment, he accepts the currency of an alternative, divine realm and offers tacit acknowledgement of the sovereign who is represented by the coinage. By receiving the coin, he enters into circuits of indebtedness and obligation to the issuing center and must ultimately render back to that center its very token.

Divine moneylending and taxation

We saw that the excess of Christ as payment to the devil functions like the compounding interest of a loan that ensnares the borrower and is ultimately his undoing. What is more, here we see that such payment functions like the issue of sovereign tokens of exchange that must be rendered back through tax or tribute obligations. The logic is analogous and the sovereign issuing center functions like a moneylender, providing loans of sovereign currency and bringing all who accept these tokens into relations of obligation with it. Christ is the sovereign token that must find its ultimate destination back into the hands of the king who issued it. Following the circuit of Caesar's coin in the gospel stories, the devil, too, had to render to God the things that are God's. Christ, as the chief coin of the Father, was always monetarily destined to find his way back to God as sovereign minter and to the royal treasury in heaven.

In his sermon on usury, Gregory of Nyssa offers a glimpse of something like a formal model of God that underlies his account of God's economic dealings. Echoing the scriptural claim that "whoever is kind to the poor lends to the Lord" (Prov 19:17), Gregory develops the remarkable image of God as the guarantor of humanity's loans when such are offered instead as gifts to the poor. He reminds the potential moneylenders in his congregation that:

the entire world is the possession of a fair Debtor (*chreôstês*) who wisely takes care to obtain abundance and wealth. The whole earth is gold and belongs to your Debtor; silver, copper and every other material are subject to his authority (*despoteias*). Consider the sky's expanse, examine the boundless sea, learn from the earth's magnitude and count the living beings which it nourishes. All are subject and belong to him who transcends your comprehension. Oh man, pay close attention. Do not insult God nor reckon him to be worse than a money-changer. Make a pledge to him who is immortal and believe in his reliable bond (*cheirographoi*) which can never be sundered. Do not demand gain but give bountifully and without corruption. Then you will see God who abundantly dispenses his grace. (*Against Those Who Practice Usury*)[20]

Gregory's image here is striking for how it juxtaposes notions of God as moneylender as well as a sovereign who rules all and possesses all, invoking both a notion of indebtedness to a creditor and a sense of tax or tribute owed to the king. Believers are called to enter into debt obligations to such a king and to trust in his universal ownership and copious provision, which exceeds the terms of exchange. God is not like a typical moneychanger, exacting harsh terms on the loan; God expects repayment in the form of human generosity and largesse and rewards this with superabundance. God as creditor thus functions with a system of debt obligation in the name of one who cleared all debts.[21] That such a nearly tautological circuit can exist is enabled in part by the dynamic that debt cancellation operates side by side with reentrenched indebtedness. Divine deliverance and ransom from debt by debt lead not to a removal of obligation upon those set free but to a transference of ownership of the bond. Liberated humanity remains bound to God.

The faithful are enjoined to serve God by giving gifts to the poor, with the promise that they will eventually be repaid for these duties. Lenders may not demand interest, fearful of God who owns all and is lord of all. Repayment is deflected and deferred, however, relegated to an eschatological dimension, or at least one that is tenuous and thus requires faith. What must be hoped for is eventual repayment by treasure in heaven. This ruler who achieved victory over enemies through strategic economic conquest and who asserts benevolent reign over rescued humanity thus occupies a structurally similar position to the monetary sovereign. When addressing moneylenders, Gregory posits God as the ultimate moneylender, who carries out such transactions generously as a model for Christian lenders to follow.

This idea of lending as a gift is one contribution by Gregory to the discourse of almsgiving so prevalent in his time. Giving in order to gain eternal reward is here contextualized to address those who would lend money. Such loans should be converted to gifts to the poor, with the expected repayment to be deferred according to God's timing. In this way, Gregory secures generosity toward the poor as well as resources for congregations. Pastoral economy is cognizant of the divine economist and also, as we see now, the divine creditor who loans to all since he is the owner and sovereign of all. It is this sovereign who toppled the devil by economy, through a loan so great and generous that it ensured the obligation of the satanic recipient. In parallel fashion, God is displayed as sovereign over the devil, inducting the devil into the territory of divine economy such that the devil, like all subjects, must render tax tribute to the heavenly Caesar.

Counterintuitive as it may seem, to receive money from the sovereign issuing center is to receive a burden, a token of obligation. Reflecting on various historical instances of taxation, Alfred Mitchell Innes observes:

> Every time a coin or certificate is issued a solemn obligation is laid on the people of the country. A credit on the public treasury is opened, a public debt incurred. It is true that a coin does not purport to convey an obligation, there is no law which imposes an obligation, and the fact is not generally recognized. It is nevertheless the simple truth. A credit, it cannot be too often or too emphatically stated, is a right to "satisfaction." This right depends on no statute, but on common or customary law. It is inherent in the very nature of credit throughout the world.[22]

The issuance of currency betrays the imposition of debt by a governing power. The burden is shared and passed around to all of the governed, who labor and exchange under the mark of the king. Recognition is given that the power center has rightful claim to determine the weights and measures for transaction, and tacit thanks and honor are rendered to the one whose image is on the circulating token. Like Gregory of Nyssa, Innes asserts that the right or justice of monetary obligation here needs no external law or statute. It is justice unto itself. In this case, it is right and just that the one who oversees economy, the one whose very image makes possible transaction and resource allocation, should be the ultimate destination of value that is returned through the praises of tribute, tithe, and taxes.

God's ransom payment to the devil therefore serves to conquer the enemy by bringing him into economic circuits with God. The transaction is governed by the "just" logic of monetary exchange and debt obligation. The devil has no recourse to protest. Had God invaded satanic territory and pulled humanity back into the divine kingdom by force, Satan could

have accused God of foul play. By accepting the initial satanic loan payment, humans had been brought into exchange relations with the devil.
They had acknowledged him as the standard bearer of value, and their
debt servitude was as to a foreign lord. Satan's acceptance of the divine
counterloan served, in turn, as the devil's own unknowing acknowledgement of the superiority of divine currency and as a submission to God's
weights and measures. God came to Satan and offered him the currency
of the kingdom. When he accepted it, his territory was economically colonized by the divine (conquered via *oikonomia*), bringing his space under
the reign of God.

Indeed, many accounts of colonization note the imposition of a sovereign currency and tax requirement upon occupied territory.[23] Infusing a
colony with new currency achieves many tasks. Ideologically speaking, it
circulates the image of the ruling center among the populace. New subjects are gradually conditioned to associate such images with the means
of payment and acquisition of the basics of life. They are reminded of the
lord by whose mark it is they buy and sell. Figuratively speaking, they
must prostrate themselves before the image in order to prolong physical
life, accepting its terms and regime of value. The imposition also inserts
the particular weights and measures established by the power, permeating
exchange relations with certain denominations of worth. This provides
new sovereignly determined methods of categorizing and evaluating reality. Most centrally, perhaps, establishing a new monetary space draws all
participants into relations of obligation with the colonizing center. They
must now render back to the authority a portion of these circulating
tokens, reclaimed in taxes.

Annexation and colonization

In describing this encounter between God and the devil, Marion
Grau invokes a colonization metaphor: the devil is the colonizer of old
who has exerted dominion over humankind, which Christ undoes. Grau
deploys colonization in a one-sided fashion, however, attributing such a
role to the devil alone. Drawing on a notion of postcolonial mimicry,
Grau places Christ in the position of subversive trickster, exhibiting weak-
ness and subservience in the veil of humanity, while implicitly defying

Satan's rule.[24] The end result is that "[t]he devil, that colonizer of humanity, is tricked by divine mimicry."[25]

The "justice" and balance of Gregory of Nyssa's account, however, require that God's tactics *reciprocally mirror* those of the devil. Here the colonizer is colonized, the deceptive conqueror is in turn conquered through deception, and an original debt that enslaved humanity is countered with a new loan that brings the devil into indebted subservience. God is not any more a trickster than the devil originally was, although God is depicted as a better one. Likewise, God is *not any less a colonizer* than Satan and is, again, superior in such acts. Economic colonization is given divine legitimation in such an account. As the logic of an early ransom narrative such as Gregory's requires God to mime and outdo the devil at his own game of debt entrapment and economic conquest, we see the roots of a troubling eventual theological reversal: as Kotsko notes in light of Anselm's more developed salvation account centuries later, itself preoccupied with balance and reciprocal mirroring, "God becomes the devil."[26]

We glimpse here the problems with construing ransom accounts, as J. Denny Weaver has, as "nonviolent atonement."[27] To be sure, Gregory's account laudably does not center on the suffering and slaughter of God's Son at the altar of sacrifice. Departing from notions of sacrifice, with their troubling displays of the Father approving of the murder of the Son on the cross, Weaver invokes ransom as a nonviolent alternative. Focusing on themes of divine duplicity and toppling of Satan's kingdom via this cloaked payment, Weaver considers ransom an improvement for the ethic it commends and the narrative it upholds. But is it?

Aside from the fact that Satan swallowing the bait of Christ is code for Christ's suffering, death, and descent into hell—in other words, we have not really escaped the cross here—what are the possible ramifications of this vision of divine economic conquest? God's acts may not endorse those of a Father requiring the death of his Son as atonement, but they do appear to validate the use of economic means to overcome a foe. Perhaps this alternative is agreeable here since it is the devil and not the Son who is the victim? This is certainly how Gregory's ancient critics responded: God's deception of the devil was lauded as a sign of divine supremacy.

Regardless of whether or not the devil should be considered an acceptable victim, we should attend to the themes of imposed debt obligation and the violence of economic conquest as carried out by God. Since God becomes the ultimate standard and model to follow for pastoral economy and imperial governance, the implications of God's acts as here narrated for sociopolitical application require analysis. More to the point, we need to consider the dynamics of economic annexation and colonization that are modeled in such a narrative.

The emperor Constantine, depicted as he was by Eusebius as theopolitical redeemer, operates as an implicit trope in the ransom account as well. In the midst of conquest, Constantine made use of monetary payment to save lives of enemies. Soldiers aligned with opposing forces justly deserved condemnation and death in this struggle, but they received mercy through a means of payment. The details are different, for here Constantine is seen as bargaining with—or, better yet, providing incentives to—his own soldiers. He is not undertaking exchanges with the enemy captain in order to spare the lives of combatants. Yet, when one of his soldiers achieved victory over an enemy in the midst of battle, that enemy was at the mercy of—enslaved to—that Constantinian soldier. The latter now had authority over the enemy soldier's life, having won it "justly" in the course of battle. The enemy had entered willingly and knowingly into a contest of strength and skill and had lost. His life was justly forfeit, and as a prisoner of war he could be enslaved or killed. Yet Constantine, mirroring divine compassion, uses money to intervene, paying his soldiers in exchange for sparing the lives of prisoners. He thus gains additional conscripts and subjects. His redemptive payments function within a larger framework of advancing his territorial rule. The ransom works together with his claim of lordship over those who are saved, as he overcomes their lord and conquers their enemy realm.

A key parallel to the divine conquest of Satan through economy is glimpsed in Constantine's subjugation of barbarian tribes. Eusebius routinely correlates such peoples to the demons vanquished by Christ. Constantine's expansive victory over such tribes corresponds to Christ's advance of the kingdom of God against all demonic opponents.[28] Non-Romans—and therefore non-Christians, as far as Eusebius is concerned—are quite literally demonized. Constantine's victory over such peoples is therefore to be celebrated. As Eusebius recalls: "What need is there for me to mention even incidentally how he *subjected* barbarian races to Roman *rule*, how he was the first to *subjugate* the Gothic and Sarmatian tribes which had never before *learnt to serve*, *compelling* them to accept the Romans as their *masters* even *against their will?* Previous rulers had even paid tribute to the Goths, and Romans served barbarians with yearly payments" (*Life of Constantine* 4.5.1, emphasis added). Such encounter involves economy.

For Eusebius, the fact that Rome had offered tribute payments to the barbarians was the consummate sign of a failure to subdue such groups. The payments demonstrated an inability to establish sovereignty such that one might even speak, shamefully, of domestic subservience to foreign authorities. Barbarian freedom was sustained through economic independence, and foreign authority was tacitly acknowledged by Rome through tribute it paid. This disgraceful situation was rectified in Constantinian victory:

> Such a reckoning was not acceptable to the Emperor, nor did it seem good enough to the Victor to make the same payments as his predecessors. Confident in his Saviour and brandishing the victorious trophy over them too, he very soon *subdued* them all, sometimes *taming* the refractory with the military arm, sometimes *pacifying* the rest by reasonable negotiations, *converting* them from a lawless animal existence to one of reason and law. In this way the Goths *learnt at last to serve* Rome. (*Life of Constantine* 4.5.2, emphasis added)

Roman tribute payments to foreign lords cease. Constantine uses military force but more significantly employs "reasonable negotiations" to subdue opposition. All this is done while exhibiting the glorious sign, symbol, and image of Christ's authority, which figuratively indicates Constantine's confessed allegiance to the God of Jesus Christ and literally meant brandishing of the sign of the cross in battle and impressing its stamp upon his coinage.

The "reasonable" methods here employed resemble the "just" dealings of God with Satan, although Constantine is also granted full rights to exert force and fiat in extending authority. Negotiations might involve discourse or economic transactions such as gifts and other pacifying gestures. Indeed, we are told later that Constantine's typical reaction to foreign diplomatic gifts of tribute was to respond "with equal gifts, so as to make the bearers very rich all at once. He honoured the most distinguished of them also with Roman titles, so that very many now longed to remain [there], forgetting any thought of returning to their homes" (*Life of Constantine* 4.7.3). With winsome and appropriately crafty transactions, as fitting the righteous *oikonomia* and exemplifying the peaceful ideal of transactional payments held up by Irenaeus, Constantine managed his relations with barbarians so as to maintain his sovereign status and position of rule. Although not explicitly stated, we can assume that the Goths were absorbed into economic relations with Constantinian administration, rendering tribute or taxes to him like all subjects. This reversal would at least follow Eusebius's logic in these passages. Whereas tribute once flowed outward, the subjugated barbarians now render to the Christian emperor his due. Such subjugation is glorified for the ways it has "converted" barbarian society from "lawless animal existence to one of reason and law."

Echoes of similar economic conquest and colonization are discernible in Gregory's account, whether or not he had Eusebius's depiction of Constantine in view. Once a rogue or outlaw holding humanity captive outside of divine allegiance, the devil has been brought into the territory of the sovereign and demoted. Through exchange, through an economic interface that is simultaneously a conquest, God brings the devil into the sphere of divine sovereignty. This is not to ignore more perennial theological claims that God is always already sovereign over the devil and that no territory exists outside of divine authority. Rather, it works within the dramaturgical and narrative structure of salvation accounts that indicate a progression and change in the relations and statuses of those involved. Because of the exchange and payment with the Christ coin, the one who accepts the currency of the sovereign center is drawn into a web of obligation to that power. As in accounts of colonization, where an invading or occupying power distributes its currency into a new territory and in so doing brings the resident population into exchange relations and eventual obligation, here God annexes or colonizes satanic territory.

Ransom is thus an integral mechanism in *oikonomia* and functions within Gregory's ancient account of divine conquest. *Christus Victor* is Christ as payment. In offering Christ as compensation, God is not kowtowing to the devil's demands. God gets the devil to accept divine currency and to receive it as an exchange medium. God also imposes a debt obligation upon the devil, a contract that generates eternal interest and forever subjugates the devil to God. Satan unwittingly allows the realm of death to be colonized and annexed by divine power through the channels of economy. The satanic sphere becomes economically linked by this standard of account to God's center of value and seat of authority, and the overthrow of death turns on a dime, as light instantaneously drives away darkness and divine excess overcomes diabolical surplus.

The parallels we saw Eusebius draw between Roman political and economic unity and divine monarchy are here deepened. As Rome expanded into new territories, toppling opposing powers and barbarian hordes, it created a (symbolically) unified economic space. In the face of persistent provincial coinage, Rome asserted the ideological standard of a single, unified monetary zone. Rome conquered new lands, inserting its currency and measures of value into such realms in order to bring them into economic communion with the center. Expansion and unification are seen by Eusebius as the overthrow of demons, as pagan deities in their plurality were brought to submission under Rome's one God, made manifest in inchoate form under Augustus and not universally acknowledged until Constantine.

Whereas Eusebius moved back and forth almost schematically between Roman and Constantinian patterns and those of God's rule, the correlations in Gregory are more implicit. Gregory's account demonstrates in a cosmic drama what a divine victory over demonic forces might entail when considered in parallel to Rome's economic conquest. Through strategic, monetary economic warfare, God brings the devil into submissive union with the divine realm. Gregory gives no evidence that he is attempting to provide a theopolitical counterpart to Eusebius's tale. Neither do I claim that he necessarily has a thoroughgoing conception of political conquest through money that he then applies to God.[29] Yet all the pieces are present in his ransom account and operate together in a way that gives the narrative its force. Through discourse of tyranny, slavery, and rightful lordship, Gregory indexes themes of sovereignty and authority in the political realm and applies them to God and Satan. Through reflection on moneylending and debt slavery, he invokes the struggles for power and acts of aggression inherent in these relations, again attributing the deeds to God and the devil.

These political and economic dynamics coalesce in a tale of victory over the forces of darkness that oppose the church and oppress the believer. *The operative logic in this account of efficacious* oikonomia *is one of divine, theopolitical conquest, at the heart of which occurs a monetized transaction that helps secure freedom and victory, overturn a foe, and bring that enemy into subjection.* It is this narrative that is celebrated in various forms as a tale of salvation, as the soteriological core that drives declarations of divine grace, makes pastoral exception possible, and shapes relations within the ecclesial community and throughout wider Christian empire and at its borders.

As this ransom tale develops historically, there is a change in— not a loss of—the dealings with the devil motif inherited from patristic authors. Subsequent formulations of this account in medieval Christian tradition will foreground the dual submission of humanity and Satan to God. Downplayed is the notion of the "devil's rights" seen in Gregory of Nyssa, the idea that God must or chooses to deal justly with the devil in redeeming humanity. Rather, the emerging narrative will decree that the devil held humanity based on a permission granted by God, since both humanity and the devil are under divine sovereign control.

Remarkably, medieval interpretive tradition even presents the devil as a servant in God's house (*oikos*) alongside humanity. Furthermore, as C. W. Marx notes, "In the new formulation the Devil is conceived as a figure within a model of society: the Devil is a servant of the king; he is a jailer, one who must do the will of the king and one who is treated in law like any of the king's servants."[30] As a participant in the divine *oikonomia* and, hence, as an indentured domestic servant, the devil is unable now to steal away the allegiance of other servants—namely, humans. Within the *oikonomic* family of Christendom, where empire and divine household coincide, the devil thus assumes a submissive role as a tool of the king or father.

That such a formulation is possible centuries later can be seen as an outgrowth of a Nyssen-like narrative as its implications are extended and developed. Through ransom exchange, God conquers the devil and brings him into the divine *oikos*. Satan now enjoys or endures a formal position of submissive exchange relations with God as *oikodespotês* or master of the house. The colonization of Satan here leads to the devil's forced adoption into God's household, a move justified because of the devil's eventual salvation.

Governmental economies of redemptive conquest

The various themes of salvation explored in this and the foregoing chapter combine to support an account of God's economic (re)assertion of sovereignty, where all opposition is vanquished. Inasmuch as ransom narratives tell a tale of divine kindness and graciousness toward humanity, they index a conceptual system that proclaims the reign of the sovereign and the expansion of governed territory through economy. The theological frameworks surveyed appear to be informed by, or evocative of, mechanisms of monetary administration and rule by governmental authorities in the wider culture. The theological, political, and economic are here intertwined. Various political practices of monetary governance become associated with theological discourse about divine grace, benevolence, and liberation. This may provide a clue to the increasing centrality of economic administration in the state management of society, implicitly legitimated as such administration can become by these divine models.

Exceeding the trope of a mere moneylender—even moneylenders are subject to the rulers in whose economic space they carry out their distasteful activities—God and the devil are theopolitically portrayed. They are lords of their respective domains as monetary sovereigns, the devil being at least a would-be authority. The devil as recipient of a divine loan and coin finds his political economic power undermined. By accepting the currency of the king and transacting with it, he accepts the disciplinary power of money, for to trade with the king's currency is to acknowledge the king's authority. Just as *oikonomia* supports a view of the sovereign God's power over and governance of creation and the redemptive economy, here ransom payment vindicates that rule. Administrative management and financial conquest work together.

Satan's domain is an internally emergent—and potentially destabilizing—alternative economy and realm of governance. It represents an incipient attempt to establish a different sphere of sovereignty, accomplished through economy. While God could assert total sovereignty, declaring that the territory and goods—namely, humanity—claimed by Satan are ultimately God's, the divine sovereign chooses instead to deal with the devil in a manner by which a king might interact with a foreign lord: through economic negotiation. Trade relations are opened and a deal is brokered. God is the savvier dealer, however, and understands the nature of monetary economy. The terms that are settled serve to bring Satan and his insurgent economic territory into communion with God's, and it is the divine standard of account that establishes parameters for exchange. God subdues the foe with an excess, a loan of eternal value that obligates the satanic recipient and, denominated as it is in the royal currency as God's very coin and standard, unites the subjected foe to the sovereign monetary center.

In terms of earthly imitation, God's participation in the devil's demands for payment need not validate the use of monetary transactions or economic conquest any more than Christ's submitting to the cross valorizes crucifixion. In other words, divine accommodation and conformity to the strictures of financial exchange do not necessarily endorse these practices as an ideal pattern to emulate. Yet the transposition of such models onto earthly practice is not only possible but likely. Although one can argue that, theoretically, Christ's crucifixion should eliminate any need for others to follow suit—since the tradition claims that Christ died once and for all so that others need not die—early martyrdom ideology certainly claimed the example of Christ's death as a mode of discipleship.[31] Divine activities present themselves with a kind of irresistible force and allure within ecclesial tradition, compelling duplication or at least serving as the horizon against which human activities are measured.

In our case, the practices of economy may be implicitly commended, particularly since monetary dealings turn out to be victorious for God and serve to further the divine kingdom. Given that earthly authorities, following a Eusebian model, are under an injunction to pattern their rule and administration after God's, economy may be put to creative use in the service of maintaining and expanding kingdoms. Constantine remains one paradigmatic instance, as Eusebius interweaves images of imperial rule and economic administration used to save lives and annex barbarian territory. Benevolent, salvific ends legitimate forms of economic conquest. The philanthropy of the divine lender serves as a concrete exemplar for pastoral economy, further entrenching it as a model for praxis. As pastoral arts and governmental techniques intermingle, divine valorization of economic annexation in the name of saving grace provides tacit legitimation of governmentality, of the management of territories and populations via resources and exchanges in the name of economic growth and human flourishing.

The language of economic incursion can eventually be wedded to talk of betterment, liberation, and even salvation. An empire's markets breaking into new lands might then fit a story of such foreign lands' deliverance when told from the master narrative of the sovereign center. Such storytelling has been typical at least since the early modern colonial project up to its present iteration in globalization under late capitalism. People toiling in darkness under oppressive regimes, unable to enjoy the fruits of their labors due to the severity of this rule and impositions of obligation, can be set free toward authentic productivity. Liberation here essentially involves economic annexation, being made tributaries of the center by integration into a unified economic space. Not only are conquered peoples "convert[ed] . . . from a lawless animal existence to one of reason and law" (Eusebius of Caesarea, *Life of Constantine* 4.5.2) through a new type of market discipline, such subjects are more fundamentally "rescued from death" and their "nature is purified and benefitted" (Gregory of Nyssa, *Address* 25, 26). They are set free not for themselves but to labor and serve a new governing center. Their debts to a foreign lord cancelled, they enjoy another indebtedness to the conquering sovereign.

Conclusion

This exploration of religious language—of certain metaphors and concepts used to describe what God is like, how God interacts with creation, and what salvation entails—has been tied to assumptions about a wider social imaginary, to a backdrop of political, economic, and cultural practices that give meaning to the linguistic signs employed. I have endeavored to highlight these signs and point to the wider context in which they are vivified and deployed. While I am convinced of the significant impact of monetary economic ideas and institutions upon early theological formulations, as well as the resultant legitimation that theological language could then provide to pastoral and political practice, further historical work is needed to demonstrate how such processes actually played out. It is my hope that this study will spur this type of work, motivating efforts to both corroborate and contest the links I have posited.

I have labeled my approach "re/constructive," intentionally taking up the ambiguity and peril of archaeological practice that fashions a past inasmuch as it attempts to recollect it. Yet my effort has been primarily conceptual and theoretical, and I make no pretensions to have offered a rich, historical depiction of early Christian contexts or practices, let alone to have provided a study of the ancient economy. Situated among modern inquiries into the sources of a theopolitical imagination and responding to claims about modern economy's theological provenance, I have endeavored to *construct* a theoretical schema for thinking about discourse on the divine in relation to monetary economy even as I have attempted to *reconstruct* aspects of what I claim is an implicit theology operating in many patristic contexts. The divine economist and Christ as currency are analytically useful tropes for assessing ancient and contemporary discourse and institutions. The challenge remains to provide richer depictions of the interactions between the theological systems I have outlined and the diverse practices—ecclesial, economic, and political—that have been conveyed to Western modernity. As a step in this direction, I conclude here with gestural reflections on what legacy this monetary theological conceptual nexus may have bequeathed to the modern West.

According to Michel Foucault, Christian pastoral practice is characterized by networks of simultaneous concern for and oversight over the whole community and the individual. The pastor as shepherd is portrayed as in charge of a flock and called to be devoted to each sheep and to the multiplicity. This mobile multiplicity, the individual and flock—which gets expanded to include all of Christendom—is the object of focus rather than the territory of the city-state as in Greco-Roman thought. Such care is purposeful and has the good and salvation of each and all as its ultimate goal and justification. It is also vigilant and watchful, observing the minute details of the life of the whole and of each member. Furthermore, the care is sacrificial, and the good pastor must be prepared to lay down his life for the sheep. This attention lends itself to relations of obligation and obedience, for directing and being directed are neither optional nor temporary but are oriented to an entire way of life whose ultimate goal is to learn obedience and is hence self-referential.

Already in his lectures, Foucault associated this work of shepherding with a type of economic activity that prefigured modern government, since "the essential issue of government will be the introduction of economy into political practice."[1] Attentive pastoral concern for one and all, directed toward a specific goal, involves modulating relations of merit and fault. This is manifested in a "series of relations of reciprocity" that is "complex and elaborate."[2] Overseeing a series of networks and exchanges of value, the pastor functions as a steward and administrator managing these credits and faults in addition to, as we saw, very real church resources.

Crucial among the tenets of pastoral government is the conviction that, although the pastor must oversee "precise elements, mechanisms of transfer, procedures of reversal," and "conflicting elements," he cannot guarantee the outcome of salvation toward which the economy strives. While he "has to manage the trajectories, circuits, and reversals of merit and fault," the global perspective is such that "in the end, the actual production of salvation eludes one's grasp; it is entirely in God's hands."[3] The pastor cannot actually make spiritual growth happen but simply facilitates exchanges and exhorts members and the flock in the direction of merit. "The Christian pastorate is [therefore] a form of power that, taking the problem of salvation in its general set of themes, inserts into this global, general relationship an entire economy and technique of the circulation, transfer, and reversal of merits, and this is its fundamental point."[4] It is a form of power that, while maintaining a general relationship to salvation (since it is in God's hands), can develop techniques of management, discipline, and direction in minute detail. Precisely because final pastoral outcomes are left up to God, practices of oversight and discipline can, counterintuitively, receive full attention, and elaborate systems of spiritual obligation, credit, and debt can be designed.

These dynamics prefigure the central problem of liberal governance identified by Foucault in subsequent lectures—namely, the inability of the sovereign adequately to manage and ensure the fruitful outcome of the economy proper.[5] Once centralized sovereignty is displaced or diffused, the governmental administration inherits this dilemma. The original sin in liberal theories of statecraft becomes the attempt by the state to achieve a God's-eye view of the economy and direct its course. Rather, a distance must be maintained that recognizes that an "invisible hand" ultimately manages the complexities of economic exchanges. The pastoral government's role recedes to strategic interventions and modulations, as well as to protection of the flock and each member through techniques of security.

The state is also called, biopolitically, to care for each and all, which then frees up and empowers each member to participate in a providentially managed network of exchanges. In modern economy, the state's loose hold on economic direction also allows, counterintuitively as in pastoral economy, the growth and diffusion of elaborate instruments of exchange and measures of value. Endless networks and relays of productive power lead to innovations in modern economy's own system of merits and faults, or credit and debts. In recent history, for example, the mass proliferation of derivatives and debt-based financial commodities, opposed by rhetoric of government regulation to rein in innovations and stave off future financial crises, exhibits this logic.

As we have seen, ideas of the pastor as economist or steward (*oiko-nomos*) are profoundly tied to ideas of God as economic manager and administrator. The divine economist and divine shepherd operate together. While Giorgio Agamben helps us retrieve this theology, he does not do the work of relating it in any extended sense to the pastorate, nor does he tie themes of economic governance, whether earthly or divine, to an economy proper of goods and money. One crucial task that remains, therefore, is to relate the more robust sense of divine, monetary economic administration contributed by this study to Foucault's focus on the pastorate as the key site for emergent governmentality. The "idea of pastoral power, which is entirely foreign, or at any rate considerably foreign to Greek and Roman thought," brings with it entire symbolic systems of legitimation. If the "Christian Church coagulated all these themes of pastoral power into precise mechanisms and definite institutions, [and] . . . implanted its apparatuses within the Roman Empire," what does this potent nexus of theology, pastoral practice, monetary economy, and ever-attendant political institutions convey to Western society?[6]

Implied in Agamben's critique of Foucault is that the very real alterations in patterns of governance that "suddenly break out" in the sixteenth century should be understood together with the ways in which patristic theology and ensuing theological tradition are redeployed in these contexts. Agamben's location of the fissure between sovereignty and governance managed by *oikonomia* in the earliest of Trinitarian formulations means little for the transformations in early modern Europe if such thought was not continually being accessed by these later communities. Manifestations of pastoral "counter-conduct" and the "great revolts around the pastorate, around the right to be governed and to know how and by whom one will be governed" were, Foucault claims, less about doctrine than about ways pastoral power was exercised.[7] Yet the reorganization and its symbolic motivators can be understood fully only in light of an inheritance of theological ideas and pastoral applications. While Foucault's work helpfully elucidates the level of social *practice*, these historical actors everywhere coordinated their activity to symbolic systems and operative theologies that also merit exposition and analysis.

Peter Brown issues the caveat that the changes and upheaval in late antiquity are not comparable to the massive social and industrial transformations in early modern Europe. The latter were of "a different order of magnitude." He cites the use of sermons by fourth-century theologian Gregory Nazianzen on the love of the poor in sixteenth-century Lyon, cautioning against concluding a parallelism of context: "[T]hese were distant ghosts from an unimaginably distant past. The early modern cities to which their message was applied bore no relation whatsoever to the world of late antiquity."[8]

Brown's point is well taken as a historiographical word of caution, yet it neglects one crucial factor: these two contexts, separated as they are by the centuries, exist in significant relation precisely in the very redeployment of this discourse. There were apparently those in Lyon who imagined themselves as standing in continuity with communities to which Gregory spoke, and there is a symbolic transfer of the notion of the poor from ancient to early modern spaces. To be sure, Gregory's words were received and interpreted differently and had distinct outcomes. But these two worlds are connected in the least by this volitional structure of willing receptivity, affective solidarity, and discursive (re)application. They are also linked in that the same theological images and concepts, however differently interpreted, are at play and are taken up to inform new thought and action. This is not a question of identity of context. Of course these communities are vastly different. But the symbolic continuity is important, and genealogical relations are made evident in part through such a theological legacy. The links are very real and are of material consequence.

We must therefore consider the operative role of theology in the evolution and development of attitudes, practices, and institutions of monetary economy in Europe as the context of emergent capitalism, the managerial state, and liberal forms of governance. A multiplicity of factors are certainly involved, and a variety of studies and perspectives are required in order to develop a rich and composite picture. In light of the growing awareness that theology cannot be neglected in regard to the development of modernity, more work is needed to examine its presence and influence.

Just as the break-up of large, agrarian empires in the ancient Near East precipitated new forms of sovereignty, government, and concomitant monetary innovations in ancient Greece, so did the collapse of the Roman Empire facilitate important transformations borne out in emerging politics and economies across Europe. Monetary anarchy reigned for years throughout the Middle Ages and broke out periodically through the tumultuous period that witnessed the founding of the modern nation-state. Varieties of money and competing methods of account circulated. Such differing standards of value were erected by regional powers as statements of sovereign self-determination. A correspondence can be seen between strong monarchies, such as Charlemagne's, and stable currencies, i.e. a unified form of money representing a widely recognized and enforced abstract money of account.[9]

Conversely, as various chieftains and local warlords struggled for power, new currencies multiplied. The same monetary struggle we witnessed between God and Satan, told by Gregory of Nyssa as a cosmic battle, drew on long-standing patterns in the ancient world that remained present in the Middle Ages. Diverse exchange systems emerged, and the role of moneychangers proved crucial as systems of proportions were established to negotiate transferences between different currencies. Furthermore, when currency systems faltered in state power vacuums, merchant classes rose in influence, with strong kinship bonds and forms of localized trust enabling them to engage in trade based on bills of exchange. Rather than use cumbersome and constantly changing currency, guilds made payments with bills drawn up based on relational networks of bankers and traders spread across diverse territories.

According to Geoffrey Ingham, capitalism is facilitated by an ongoing delinking of the form of payment—the money form itself—from the abstract money of account—or set of weights, measures, and proportions—that creates space for innovations such as the bill of exchange. New early capitalist developments include the emergence of the private deposit bank and formation of public banks, the use of bills of exchange by an international merchant class, and "the very gradual *depersonalization and transferability of debt* in the major European states during the seventeenth and eighteenth centuries, which transformed the private promises to pay into 'money.'"[10] These culminate in the development of capitalist credit-money. Essentially this money represents the wedding of private forms of debt and payment, like the bill of exchange drawn on a private bank, with the state regulated monetary system. Coins and currency merge with paper bills of payment, and personal debt becomes transferable to third parties. Notions of sovereignty are reconfigured (and power is disbursed) as the governing system merges with interpersonal systems of payment and obligation. Yet two key elements of money, representing sovereignty and marking relations of credit and debt, remain crucial in these monetary economies.[11]

Of particular theological interest is this reconfiguration in the symbolic imaginary of relations of credit, debt, and obligation taking place in this period of early capitalism. The state comes to support, and in turn be supported by, private credit-debt relations, and debts soon become transferable and anonymized in a way not previously seen. "[T]he issue and circulation of bank notes independently of any particular individual's deposit or, indeed, of particular aggregate level of deposits requires the impersonal or *universalistic transferability of debt* as a means of payment. This social relation was *entirely absent* from both the ancient and . . . classical economies."[12] In the merger of private and personal debts with state-backed and anonymous debt mechanisms, we see one source of the eventual liberal tension between firsthand and personal transactional knowledge versus direction and oversight by superiors in matters of merit and fault. For, while the state will assume the place as guarantor of the myriad individualized debts by underwriting all such bills with its fiat currency, it will not have access to the intricacies of what these exchanges entail on the ground.

We have seen that the pastoral inability to manage the salvific outcomes of the flock may prefigure the supposed inability of the sovereign or the administration to direct the growth of the economy. Similarly, the position of the pastoral governor as confessor over the flock provides an equalizing function where the sins of each member elide with the sins of the whole. Christianity's concepts of the universal equality of all as debtors before God and of a cosmic credit and debt settlement via Christ as payment inform pastoral practice in this regard. Before the infinite God as shepherd, economist, and judge and before his earthy ministers, the offenses of each recede in specificity and become a general position of debt before the cosmic creditor, a debt that has been repaid and accounts credited by Christ as God's coin, providing the funds to invest in new forms of life. The sins of each and of all have one ultimate remedy in Christ, rendering them ultimately of a piece—although, as we know, pastoral economy devoted its energy to the minutia of such infractions and corresponding forms of penance and absolution.

This pastoral economy where one's debt is borne by another and dissipated amidst a wider body appears central to theological discourse and new pastoral practices being shaped in the highly public and contentious exchanges between the Catholic Church and emergent Protestant sects. Protestants retrieved notions of Christ as redeemer, ransom, and payment for sin in their diatribe against Catholic indulgences and other modes of spiritual debt management. Protestant theology reemphasized the single, universal, divine creditor and proffered a competing set of practices of obligation, reversal, and exchange. Eschewing the layers of pastoral management that had proliferated under Catholicism, Protestants advocated direct access to the divine creditor and to the appropriation of saving grace made possible through the ransom exchange. The personalized exchanges with priests were circumvented, and Protestants magnified the inchoate conviction that pastors were powerless over the ends of salvation.

Such transformations are everywhere related to inquiries into pastoral power and developing governmentality. Foucault recognizes the pastorate as the "hinge or pivot" for mediating disparate elements in this period: "Fundamentally, the problem is why and how political and economic problems that arose in the Middle Ages, such as the movements of urban revolt and peasant revolt, the conflicts between feudalism and the merchant bourgeoisie, were translated into a number of religious themes, forms, and concerns that finally result in the explosion of the Reformation, of the great religious crisis of the sixteenth century."[13] The pastorate proves to be a key "field of intelligibility" for analyzing these "economic crises on one side and religious themes on the other." What remains to be explored are the ways in which pastoral governance and Christian communities, these economies of merit and fault, play a role in conceptual reconfigurations of credit and debt. The pastor-shepherd is the steward over an economy of souls. This economy involved networks of merit and fault, or credit and debt, modulating between community, pastor, and God. There is a sense in which the guilt or debt of one is the debt of all, and the pastor, too, in singular fashion, takes on or bears responsibility for it before God. These communities thus reveal a certain type of debt sharing, one that, with the extension of the flock ideal into all of Christendom, can be extrapolated onto European society.

Subsequent revolts of pastoral counter-conduct were in part protests against how this economy had evolved and amount to proposals for its alteration. Models of the divine as a particular type of economist are brought into the fray to aid the legitimation of claims. Protestants challenge the very position of the bishop/pastor as the representative of an economy of merit, as a conduit of its reversals between the flock and God. Thus, questions of economic representation, of who has the authority and right not only to govern but to receive and dispense spiritual value and to make alterations in systems of obligation (through, e.g., absolution) remain front and center. Given our recollection that Eucharist functions as a symbol for the ransom exchange, it is no surprise that the nature of such communion is a primary site of contention. Foucault notes that the pastor's sacramental power was a key flash point of debate.[14] Although he does not relate it explicitly to themes of economy, sacramentality is without a doubt operative as a question of control over economic exchanges and belonging to the institution of the church. In Protestant economic governance, then, responsibility for debts and obligations circumvents the pastor (and with him the church hierarchy and bureaucracy), being recalibrated in terms of the individual believer and God.

Such developments in pastoral economy, I suggest, affect the social consciousness and quite possibly make institutions and practices of shared, public monetary debt more viable. There emerges the possibility that such innovations come to shape the social imaginary, the theological and cultural fabric, in which the seeds of capitalism could develop. Max Weber famously highlighted the connections between Calvinist desires for assurance of elect status before the inscrutable divine sovereign and financial or entrepreneurial success as one marker of this predestination. To such an inquiry we must add consideration of novel conceptions of the divine economist and currency in terms of managing spiritual credit and debt and the new patterns of politics and possibilities for exchange that result.

Given the apparently novel capacity to think of debt as general, universal, and impersonal—or at least as capable of being borne by another without violations of justice—energies could be devoted, after the manner of pastoral techniques, to proliferating mechanisms and methods to manage the flows of credit and debt in this anonymized milieu. With the political control of the Holy Roman Empire undermined, emerging nation-states stepped into the vacuum of social governance, and history witnessed dramatic alterations in relations of production and exchange. As secular states took on the governmental role of pastoral oversight and management of populations, merging with networks of bankers and lenders who assumed the role of priests granting access to credit, this fusion faces the eventual challenge of blindness before the inscrutable salvific ends of the divine economy. Like pastors before them, the meshing of state power and capitalist credit into secular, governmental caretakers could not make economic salvation happen. Instead, we witness the increase in techniques for the transmission of credit and debt, coupled with a refusal to regulate too closely the directions this economy takes.

Furthermore, much of the Reformation's adversarial struggle was economic—in terms of both governance and concerns over property, wealth, and demarcations of value. Indeed, terminologically, the notion of "secularization" associated with the period precisely signifies the forceful transmission of ecclesial property and land holdings into state control. How might the patristic trope of God engaging in economic warfare with Satan inform these adversarial, political economic struggles? Protestants portrayed the pope as antichrist or devil in a contest over economic governance and understandings of how (spiritual) value and power were to be allocated.

This is one instance of a longer heritage of demonizing Europe's socioeconomic others: Jews exhibit something of a proverbial pride of place in this regard, even as Islamic empires, ever at Europe's gate, also retained a special designation as Christendom's satanic foes. In analyzing representations of certain others as enemies in struggles that partake not only of the religious or political but also of the economic, theological considerations raise the possibility of an implicit narrative of cosmic battle that makes economy central and that uses the shifts in debt as a means to gain power. Christ is simultaneously the payment that takes on and bears debt and the means to entrap and topple an adversary through such exchange.

Indeed, as Jacques Le Goff recounts, the medieval world included at least one special role for accursed usury or moneylending.

Romano-canonical legislation forbade moneylending among Christians, as those considered of the same house, drawing upon the biblical injunction against usury within the people of Israel. Yet moneylending and charging interest with foreigners was permitted. Extending this, medieval thinkers "likened their enemies to foreigners and, in the event of war, considered usury lawful if it would harm the adversary." Such a posture was codified in law: "Gratian's *Decretium* of circa 1140, the die from which Canon Law was cast, employed St. Ambrose's formula: '*Ubi ius belli, ibi ius usurae*,' that is, 'Wherever there is the law of war, there is the law of usury.'"[15] The antagonistic relations of moneylending, seen as a contest of power and domination, are here remarkably brought into and included among the arts of war. Whether or not these later canon lawyers had God's cosmic struggle with the devil directly in mind, the antagonistic heavenly exchange, as Gregory of Nyssa depicts it, provides a paradigmatic instance of moneylending as adversarial political struggle and as warlike conquest, one implicitly validated by divine example.

The logic of the economic other as a spiritual enemy is also extended and transformed in colonial expansion. Annexing new territories in the name of the crown, and simultaneously in the name of the divine one who used economic means to conquer foes, can be imagined as an earthly outworking of an archaic cosmic drama of redemption. Colonial projects, with specific political economic interests at their heart, invoke the language of evangelization and civilization—in short, spiritual and cultural salvation. A potential key anchor in the symbolic legitimation of these endeavors is a particular theology of divine conquest through money and economy.[16]

In early modern colonialism, the language of battle for purification through pastoral economies of discipline and obedience, on the one hand, and state needs for new lands and resources, on the other, meet in potent and destructive synthesis. This merger is combined with a redeployment of the (debt) slave, the figure lurking behind the cosmic narratives of bondage and liberation, as chattel slavery becomes a grounding and necessary logic to colonial expansion and capitalist growth. As we saw, although ransom narratives are posed as redemption from slavery, the logic of enslavement by debt remains operative, as God annexes satanic territory and brings Satan into God's *oikos* as an indebted bondservant.

Humans, likewise, remain as slaves, with their ownership transferred into God's hands as purchaser of the bond. Such slavery is construed as salutary and salvific. The proximity of tropes of slavery and salvation may give a clue to the paradoxical persistence of brutal enslavement alongside both pacifying missionary practices and purportedly beneficial economic growth as core features of modernity.[17]

Given the logic of economic salvation in the colonial legacy, it is perhaps no coincidence that the prosperity gospel—a Christian movement dedicated to the proliferation of material wealth as a sign of divine blessing—has developed in former colonies, both in the United States and throughout the global South. Strikingly, such movements are at their most popular among formerly enslaved or subjugated peoples, as well as among poorer, working class whites. In the diverse outworkings of the theopolitical and monetary transcript communicated in coloniality, that of the economy supposedly forging peace while subduing adversaries, we might here discern the literal manifestation of such claims: poor communities proclaim monetary growth and economic returns as marks of divine blessing and victory over demonic and material oppression.[18]

The fact that prosperity churches proclaiming the centrality of money and wealth can take root and develop alongside Christian communities advocating poverty and simplicity, such as Latin American base communities, speaks to the broad and ambivalent spectrum of monetary economic theology within Christian tradition. Both extremes can lay claim to scriptural witness and authenticity despite attempts by many to decry one or the other as heterodox. The middle class in the West desires a middling theology, one that prescribes balance in the use of money under the auspices of a balanced and reasonable heavenly administrator.[19] Yet, as we have seen, the same God who apparently advocates divestment, downward mobility, and poverty for the sake of salvation also strategically and calculatively stewards cosmic resources, seeks a return on the investment of such goods, and makes use of economic transactions in the service of greater gain and victory. The prosperity gospel, like early Christian communities, literalizes the cosmic struggle in *oikonomia* into concrete uses of money, strategy, and surplus. While many would argue that such modern manifestations have forgotten the exhortation toward saving treasure in heaven by claiming such wealth in the present, clearly such traditions are drawing upon long-standing monetary economic tropes within orthodoxy, deploying them toward novel ends, as is the case with any Christian movement over time.

More challenging but arguably even more needed is to trace out how the logic of victory and salvation through economy and exchange has shaped financial institutions and market practices in the modern West. How does the quest for salvific wealth, seen literally in prosperity churches, align with the quest for economic salvation, manifest figuratively on Wall Street and in the halls of economic orthodoxy? Does the "American style" fusion of Christianity and capitalism speak to a deeper and implicit link, even in secular form, between the theologies forged in late antiquity and the contemporary "market as God"?[20] It is my contention that they are profoundly related. While I have noted studies that gesture to this assemblage, the difficult work of tracing the actual connections, of playing out this founding fusion of divinity and currency in such modern practices and institutions, remains to be done.[21]

Attempting to trace the vast and multifaceted networks through which money and economic power operate in the development of the West is a Leviathan task, requiring a variety of methodological lenses and theoretical paradigms. I have argued that the theological dimension persists as a critical layer for consideration. Money is best grasped in its political and institutional dimensions and is elucidated in reference to ideas of sovereignty and administrative governance. This conceptual matrix demonstrates analogous and homologous resonances with theological systems delineating God's reign and redemptive work. A type of mutual influence takes place throughout the history of both conceptual economies—money and theology—in Western context.

As a formative period of early Christian tradition, late antiquity was a setting of great upheaval and social, cultural, political, economic, theological, and symbolic transformation. It established certain parameters within which European civilizations developed and offered a fund of conceptual and practical resources from which to draw, as the West told itself stories about itself, fashioning an identity out of a distant and reconstructed past. As Western societies continue the process of self-examination that is always also self-formation, the relations among the monetary economic, the political, and theological persist as a deposit whose books and records require auditing. For this reserve has not ceased to generate interest, compounding in the form of theoretical and social returns, paying dividends both productive and destructive, life-giving and death-dealing. This is an inheritance that calls us to account.

Notes

Introduction

1. The distinctions among such terms are explored in, e.g., Friedrich Nietzsche, *On the Genealogy of Morals and Ecce Homo*, trans. and ed. by Walter Kaufman (New York: Random House, 1967); Michel Foucault, "Nietzsche, Genealogy, History," in *The Foucault Reader*, ed. Paul Rabinow (New York: Pantheon, 1984), 76–100; Michel Foucault, *Archaeology of Knowledge* (London: Routledge, 2002); Giorgio Agamben, *The Signature of All Things: On Method*, trans. Luca D'Isanto and Kevin Attell (Cambridge, MA: Zone Books, 2009).

2. For the market's supposedly religious structure, see, e.g., Dwight N. Hopkins, "The Religion of Globalization," in *Religions/Globalizations: Theories and Cases*, ed. Dwight N. Hopkins et al. (Durham, NC: Duke University Press, 2001), 7–32; Harvey Cox, *The Market as God* (Cambridge, MA: Harvard University Press, 2016). On modern economic attitudes and practices as purportedly religious, see, e.g., Philip Goodchild, *Capitalism and Religion: The Price of Piety* (London: Routledge, 2002); Philip Goodchild, *Theology of Money* (Durham, NC: Duke University Press, 2009); D. Stephen Long and Nancy Ruth Fox, *Calculated Futures: Theology, Ethics, and Economics* (Waco, TX: Baylor University Press, 2007). On the discipline of modern economics as somehow implicitly religious or theological, see Robert H. Nelson, *Reaching for Heaven on Earth: The Theological Meaning of Economics* (Savage, MD: Rowman & Littlefield, 1991); Robert H. Nelson, *Economics as Religion: From Samuelson to Chicago and Beyond* (University Park: Pennsylvania State University Press, 2001).

3. The tendency is rightly problematized in Hent de Vries, "On General and Divine Economy: Talal Asad's Genealogy of the Secular and Emmanuel Levinas's Critique of Capitalism, Colonialism, and Money," in *Powers of the Secular Modern: Talal Asad and His Interlocutors*, ed. David Scott and Charles Hirschkind (Stanford: Stanford University Press, 2006), 113–33. See also Kathryn Tanner, "Is Capitalism a Belief System?" *Anglican Theological Review* 92, no. 4 (2010): 617–35.

4. The recent critique of market faith by Cox, *Market*, 8 is an example of this approach: Cox describes the market as an "*ersatz* religion" because it "exhibits the

characteristics of classical faith," and "because the market, like the graven idols of old, was constructed by human hands." Here he curiously implies that classical (read: authentic) religion somehow falls outside the bounds of human construction despite clearly being an element of human culture and society. Furthermore, if social construction is the criterion for designating something as *ersatz*, apparently all other elements of human culture qualify and are, hence, somehow disingenuous. We also see here the familiar specter of idolatry loosely applied to the economic realm before grounds for such attribution and implied critique have been established. The parallels Cox goes on to draw among the market, religion, and the biblical God remain as allusions and appear as a form of *jouissance*, and are thus mitigated in persuasive power.

5. In this regard, analyses associated with so-called Radical Orthodoxy rightly demonstrate the theological precursors to the modern order, while unhelpfully maintaining a predetermined fixation on orthodoxy versus heresy. Such approaches think that if theology has contributed to present economic regimes, it has done so only as a "perversion" of "authentic" Christian thought and practice. Yet this occludes analysis of how mainstream, apparently orthodox theology and ecclesial institutions have, in fact, shaped the contemporary economic order. It certainly also excludes the possibility that orthodox theology is informed by the economic sphere, lest this render theology "impure." See, e.g., John Milbank, *Theology and Social Theory: Beyond Secular Reason*, 2nd ed. (Oxford: Blackwell, 2006); D. Stephen Long, *Divine Economy: Theology and the Market* (London: Routledge, 2000); Daniel M. Bell, *The Economy of Desire: Christianity and Capitalism in a Postmodern World* (Grand Rapids, MI: Baker Academic, 2012). The work of Adrian Pabst represents a more sophisticated and nuanced development in this line of analysis and laudably engages in genealogical critique of the West in light of theology's relations to economy and politics. It does, however, invoke the specter of orthodoxy in maintaining that theology, when "properly figured," provides a radical alternative to current social order. See, e.g., Adrian Pabst, "Modern Sovereignty in Question: Theology, Democracy and Capitalism," *Modern Theology* 24, no. 4 (2010): 570–602.

6. The basic template for this approach was first laid down in the pathbreaking M. Douglas Meeks, *God the Economist: The Doctrine of God and Political Economy* (Minneapolis, MN: Fortress Press, 1989). More nuanced and recent developments include Kathryn Tanner, *Economy of Grace* (Minneapolis, MN: Fortress Press, 2005) and Nimi Wariboko, *God and Money: A Theology of Money in a Globalizing World* (Lanham, MD: Lexington Books, 2008). Tanner's approach is informed by Pierre Bourdieu's methodology and to some extent by that of Jean-Joseph Goux; see Pierre Bourdieu, *Outline of a Theory of Practice* (Cambridge: Cambridge University Press, 1977) and Jean-Joseph Goux, *Symbolic Economies: After Marx and Freud*, trans. Jennifer Curtiss Gage (Ithaca, NY:

Cornell University Press, 1990). Wariboko's methodological basis is less articulated but draws in part from Paul Tillich's correlationist method; see Paul Tillich, *Theology of Culture*, ed. Robert C. Kimball (New York: Oxford University Press, 1959). Both Tanner and, in particular, Wariboko include important literature reviews of various additional approaches to theology and economy that I will not repeat here.

7. For an important critique of structuralist ahistoricism and an argument for a processual understanding of signs instead, see Samuel Weber, *Institution and Interpretation*, rev. ed. (Stanford: Stanford University Press, 2002). A unique attempt to historicize the structural operations of theological and economic signs by way of network theory is Mark C. Taylor, *Confidence Games: Money and Markets in a World Without Redemption* (Chicago: University of Chicago Press, 2004).

8. See, e.g., Geoffrey K. Ingham, *The Nature of Money* (Cambridge, UK: Polity, 2004); David Graeber, *Debt: The First 5,000 Years* (Brooklyn, NY: Melville House, 2010); John N. Smithin, ed., *What is Money?* (London: Routledge, 2000); L. Randall Wray, ed., *Credit and State Theories of Money: The Contributions of A. Mitchell Innes* (Cheltenham, UK: Edward Elgar, 2004); Georg Friedrich Knapp, *The State Theory of Money*, abr. ed., ed. H. M. Lucas and James Bonar (London: Macmillan, 1924); and John Maynard Keynes, *The General Theory of Employment, Interest, and Money* (New York: Harcourt Brace, 1936).

9. This very preliminary sketch was first outlined in Devin Singh, "Incarnating the Money-Sign: Notes on an Implicit Theopolitics," *Implicit Religion* 14, no. 2 (2011): 129–40. The idea of such potential parallelism is not new. Marx, for instance, briefly explores the similarities between money as a representation of value and Christ as a representation of God, considering the forms of alienation that result from both systems. The logic of incarnation proves useful for him in explaining the logic of capital and credit; see his "Comments on James Mill's *Éléments D'économie Politique*" in Karl Marx, *Selected Writings*, ed. Lawrence Hugh Simon (Indianapolis, IN: Hackett, 1994), 42; see also Enrique Dussel, *Las metáforas teológicas de Marx* (Estella: Editorial Verbo Divino, 1993). On the centrality of desire in monetary economy, see Noam Yuran, *What Money Wants: An Economy of Desire* (Stanford: Stanford University Press, 2014).

10. George Tyrell, *Christianity at the Crossroads* (London: Longmans, 1910), 44.

11. As Foucault, "Nietzsche, Genealogy, History," 83 claims: "Genealogy does not oppose itself to history as the lofty and profound gaze of the philosopher might compare to the molelike perspective of the scholar; on the contrary, it rejects the metahistorical deployment of ideal significations and indefinite teleologies. It opposes itself to the search for 'origins'." Foucault's essay appears to be more a close analysis of Nietzsche's own views, transformed as they necessarily are by Foucault's paraphrasing, than a programmatic statement of his own methods.

12. Ibid., 90.

13. Dipesh Chakrabarty, *Provincializing Europe: Postcolonial Thought and Historical Difference* (Princeton, NJ: Princeton University Press, 2000), 47–71, 237–56 demonstrates this sensitivity when he assesses the "two histories" of capitalism, attending to the master narrative of progress in the agonistic modulation of modes of production as well as the residual yet vitalistic elements present in a historical epoch that seem "anachronistic," yet provide a necessary supplement to the functioning of that stage.

14. Foucault, "Nietzsche, Genealogy, History," 83.

15. On immanent criticism see, e.g., Theodor W. Adorno, *Prisms*, trans. Samuel Weber and Shierry Weber, Studies in Contemporary German Social Thought (Cambridge, MA: MIT Press, 1981), 17–34.

16. Carl Schmitt, *Political Theology: Four Chapters on the Concept of Sovereignty*, trans. George Schwab (Chicago: University of Chicago Press, 2005). Opposition between economy and the political is articulated in Carl Schmitt, *Roman Catholicism and Political Form*, trans. G. L. Ulmen (Westport, CT: Greenwood Press, 1996); and Carl Schmitt, *The Concept of the Political*, trans. George Schwab, rev. ed. (Chicago: University of Chicago Press, 2007).

17. Max Weber, *The Protestant Ethic and the Spirit of Capitalism*, trans. Stephen Kalberg, rev. ed. (New York: Oxford University Press, 2011). Albert Hirschman, *The Passions and the Interests: Political Arguments for Capitalism before Its Triumph* (Princeton, NJ: Princeton University Press, 1977) is in part an attempt to provide a complementary account of the development of capitalism through a focus on the state and statecraft, which Weber's primarily psychological account lacks. An important augmentation of Weber that evaluates the European political landscape at the time is Philip S. Gorski, *The Protestant Ethic Revisited* (Philadelphia: Temple University Press, 2011).

18. This is not to minimize the undeniable import of liberation theology, assessing as it does the interconnection of theological, economic, and political spheres. As a general rule, however, liberation theology lacks genealogical exploration of theology's role in contributing to the legacy it criticizes. Indeed, theology remains the privileged locus of reflection, such that it provides the objective point of value assessment and the controlling source for solutions to social plight. Furthermore, liberation theology's debt to Marxist analysis means that diagnosis occurs primarily in the economic realm, with the state often reduced merely to an agent of capital. Admittedly, integration of dependency theory and world systems analysis does render some liberationist critiques more nuanced, considering broader institutional and political factors that engender situations of economic exploitation.

19. Zones of indistinction are explored extensively in Giorgio Agamben, *Homo Sacer: Sovereign Power and Bare Life*, trans. Daniel Heller-Roazen (Stanford: Stanford University Press, 1998).

20. Hans Blumenberg, *The Legitimacy of the Modern Age*, trans. Robert M. Wallace (Cambridge, MA: MIT Press, 1983) and Karl Löwith, *Meaning in History* (Chicago: University of Chicago Press, 1957). Modernity's theological heritage has been explored in, e.g., Charles Taylor, *A Secular Age* (Cambridge, MA: Belknap Press of Harvard University Press, 2007); Michael Gillespie, *The Theological Origins of Modernity* (Chicago: University of Chicago Press, 2008); and Brad S. Gregory, *The Unintended Reformation: How a Religious Revolution Secularized Society* (Cambridge, MA: Belknap Press of Harvard University Press, 2012).

21. Studies examining the enduring relevance of theopolitics include Hent de Vries and Lawrence Eugene Sullivan, eds., *Political Theologies: Public Religions in a Post-Secular World* (New York: Fordham University Press, 2006); Creston Davis, John Milbank, and Slavoj Žižek, eds., *Theology and the Political: The New Debate* (Durham, NC: Duke University Press, 2005); Clayton Crockett, *Radical Political Theology: Religion and Politics after Liberalism*, Insurrections: Critical Studies in Religion, Politics, and Culture (New York: Columbia University Press, 2011); Paul Fletcher, *Disciplining the Divine: Toward an (Im)political Theology* (Farnham, UK: Ashgate, 2009); and Vincent W. Lloyd, *The Problem with Grace: Reconfiguring Political Theology* (Stanford: Stanford University Press, 2011). Attending to a theopolitical zone requires consideration of links between the ostensibly separate religious and secular spheres. Theorists note the co-construction of "religion" and "the secular," such that these terms presume and require each other; see Talal Asad, *Genealogies of Religion: Discipline and Reasons of Power in Christianity and Islam* (Baltimore: Johns Hopkins University Press, 1993); Talal Asad, *Formations of the Secular: Christianity, Islam, Modernity* (Stanford: Stanford University Press, 2003); Tomoko Masuzawa, *In Search of Dreamtime: The Quest for the Origin of Religion* (Chicago: University of Chicago Press, 1993); Tomoko Masuzawa, *The Invention of World Religions, or, How European Universalism was Preserved in the Language of Pluralism* (Chicago: University of Chicago Press, 2005); and José Casanova, *Public Religions in the Modern World* (Chicago: University of Chicago Press, 1994).

22. This is not to deny that alternative forms of money can be *theorized*, as done admirably by Nigel Dodd, *The Social Life of Money* (Princeton, NJ: Princeton University Press, 2014). It is rather to recognize that in its various *historical* manifestations thus far, money has always been associated with sovereignty, with some structure of centralized and hierarchical power.

23. Moira Fradinger, *Binding Violence: Literary Visions of Political Origins* (Stanford: Stanford University Press, 2010), 6. The imbrication of the West with colonial others is explored in Enrique Dussel, *The Invention of the Americas: Eclipse of "The Other" and the Myth of Modernity*, trans. Michael Barber (New York: Continuum, 1995); Walter Mignolo, *The Darker Side of the Renaissance:*

Literacy, Territoriality, and Colonization (Ann Arbor: University of Michigan Press, 1995); and Walter Mignolo, *The Darker Side of Western Modernity: Global Futures, Decolonial Options* (Durham, NC: Duke University Press, 2011).

24. Fradinger, *Binding Violence*, 6.

25. Martin Bernal, *Black Athena: The Afroasiatic Roots of Classical Civilization*, 3 vols. (New Brunswick, NJ: Rutgers University Press, 1987) and Cedric Robinson, *An Anthropology of Marxism* (London: Ashgate, 2001).

26. Chakrabarty, *Provincializing Europe*; Devin Singh, "Provincializing Christendom: Reviewing John Milbank's *Beyond Secular Order*," *Syndicate: A New Forum for Theology* 2, no. 6 (2015): 177–83.

27. My project speaks to the perception, for instance, that we must assess contemporary American politics in light of the peculiar fusion of economic ideas and conservative Christian values as studied in William E. Connolly, *Capitalism and Christianity, American Style* (Durham, NC: Duke University Press, 2008). It is also intended to aid studies of the curious merger of Christianity and capitalism in colonial contexts as examined in, e.g., Jean Comaroff and John Comaroff, "Millennial Capitalism: First Thoughts on a Second Coming," *Public Culture* 12, no. 2 (2000): 291–343 and Webb Keane, *Christian Moderns: Freedom and Fetish in the Mission Encounter* (Berkeley: Unversity of California Press, 2007). My study provides a deep archeology of ancient concepts that make themselves felt in novel ways in such modern contexts. Further work is necessary to relate these ancient realities to postcolonial contexts and discourses and to escape the so-called Eurocentric critique of Eurocentrism that persists in attempts to relate ancient Greece and Rome to the modern West; see Enrique Dussel, *Postmodernidad y transmodernidad: Diálogos con la filosofía de Gianni Vattimo* (Mexico City: Universidad Iberamericana Plantel Golfo Centro, 1999); Walter Mignolo, "Delinking," *Cultural Studies* 21, no. 2 (2007): 449–514; Walter Mignolo, "The Geopolitics of Knowledge and the Colonial Difference," *South Atlantic Quarterly* 101, no. 1 (2002): 56–97; and Robert Bernasconi, "African Philosophy's Challenge to Continental Philosophy," in *Postcolonial African Philosophy: A Critical Reader*, ed. Emmanuel Chukwudi Eze (London: Blackwell, 1997), 183–196.

28. Michel Foucault, *Security, Territory, Population: Lectures at the Collège de France, 1977–1978*, ed. Michael Senellart and Arnold I. Davidson (New York: Palgrave Macmillan, 2007), 184.

29. Ibid., 95. On the nature of sovereignty, see F. H. Hinsley, *Sovereignty*, 2nd ed. (Cambridge: Cambridge University Press, 1982); Jo-Anne Pemberton, *Sovereignty: Interpretations* (Basingstoke, UK: Palgrave Macmillan, 2009); Cynthia Weber, *Simulating Sovereignty: Intervention, the State, and Symbolic Exchange* (Cambridge: Cambridge University Press, 1995); Kathryn A. Morgan, ed., *Popular Tyranny: Sovereignty and its Discontents in Ancient Greece* (Austin: University of Texas Press, 2003); and Schmitt, *Political Theology*.

30. Giorgio Agamben, *The Kingdom and the Glory: For a Theological Genealogy of Economy and Government*, trans. Lorenzo Chiesa and Matteo Mandarini (Stanford: Stanford University Press, 2011) and Giorgio Agamben, *"What is an Apparatus?" and Other Essays*, trans. David Kishik and Stefan Pedatella (Stanford: Stanford University Press, 2009).

31. This orientation comes from his sustained engagement with Carl Schmitt over the question of political theology; see Agamben, *Homo Sacer* and Giorgio Agamben, *State of Exception*, trans. Kevin Attell (Chicago: University of Chicago Press, 2005).

32. While I will at times refer to what I term "lacunae" in Agamben's study that relate to his neglect of properly economic themes that circulate in the work, my reading can be seen more charitably as a development of the "potentiality" latent in what remains unsaid in his own, as noted by Leland de la Durantaye, *Giorgio Agamben: A Critical Introduction* (Stanford: Stanford University Press, 2009), 9: "For Agamben, the philosophical element—rich in potentiality—is that which, while present, goes unstated in a work and is thereby left for others to read between the lines and formulate in their own."

33. See Tero Auvinen, "At the Intersection of Sovereignty and Biopolitics: The Di-Polaric Spatializations of Money," *Foucault Studies* 9 (2010): 5–34.

34. On the ways in which such biological metaphors have structured biblical criticism of textual relations, "families," and "offspring," and concomitant quests for purity, see Yii-Jan Lin, *The Erotic Life of Manuscripts: New Testament Textual Criticism and the Biological Sciences* (New York: Oxford University Press, 2016).

35. Agamben, *Signature*, 84–90.

36. Seminal texts include Marc Shell, *The Economy of Literature* (Baltimore: Johns Hopkins University Press, 1978); Marc Shell, *Money, Language, and Thought: Literary and Philosophical Economies from the Medieval to the Modern Era* (Berkeley: University of California Press, 1982); and Goux, *Symbolic Economies*. An excellent introduction to the movement and collection of representative essays is Martha Woodmansee and Mark Osteen, eds., *The New Economic Criticism: Studies at the Intersection of Literature and Economics* (London and New York: Routledge, 1999). Also important is the critique and modification of the homological method in Fredric Jameson, *The Political Unconscious: Narrative as a Socially Symbolic Act* (Ithaca, NY: Cornell University Press, 1981).

37. Woodmansee and Osteen, *New Economic Criticism*, 11.

38. Shell, *Economy*, 7.

39. George Lakoff and Mark Johnson, *Metaphors We Live By* (Chicago: University of Chicago Press, 2003); Paul Ricœur, *The Rule of Metaphor: The Creation of Meaning in Language*, trans. Robert Czerny (London: Routledge, 2003); Paul Ricœur, *Figuring the Sacred: Religion, Narrative, and Imagination*, trans. David Pellauer, ed. Mark I. Wallace (Minneapolis, MN: Fortress Press, 1995); and

Kevin J. Vanhoozer, *Biblical Narrative in the Philosophy of Paul Ricoeur: A Study in Hermeneutics and Theology* (Cambridge: Cambridge University Press, 1990).

40. As Friedrich Nietzsche, "On Truth and Lying in an Extra-Moral Sense (1873)," in *Friedrich Nietzsche on Rhetoric and Language*, trans. and ed. by Sander L. Gilman, Carole Blair, and David J. Parent (New York: Oxford University Press, 1989), 250 infamously suggested, it is assemblages of dead metaphors that constitute truth. Without entering into the broader debate about epistemology that such a claim raises, what we can draw from it are the importance and centrality of metaphorical ascription in the thought systems we inherit and create. Remarkably, Nietzsche described such dead metaphors as "coins (*Münzen*) which have lost their pictures and now matter only as metal, no longer as coins." I would characterize dead metaphors as coins that have lost their pictures yet *still* function and circulate as coins, a common reality in the ancient world. They continue to enable transactions (of meaning) but have lost their distinctive imagery and evocative power.

41. Kathryn Tanner, "Trinity," in *The Blackwell Companion to Political Theology*, ed. Peter Scott and William T. Cavanaugh (Malden, MA: Blackwell, 2004), 320, emphasis added. Tanner is careful to note, however, that such use may also provide "a critical commentary on what is problematic about the social and political practices of the times" (ibid.). The theological impact of metaphor has been extensively explored by Sallie McFague, *Metaphorical Theology: Models of God in Religious Language* (Philadelphia: Fortress Press, 1982).

42. On the broader implications of sound and vibration in the intellectual life and for communal transformation, see William Cheng, *Just Vibrations: The Purpose of Sounding Good* (Ann Arbor: University of Michigan Press, 2016).

43. Agamben, *Signature*, 20.

44. Connolly, *Capitalism and Christianity*, 4–5, 40–41.

45. The role of affect in monetary economy as a site of "secular faith" has been helpfully explored in Martijn Konings, *The Emotional Logic of Capitalism: What Progressives Have Missed* (Stanford: Stanford University Press, 2015).

Chapter 1

1. Of the many studies, see, e.g., Mitchell Dean, *Governmentality: Power and Rule in Modern Society*, 2nd ed. (London: SAGE, 2010); Jack Z. Bratich, Jeremy Packer, and Cameron McCarthy, *Foucault, Cultural Studies, and Governmentality* (Albany: State University of New York Press, 2003); and Graham Burchell, Colin Gordon, and Peter Miller, eds., *The Foucault Effect: Studies in Governmentality* (Chicago: University of Chicago Press, 1991).

2. For a brief review of such trends, see Devin Singh, "Disciplining Eusebius: Discursive Power and Representation of the Court Theologian," in *Studia Patristica LXII.10*, ed. Markus Vinzent (Leuven: Peeters, 2013), 89–102.

3. Carl Schmitt *Political Theology II: The Myth of the Closure of Any Political Theology*, trans. Michael Hoelzl and Graham Ward (Cambridge, UK: Polity, 2008) invokes the "Modern Eusebius" in his arguments with Erik Peterson about the enduring relevance of political theology to modern statecraft, partly in response to Peterson's own use of Eusebius as a central foil in denouncing the possibilities of political theology, both ancient and modern, in Erik Peterson, "Monotheism as a Political Problem: A Contribution to the History of Political Theology in the Roman Empire," in *Theological Tractates*, trans. and ed. by Michael J. Hollerich (Stanford: Stanford University Press, 2011), 68–105. Eusebius is also invoked polemically in modern German debates about religion and politics, e.g., Franz Overbeck, *Kirchenlexicon. Materialien. "Christentum und Kultur"*, vol. 6.1, *Werke und Nachlaß*, ed. Barbara von Reibnitz (Stuttgart: J. B. Metzler, 1996), 246 and much more recently to critique US presidential speech writing in Stephen H. Webb, "Providence and the President (or, The New Eusebius)," *Reviews in Religion and Theology* 15, no. 4 (2008): 622–29. One can observe the long shadow of Eusebius in medieval political theology, as richly documented in Ernst Kantorowicz, *The King's Two Bodies: A Study in Medieval Political Theology* (Princeton, NJ: Princeton University Press, 1957).

4. Following Foucault, Agamben's preferred term is *dispositif*, often rendered "apparatus" or "dispositive." For his initial reflections on *oikonomia* as a dispositive, see Giorgio Agamben, *"What is an Apparatus?" and Other Essays*, trans. David Kishik and Stefan Pedatella (Stanford: Stanford University Press, 2009). The term denotes not merely a concept but also the related complex of practices and social mechanisms that arrange power in a given context, as "literally anything that has in some way the capacity to capture, orient, determine, intercept, model, control, or secure the gestures, behaviors, opinions, or discourses of living beings" (ibid., 14). For a problematization of the typical translation as "apparatus" and argument in favor of "dispositive," see Jeffrey Bussolini, "What is a Dispositive?," *Foucault Studies* 10 (November 2010): 85–107.

5. Giorgio Agamben, *The Kingdom and the Glory: For a Theological Genealogy of Economy and Government*, trans. Lorenzo Chiesa and Matteo Mandarini (Stanford: Stanford University Press, 2011), 20.

6. Ibid., 17, 24, 43.

7. I draw substantially on the work of classicist and biblical scholar John Henry Reumann, who engaged the concept of *oikonomia* and related ideas of stewardship with remarkable depth in classical, biblical, and patristic tradition. His doctoral dissertation of more than six hundred pages offers an encyclopedic survey and catalog of all ancient usages of the term up until 100 CE, while summarizing all major modern surveys of the term to the point of his study in 1957; see John Reumann, "The Use of Οἰκονομία and Related Terms in Greek Sources to about A.D. 100, as a Background for Patristic Applications" (Ph.D. diss., University of

Pennsylvania, 1957). Although it unfortunately remained unpublished as a monograph, its insights were disseminated in a variety of scholarly articles and a book for a general audience; see John Reumann, "'Stewards of God': Pre-Christian Religious Application of Oikonomos in Greek," *Journal of Biblical Literature* 77, no. 4 (1958): 339–49; John Reumann, "Οἰκονομία as 'Ethical Accommodation' in the Fathers, and its Pagan Backgrounds," in *Studia Patristica III*, ed. F. L. Cross (Berlin: Akademie Verlag, 1961), 370–79; John Reumann, "Oikonomia-Terms in Paul in Comparison with Lucan *Heilsgeschichte*," *New Testament Studies* 13, no. 2 (1967): 147–67; John Reumann, "'Jesus as Steward'. An Overlooked Theme in Christology," in *Studia Evangelica V: Papers Presented to the Third International Congress on New Testament Studies Held at Christ Church, Oxford, 1965*, ed. F. L. Cross, (Berlin: Akademie Verlag, 1968), 21–29; John Reumann, *Stewardship and the Economy of God* (Grand Rapids, MI: Eerdmans, 1992). Agamben, *Kingdom*, 2 acknowledges the recent encyclopedic survey of *oikonomia* in Gerhard Richter, *Oikonomia: Der Gebrauch des Wortes Oikonomia im Neuen Testament, bei den Kirchenvätern und in der theologischen Literatur bis ins 20. Jahrhundert*, Arbeiten zur Kirchengeschichte 90 (Berlin: De Gruyter, 2005), although he finds it wanting in light of its more "theological and not linguistic-philological" orientation. Reumann's work, while neglected by Agamben, provides precisely such a focus. To locate the notion of *oikonomia* and *oikonomos* in Greco-Roman patronal context and situate it within the dynamics of status and master-slave relations, I draw on Dale B. Martin, *Slavery as Salvation: The Metaphor of Slavery in Pauline Christianity* (New Haven, CT: Yale University Press, 1990).

8. Xenophon's memoirs of Socrates depict the old master as claiming that the best generals come from the ranks of businessmen: "since he knows that nothing pays off like a victory in the field, the businessman-turned-general will be eager to provide all the aids for victory" (Xenophon, *Memorabilia* 3.4.11–12, referenced in Reumann, "Use," 159–60 n. 15).

9. Polybius, *The Histories* 2.2.9–11 and 4.86.4, referenced in Reumann, "Use," 212.

10. Referenced in Reumann, "Use," 164.

11. Reumann, "Use," 177.

12. Ibid., 186 n. 87.

13. As Reumann, "Oikonomia-Terms," 150 claims, "οἰκονομία and its related terms (οἰκονόμος, οἰκονομεῖν, διοίκησις, etc.) were 'in the air' with a variety of meanings in the first-century A.D. world. There had been a steady development of usages from the root meaning of 'management in a household (οἶκος)' to management of a city-state (πόλις) to management of the world (κόσμος). Especially important is the fact that by late Hellenistic times οἰκονομία was regularly applied to God's ordering and administration of the universe."

14. Reumann, "Use," 192–97.

15. Ibid., 220, 222, 226–28.

16. Of the many studies on these doctrinal developments, see, e.g., Lewis Ayres, *Nicaea and its Legacy: An Approach to Fourth-Century Trinitarian Theology* (Oxford: Oxford University Press, 2004); R. P. C. Hanson, *The Search for the Christian Doctrine of God: The Arian Controversy 318–381* (Edinburgh: T & T Clark, 1988); G. L. Prestige, *God in Patristic Thought*, 2nd ed. (London: SPCK, 1969); and John Behr, *The Nicene Faith*, 2 vols. (Crestwood, NY: St. Vladimir's Seminary Press, 2004). Agamben's use of *oikonomia* to relate divine sovereignty and governance is explored in, e.g., Devin Singh, "Anarchy, Void, Signature: Agamben's Trinity Among Orthodoxy's Remains," *Political Theology* 17, no. 1 (2016): 27–46 and Sean Capener, "Being and Acting: Agamben, Athanasius, and the Trinitarian Economy," *Heythrop Journal* 57 (2016): 950–9.

17. Marie-José Mondzain, *Image, Icon, Economy: The Byzantine Origins of the Contemporary Imaginary*, trans. Rico Franses (Stanford: Stanford University Press, 2005), 21.

18. See Dotan Leshem, "Oikonomia in the Age of Empires," *History of the Human Sciences* 26, no. 1 (2013): 29–51.

19. Mondzain, *Image, Icon, Economy*, 19.

20. Ibid., 18.

21. Ibid., 19, citing the pseudo-Aristotelian *Economics* II.1.

22. See Dotan Leshem, "Oikonomia Redefined," *Journal of the History of Economic Thought* 35, no. 1 (2013): 43–61.

23. Mondzain, *Image, Icon, Economy*, 19.

24. Dotan Leshem, *The Origins of Neoliberalism: Modeling the Economy from Jesus to Foucault* (New York: Columbia University Press, 2016), 87–96.

25. This Christian focus on limitless growth in light of humankind's eternal nature and relation with the infinite God clashes with recent reflections on the market by Harvey Cox, *The Market as God* (Cambridge, MA: Harvard University Press, 2016), 21: "There is, however, one contradiction between the religion of The Market and the traditional religions that seems to be insurmountable. All of the traditional religions teach that human beings are finite creatures and that there are limits to any earthly enterprise." Such a sweeping claim about *all* religions is already tendentious, and here we see that it misses a key dynamic in Christian thought that holds creaturely finitude together with apotheosis and the eternal development and destiny of humanity, tenets that, according to Leshem, *Origins*, 87–96 at least, contributed to Western economy's focus on limitless growth.

26. Agamben, *Kingdom*, 99.

27. Gregory of Nyssa, *Address on Religious Instruction*, 20–26.

28. For a review and problematization of the anxieties around Eusebius's relation to politics, see Singh, "Disciplining Eusebius." Eusebius is the central foil in

Erik Peterson's rejection of Carl Schmitt's notion of political theology, a debate that Agamben reviews. For a critique of Peterson's caricatures of Eusebius in this debate, see Devin Singh, "Eusebius as Political Theologian: The Legend Continues," *Harvard Theological Review* 108, no. 1 (2015): 129–54. For an elegant and trenchant defense of Peterson, see György Geréby, "Political Theology versus Theological Politics: Erik Peterson and Carl Schmitt," *New German Critique* 105, no. 3 (2008): 7–33.

29. See Origen, *Against Celsus* 2.30. Harry O. Maier, "Dominion from Sea to Sea: Eusebius of Caesarea, Constantine the Great, and the Exegesis of Empire," in *The Calling of the Nations: Exegesis, Ethnography, and Empire in the Biblical-Historical Present*, ed. Mark Vessey et al. (Toronto: University of Toronto Press, 2011), 162 notes that while Origen "distinguished between the world-wide dominion of the pagan empire and the universal proclamation of the Gospel to all nations," the later thought of Eusebius elides and conflates these two.

30. On the following points, see, e.g., Martin Goodman, *The Roman World: 44BC–AD180* (London: Routledge, 1997) and Andrew Erskine, *Roman Imperialism* (Edinburgh: Edinburgh University Press, 2010). Further references are provided below. This brief review can in no way do justice to the variation and complexity of the situation. My aim is to mention general trends in order to convey a sense of the context as ideal type in which theological claims were made.

31. As is the character of bureaucracy, such structures tended to proliferate, and they grew in layers of complexity and delegation under Constantine; see John L. Teall, "The Age of Constantine: Change and Continuity in Administration and Economy," *Dumbarton Oaks Papers* 21 (1967): 11–36. Roman bureaucracy also appears reactive rather than proactive in its development, as argued in Fergus Millar, *The Emperor in the Roman World (31 BC–AD 337)* (Ithaca, NY: Cornell University Press, 1977).

32. Kenneth W. Harl, *Coinage in the Roman Economy, 300 B.C. to A.D. 700* (Baltimore: Johns Hopkins University Press, 1996) notes that Roman coin production and dissemination took place on a scale unprecedented in the ancient world, outstripping medieval economies and remaining unrivaled until modern times. See also Christopher Howgego, "Coin, Circulation and the Integration of the Roman Economy," *Journal of Roman Archaeology* 7 (1994): 5–21 and Elio Lo Cascio, "The Early Roman Empire: The State and the Economy," in *The Cambridge Economic History of the Greco-Roman World*, ed. Walter Scheidel, Ian Morris, and Richard Saller (New York: Cambridge University Press, 2007), 627–30.

33. Richard Duncan-Jones, *Structure and Scale in the Roman Economy* (Cambridge: Cambridge University Press, 1990); Richard Duncan-Jones, *Money and Government in the Roman Empire* (Cambridge: Cambridge University Press, 1994). The conclusion of both these studies is that the empire was unevenly monetized and that many payments were made in kind rather than in money. Yet

money as abstract governing conceptual system was fully present, such that even payments in kind were denominated in a monetized account. Furthermore, the Roman Republic was already highly monetized, having discrete zones of application where in-kind payments functioned in lieu of coinage. Such monetization only increased during the Imperial period and beyond, cycles of depreciation and specie shortage notwithstanding. See David B. Hollander, *Money in the Late Roman Republic* (Leiden: Brill, 2007) and Neil Coffee, *Gift and Gain: How Money Transformed Ancient Rome* (New York: Oxford University Press, 2016).

34. Jairus Banaji, "Economic Trajectories," in *The Oxford Handbook of Late Antiquity*, ed. Scott Fitzgerald Johnson (Oxford: Oxford University Press, 2012), 597.

35. Christopher Kelly, *Ruling the Later Roman Empire* (Cambridge, MA: Belknap Press of Harvard University Press, 2004), 138–45.

36. Harl, *Coinage*, 23, 36 claims that imperialism was the driving force behind monetization of the Athenian and later Roman empires. Money was needed to fuel expansion, and new metal resources discovered in new territories were fed back into the circulating coinage. As armies spread, so did their coins and concomitant habits of exchange.

37. Colin M. Kraay, "Hoards, Small Change and the Origin of Coinage," *Journal of Hellenic Studies* 84 (1964): 76–91. See also Mark S. Peacock, "The Origins of Money in Ancient Greece: The Political Economy of Coinage and Exchange," *Cambridge Journal of Economics* 30 (2006): 637–50 and Charles Goodhart, "The Two Concepts of Money: Implications for the Analysis of Optimal Currency Areas," *European Journal of Political Economy* 14 (1998): 407–32.

38. Keith Hopkins, "Taxes and Trade in the Roman Empire (200 B.C.–A.D. 400)," *Journal of Roman Studies* 70 (1980): 102.

39. The modern ideological correlate to the connection between peace and economic integration is summed up in the infamous claim by Thomas Friedman, *The Lexus and the Olive Tree* (New York: Anchor Books, 2000) that no two countries containing a McDonald's have ever gone to war with each other. The implication is that a correspondence of free-market capitalist practices, for which McDonald's is a shorthand signifier, mitigates ideological animosity and potential for conflict. Similarly, the ideologically construed Augustan peace is partly the result of monetary economic integration. An argument for the centrality of markets as a unifying and productive force in the Roman economy can be found in Peter Temin, *The Roman Market Economy* (Princeton, NJ: Princeton University Press, 2013).

40. Kenneth W. Harl, *Civic Coins and Civic Politics in the Roman East, A.D. 180–275*, The Transformation of the Classical Heritage 12 (Berkeley: University of California Press, 1987).

41. "None of the cities should be allowed to have its own separate coinage or system of weights and measures; they should all be required to use ours," wrote

Cassius Dio, *History of Rome* 52.30.9, expressing at least one common opinion of the time. This opinion is cited by Christopher Howgego, *Ancient History from Coins* (London: Routledge, 1995), 56, who notes that the process of monetary integration and unification was not necessarily a centralized and concerted effort but often the result of various provincial and ad hoc decisions.

42. Jairus Banaji, *Agrarian Change in Late Antiquity: Gold, Labour, and Aristocratic Dominance* (Oxford; New York: Oxford University Press, 2001) and Banaji, "Economic Trajectories."

43. Following Eusebius of Caesarea, *Demonstratio Evangelica*, trans. W. J. Ferrar (London: SPCK, 1920).

44. Peterson, "Monotheism," 94: "Monotheism is the metaphysical corollary of the Roman Empire, which dissolves nationalities."

45. These Greco-Roman beliefs are explored in greater detail in Singh, "Eusebius."

46. Peterson, "Monotheism," 226 n. 136 notes in his critical reading of Eusebius on this subject: "Probably, Eusebius's formulation of the idea that the Roman Empire had improved the apostles' access to all nations is also shaped by the rhetorical topos in the encomia on Rome, according to which the Roman Empire had made free commerce possible." Eusebius does not single out Roman monetary economy specifically. Indeed, why would he, given what we know about the economy's so-called "embeddedness" in the ancient world? For the market was not typically construed as a thing-in-itself in the manner of modern discourse. On ancient economic embeddedness, see Karl Polanyi, *The Great Transformation* (New York: Rinehart, 1944); Karl Polanyi, *Trade and Market in the Early Empires* (Glencoe, IL: Free Press, 1957) and M. I. Finley, *The Ancient Economy*, rev. ed. (Berkeley: University of California Press, 1999).

47. Eusebius's *Oration in Praise of Constantine* (*De laudibus Constantini*) and his sermon *On Christ's Sepulcher* (*De Sepulcro Christi*) are separate documents that were collated by an ancient editor and will be cited here as distinct texts. For both texts, I follow H. A. Drake, *In Praise of Constantine: A Historical Study and New Translation of Eusebius' Tricennial Orations*, University of California Publications: Classical Studies 15 (Berkeley: University of California Press, 1976).

48. See the excellent discussion in Maier, "Dominion."

49. Peterson, "Monotheism," 94.

50. Arjun Appadurai, *Modernity At Large: Cultural Dimensions of Globalization* (Minneapolis: University of Minnesota Press, 1996), 116–20.

51. On taxation and sovereignty, see Geoffrey K. Ingham, *The Nature of Money* (Cambridge, UK: Polity, 2004); L. Randall Wray, ed., *Credit and State Theories of Money: The Contributions of A. Mitchell Innes* (Cheltenham, UK: Edward Elgar, 2004). Consider also Lisa Kallet, "Demos Tyrannos: Wealth, Power, and

Economic Patronage," in *Popular Tyranny: Sovereignty and its Discontents in Ancient Greece*, ed. Kathryn A. Morgan (Austin: University of Texas Press, 2003), 123, who writes: "It is a virtual topos in modern scholarship as well as in ancient literature that tyrants, having established themselves in power, increased their wealth through taxation."

52. Georg Friedrich Knapp, *The State Theory of Money*, abr. ed. (London: Macmillan, 1924).

53. Census was undertaken to facilitate extraction of *tributum capitisi* or poll tax, the per capita tax on all inhabitants of Roman provinces. The historicity of the census as depicted in the gospel story is dubious. Nevertheless, Christ's birth is discursively represented as coincident with a tax census, raising the question of why. Furthermore, this trope has been accepted and reduplicated in theological tradition, inviting consideration of its impact and ramifications.

54. Cited in Peterson, "Monotheism," 96.

55. Cited in Peterson, "Monotheism," 226 n. 138.

56. Peterson, "Monotheism," 96, 226 n. 138. *Oikothen* most broadly means "from one's own house or resources," and in fairness need not index so specifically a "financial department," although such a translation (Peterson's via Hollerich) certainly is felicitous for our purposes.

57. Ibid., 100. Peterson makes no mention of Orosius's link to Augustine, even though Peterson upholds the latter as a prized example of resistance to identifying the geopolitics of Rome with divine reign and governance.

58. Ibid.

59. Cited in Peterson, "Monotheism," 100.

60. Ibid.

61. Peterson, "Monotheism," 101. Orosius is either ignorant of or ignores the fact that Roman citizens were exempt from the poll tax and so presumably would not be numbered in such a census. Only later is taxation extended to citizens. Following Orosius's logic, however, one could argue that such timing indicates deliberate divine identification with the oppressed noncitizenry of the Roman Empire who are groaning under the burden of such imposed taxation.

62. Richard Seaford, "Tragic Tyranny," in *Popular Tyranny: Sovereignty and its Discontents in Ancient Greece*, ed. Kathryn A. Morgan (Austin: University of Texas Press, 2003), 95–116.

63. On these and related points, see, e.g., Ingham, *Nature* and John N. Smithin, ed., *What is Money?* (London: Routledge, 2000).

64. The correlation of monotheism and monarchy is a vexed debate that I do not wish to take up. Important interventions have rightly pointed out that imperial dominance does not require monotheistic ideals, with Rome's success being one such example explored in, e.g., Arnaldo Momigliano, "The Disadvantages of Monotheism for a Universal State," *Classical Philology* 81, no. 4 (1986): 285–97.

My interest here is in the rhetorical and ideological coordination of these ideas, as well as the potential place of money in such a matrix.

65. Marc Shell, *The Economy of Literature* (Baltimore: Johns Hopkins University Press, 1978); David M. Schaps, *The Invention of Coinage and the Monetization of Ancient Greece* (Ann Arbor: University of Michigan Press, 2004); and Richard Seaford, *Money and the Early Greek Mind: Homer, Philosophy, Tragedy* (Cambridge: Cambridge University Press, 2004).

66. See the brief discussion of money in Robert N. Bellah, *Religion in Human Evolution: From the Paleolithic to the Axial Age* (Cambridge, MA: Belknap Press of Harvard University Press, 2011), 370.

67. Seaford, *Money*, 175–283.

68. Ibid., 214–15.

69. Seaford, "Tragic Tyranny," 100.

70. Also worthy of consideration is Heraclitus (ca. 535–475 BCE), whose thought, claims Shell, *Economy*, 52, "defines a kind of exchange (or metaphor) that did not exist in the world much before [his] time," possibly indexing the transformations brought by coinage. Shell devotes close analysis to Fragment 90: "All things are an equal exchange for fire and fire for all things, as goods are for gold and gold for goods" (ibid.). Fire invokes an all-pervasive and fundamental cosmic element apparently transmutable into all other aspects of reality, just as gold as a medium of exchange appears as the basic constituent of economy. Shell's claims here are explored further in Devin Singh, "Monetized Philosophy and Theological Money: Uneasy Linkages and the Future of a Discourse," in *The Future of Continental Philosophy of Religion*, ed. Clayton Crockett, B. Keith Putt, and Jeffrey W. Robbins (Bloomington: Indiana University Press, 2014), 140–53.

Chapter 2

1. M. Douglas Meeks, *God the Economist: The Doctrine of God and Political Economy* (Minneapolis, MN: Fortress Press, 1989).

2. Two major interventions in this tradition are Kathryn Tanner, *Economy of Grace* (Minneapolis, MN: Fortress Press, 2005) and Nimi Wariboko, *God and Money: A Theology of Money in a Globalizing World* (Lanham, MD: Lexington Books, 2008).

3. Harry O. Maier, "Dominion from Sea to Sea: Eusebius of Caesara, Constantine the Great, and the Exegesis of Empire," in *The Calling of the Nations: Exegesis, Ethnography, and Empire in the Biblical-Historical Present*, ed. Mark Vessey et al. (Toronto: University of Toronto Press, 2011), 158.

4. Michel Foucault, *Security, Territory, Population: Lectures at the Collège de France, 1977–1978*, ed. Michel Senellart and Arnold I. Davidson (New York: Palgrave Macmillan, 2007) and Michel Foucault, *Politics, Philosophy, Culture:*

Interviews and Other Writings, 1977–1984, ed. Lawrence D. Kritzman, trans. Alan Sheridan et al. (New York: Routledge, 1988), 57–85.

5. Foucault, *Security, Territory, Population*, 95.

6. Ibid., 129–30.

7. Ibid., 192.

8. Leshem, *The Origins of Neoliberalism: Modeling the Economy from Jesus to Foucault* (New York: Columbia University Press, 2016), 6–7.

9. Agamben, *The Kingdom and the Glory: For a Theological Genealogy of Economy and Government*, trans. Lorenzo Chiesa and Matteo Mandarini (Stanford: Stanford University Press, 2011), 276, emphasis added.

10. While government falls under the auspices of the Son, its anarchic nature, *pace* Agamben, is not derived from the Son as *anarchos*. For an argument against Agamben's reading of the Son's anarchy, see Devin Singh, "Anarchy, Void, Signature: Agamben's Trinity among Orthodoxy's Remains," *Political Theology* 17, no. 1 (2016): 27–46.

11. Agamben recognizes the role of angels as bureaucratic ministers or "civil servants." The section of *Kingdom* exploring this was also separately published with the suggestive title: Giorgio Agamben, *Die Beamten des Himmels: Über Engel*, trans. Andreas Hiepko (Berlin: Verlag der Weltreligionen im Insel Verlag, 2007).

12. Marie-José Mondzain, *Image, Icon, Economy: The Byzantine Origins of the Contemporary Imaginary*, trans. Rico Franses (Stanford: Stanford University Press, 2005), 61.

13. Ibid.

14. Ibid., 63.

15. Peter Brown, *Poverty and Leadership in the Later Roman Empire*, The Menahem Stern Jerusalem Lectures (Hanover, NH: University Press of New England, 2002), 74.

16. Ibid., 7. The definitive work on the Greco-Roman practice of euergetism is Paul Veyne, *Bread and Circuses: Historical Sociology and Political Pluralism*, trans. Brian Pearce (London: Allen Lane at The Penguin Press, 1990). See also the discussion of Seneca's treatise on giving in Marcel Hénaff, *The Price of Truth: Gift, Money, and Philosophy*, trans. Jean-Louis Morhange and Anne-Marie Feenberg-Dibon (Stanford: Stanford University Press, 2010), 257–66. On wealth in Latin Christendom in particular, see Peter Brown, *Through the Eye of a Needle: Wealth, the Fall of Rome, and the Making of Christianity in the West, 350–550 AD* (Princeton, NJ: Princeton University Press, 2012). Brown extends his reflections on the centrality of almsgiving for the poor and the dead in Peter Brown, *The Ransom of the Soul: Afterlife and Wealth in Early Eastern Christianity* (Cambridge, MA: Harvard University Press, 2015).

17. Brown, *Poverty and Leadership*, 9. L. Wm. Countryman, *The Rich Christian in the Church of the Early Empire: Contradictions and Accommodations* (New

York: Edwin Mellen Press, 1980), 107 provides a concise summary of the differences: "Greco-Roman philanthropy, then, differed from Jewish [and Christian]
in being directed not to the poor as such, but to relatives, friends, fellow-citizens,
or clients. And where the Jewish almsgiver expected his reward from the hand
of God, Greek or Roman looked for a direct return from those benefited [in the
form of, e.g., return gifts or public honors]."

18. Brown, *Poverty and Leadership*, 19.

19. Ibid., 8–9.

20. Ibid., 24. Brown continues: "The bishop was presented, above all, as the
oikonomos, as the 'steward,' of the wealth of the church. This wealth was to be
used by the clergy for the benefit of the poor. In some circles, even private almsgiving was discouraged: ideally, all gifts to the poor were to pass through the
bishop and his clergy, *for only they knew* who needed support" (emphasis added).
Here we glimpse a profound early link between economic resource distribution
and panoptic aspirations.

21. On bishops' courts, see Jill Harries, *Law and Empire in Late Antiquity*
(Cambridge: Cambridge University Press, 1999), 191–211.

22. Andrea Giardina, "The Transition to Late Antiquity," in *The Cambridge
Economic History of the Greco-Roman World*, ed. Walter Scheidel, Ian Morris, and
Richard Saller (New York: Cambridge University Press, 2007), 768.

23. Unless otherwise noted, all biblical citations follow the New Revised Standard Version. On almsgiving, see the important exploration in Gary A. Anderson, *Charity: The Place of the Poor in the Biblical Tradition* (New Haven: Yale
University Press, 2013). An excellent recent sourcebook on early Christian attitudes toward wealth more broadly is Helen Rhee, *Loving the Poor, Saving the
Rich: Wealth, Poverty, and Early Christian Formation* (Grand Rapids, MI: Baker
Academic, 2012).

24. Brown, *Ransom*, 22.

25. Countryman, *Rich Christian*, 113–14.

26. Brown, *Ransom*, 30.

27. John Reumann, "The Use of Οἰκονομία and Related Terms in Greek
Sources to about A.D. 100, as a Background for Patristic Applications" (Ph.D.
diss., University of Pennsylvania, 1957), 222.

28. Numenius, *The Revolt of the Academics Against Plato*, a fragment preserved
in Eusebius, *Praeparatio Evangelica* 14.7, referenced in Reumann, "Use," 205.

29. Dale Martin, *Slavery as Salvation: The Metaphor of Slavery in Pauline
Christianity* (New Haven, CT: Yale University Press, 1990), ch. 1.

30. In designating this arrival, "*parousia* is the term sometimes employed"
(Reumann, "Use," 267). The usage here is notable if only because this term will
come to be used by Christians to denote the return of Christ.

31. Ibid.

32. Reumann, "'Jesus as Steward': An Overlooked Theme in Christology," in *Studia Evangelica V: Papers Present to the Third International Congress on New Testament Studies Held at Christ Church, Oxford, 1965*, ed. F. L. Cross (Berlin: Akademie Verlag, 1968), 23. He notes further that "it is possible that two fragments of Philo even refer to the logos as the οἰκονόμος ("administrator" or "steward") for God" (ibid.).

33. Ibid., 27.

34. Ibid., 24.

35. Both cited in Reumann, "'Jesus'," 23.

36. Reumann, "'Jesus'," 25.

37. See Wilfred Tooley, "Stewards of God: An Examination of the Terms OIKONOMOS and OIKONOMIA in the New Testament," *Scottish Journal of Theology* 19 (1966): 74–86.

38. Cited in Reumann, "'Jesus'," 29. Reumann comments: "Here God (or Christ) is called οἰκοδεσπότης; certain leaders are said to have a special οἰκονομία in the household, and the principle holds that an agent or 'one sent' (*shaliah*) is like the sender himself. In such circles it is easy to view Jesus as the οἰκοδεσπότης or οἰκονόμος in God's οἰκονομία."

39. Reumann, "'Jesus'," 29.

40. Translation from Samuel Lee, *Eusebius Bishop of Caesarea. On the Theophaneia or Divine Manifestation of our Lord and Saviour Jesus Christ* (Cambridge: Cambridge University Press, 1843).

41. Translation from *The Life of Apollonius of Tyana, the Epistles of Apollonius and the Treatise of Eusebius*, translated by F. C. Conybeare, Loeb Classical Library (New York: Macmillan, 1912), 404–605.

42. Commentary by Cameron and Hall, in Eusebius of Caesarea, *Life of Constantine*, trans. and ed. Averil Cameron and Stuart George Hall (Oxford: Oxford University Press, 1999), 186.

43. Emphasis added. See also 3.15. Translation from Eusebius of Caesarea, *On Ecclesiastical Theology*, trans. Markus Vinzent and Kelley Spoerl, Fathers of the Church (Washington, DC: Catholic University Press of America, forthcoming). Permission to cite gratefully acknowledged.

44. Numenius, *Ho Prôtos Theos*, in Eusebius *Preparation for the Gospel* 11.18, cited in Erik Peterson, "Monotheism as a Political Problem: A Contribution to the History of Political Theology in the Roman Empire," in *Theological Tractates*, trans. and ed. Michael J. Hollerich (Stanford: Stanford University Press, 2011), 205 n. 15.

45. Peterson, "Monotheism," 71–72.

46. Pierre Vidal-Naquet, *The Black Hunter: Forms of Thought and Forms of Society in the Greek World*, trans. Andrew Szegedy-Maszak (Baltimore: Johns Hopkins University Press, 1998), 224–48.

47. The demiurge as divine craftsman is also linked with precious metal discourse. Reflecting on the *Timaeus*, Pierre Vidal-Naquet (ibid., 235) draws attention

to the language of metallurgy in the work of the demiurge. In creation, the demi-urge "uses all the artisanal techniques available in Plato's time . . . What is less understood, in my opinion, is that all these skills form a meaningful hierarchy . . . At the peak of creation, the world-soul is produced by the finest metallurgy, with its techniques of refining, alloying, even lamination (*Tim.* 35a et seq.)." In response to Vidal-Naquet, Leslie Kurke, *Coins, Bodies, Games, and Gold: The Politics of Mean-ing in Archaic Greece* (Princeton, NJ: Princeton University Press, 1999), 49 n. 20 suggests that "the crafting of the world-soul by the techniques of metallurgy may be partly motivated by the archaic aristocratic discourse of self, in which the image of refining metals serves as a mastertrope." Her analysis reveals the esteem and sta-tus associated with such materials in ancient Greece, lending power to elite classes who enjoyed monopoly on their use. Such metals were constructed as precious through such privileged access and their ritual use to mark sacrality and authority. Biblical language also partakes of the esteem of precious metals, seen, e.g., where the Hebrew prophets ask for God's people to be refined and made as pure as gold and silver (Zech 13:9; Mal 3:3). The soul's worth and moral purity are compared with that of valuable metals. The language of refining metals is also taken up by early Christian thinkers to describe the purity of faith and moral standing before God (1 Pet 1:19; Rev 3:18). Within the Christian cooptation of demiurgic role and function, an exaltation of artistic production and the esteem of precious metals may thus also be conveyed. In fact, as we will consider in a subsequent chapter, the possibility emerges of conceiving of God as a minter, impressing the divine image upon the soul of humanity like coins.

48. Brown, *Poverty and Leadership*, 74.

49. Foucault, *Security, Territory, Population*, 154.

50. As Brown, *Poverty and Leadership*, 80–81 notes, "From around 300 onward, the later Roman empire was characterized by an unprecedented degree of closeness of the state to the lives of its subjects. For the first time in its long history, the Roman empire had become a presence that could not be ignored by the majority of its inhabitants." It may not have been the bulky, repressive regime that previous scholarship characterized it as, "[b]ut its representatives were now everywhere."

51. Brown (ibid., 89) highlights a phenomenological distinction between sov-ereignty and governance made by the ruled: "The reputation for being a true 'lover of the poor' was projected away from the harsh realities of governmental control on the local level to the distant figure of the emperor . . . Such a belief preserved the hope in Christian circles that, despite the abrasive methods of the emperor's representatives, a mysterious reservoir of mercy existed, at the distant center, which might soften the workings of a hard-driving imperial system."

52. Ibid., 80. Brown continues: this "novel 'master image' . . . was originally formed in the highly stratified, monarchical societies of the ancient Near East.

It accepted towering asymmetries of power and wealth between 'the poor' and those to whom they looked for help. But it also functioned in the Near East, as it would function in the later empire, as a language of claims that was calculated to bridge just such daunting social distances. It was the duty of the powerful (and, indeed, it was regarded as a special ornament of their power) to listen to 'the cry' of the poor."

Chapter 3

1. Key studies of the relation between Eusebius and Constantine include Timothy D. Barnes, *Constantine and Eusebius* (Cambridge, MA: Harvard University Press, 1981); H. A. Drake, *In Praise of Constantine: A Historical Study and New Translation of Eusebius' Tricennial Orations*, University of California Publications in Classical Studies 15 (Berkeley: University of California Press, 1976); Michael J. Hollerich, "Religion and Politics in the Writings of Eusebius: Reassessing the First 'Court Theologian'," *Church History* 59, no. 3 (1990): 309–25; and Pierre Maraval, *Eusèbe de Césarée. La théologie politique de l'empire chrétien: louanges de Constantin (Triakontaétérikos)*, Sagesses chrétiennes (Paris: Les Éditions du Cerf, 2001).

2. Dale B. Martin, *Inventing Superstition: From the Hippocratics to the Christians* (Cambridge: Harvard University Press, 2004), 220–21.

3. Erik Peterson, "Monotheism as a Political Problem: A Contribution to the History of Political Theology in the Roman Empire," in *Theological Tractates*, trans. and ed. Michael J. Hollerich (Stanford: Stanford University Press, 2011), 68–105.

4. For a critique of Peterson's dismissal of Eusebius and analysis of the distinction between sovereignty and governance in Eusebius, see Devin Singh, "Eusebius as Political Theologian: The Legend Continues," *Harvard Theoloigcal Review* 108, no. 1 (2015): 129–54. This distinction is central to the project in Giorgio Agamben, *The Kingdom and the Glory: For a Theological Genealogy of Economy and Government*, trans. Lorenzo Chiesa and Matteo Mandarini (Stanford: Stanford University Press, 2011).

5. As Alois Grillmeier, *From the Apostolic Age to Chalcedon*, vol. 1, *Christ in Christian Tradition*, trans. John Bowden, 2nd rev. ed. (Atlanta: John Knox Press, 1975), 253–54 notes, "the emperor is the image (εἰκών) of the ruler of the world. At the same time he imitates the Logos-Christ. Thus we have a twofold *mimesis*: first between the emperor and God, and second in the imitation of the *mimesis* which is to be found between Father and Son. By virtue of this twofold mimesis, the emperor enters into a kind of triadic relationship with the Father and the Logos. He occupies the position of a 'third person'. It follows almost automatically that the emperor also participates in the functions of the Logos before the Father."

6. For example, as Michael J. Hollerich, "Myth and History in Eusebius's 'De vita Constantini': 'Vit. Const. 1.12' in Its Contemporary Setting," *Harvard Theological Review* 82, no. 4 (October 1989): 421–45, at 431 argues, in the face of pagan criticism and dismissal of the exodus story as mythic, Eusebius employs Constantine's victory at the Milvian Bridge to authenticate and authorize the tale of Moses. It is as if to say, "Unnamed doubters may have scouted the credibility of the Exodus story as a *mythos*, but Constantine's triumph has removed all doubt." Political victory helps the exegesis of ancient biblical events and thus legitimates the authority of God's word.

7. For the *Life of Constantine (Vita Constantini)*, I follow Eusebius of Caesarea, *Life of Constantine*, trans. and ed. Averil Cameron and Stuart George Hall (Oxford: Oxford University Press, 1999).

8. Eusebius, *Life*, introduction by Cameron and Hall on 13. See also Aaron P. Johnson, *Ethnicity and Argument in Eusebius' "Praeparatio Evangelica"* (Oxford: Oxford University Press, 2006), 195. This purported function as a training manual for Constantine's sons is debated. Whether or not it had such a purpose, the depictions Eusebius provides are clearly idealized, and he is transparent about being selective in his reportage in order to provide a theological portrait.

9. This theme will be taken up in very similar fashion in, e.g., Athanasius, *Against the Arians* 3.5 and Basil, *On the Holy Spirit* 18.45. Such language will come to play a significant role in the iconoclastic controversy, with such passages among key citations in the florilegia employed in the debate.

10. In their commentary on this passage, Cameron and Hall note that "though Eusebius does not say so, the type recalled depictions of Alexander the Great, also a deliberate choice from 325 onwards." Eusebius, *Life*, commentary by Cameron and Hall on 315. This complicates the discussion by demonstrating additional potential motives for Constantine's self-depiction. Here the minters draw on the esteemed imperial legacy of Alexander and invoke a notion of pangeographic rule, as emperor over the East and West. That Eusebius conveniently leaves this out, assuming he recognized it, can be attributed to his rhetorical *oikonomia*, the strategic withholding of information unhelpful to his purposes of presenting the emperor theologically (*Life of Constantine* 1.10–11). While Constantine and his coiners may be appealing to the legacy of Alexander, Eusebius is careful to invoke Christian themes, both to distinguish the uniqueness of Constantinian reign and signal divine election. Drake, *In Praise*, 3 makes similar comparisons between the heavenward gazing statue of Constantine and depictions of Alexander. See also Evelyn B. Harrison, "The Constantinian Portrait," *Dumbarton Oaks Papers* 21 (1967): 81–96.

11. Dotan Leshem, *The Origins of Neoliberalism: Modeling the Economy from Jesus to Foucault* (New York: Columbia University Press, 2016), 120–23.

12. Richard Seaford, "Tragic Tyranny," in *Popular Tyranny: Sovereignty and Its Discontents in Ancient Greece*, ed. Kathryn A. Morgan (Austin: University of Texas Press, 2003), 98. Citing Sophocles, Fragment 88, Seaford continues, "What exactly is this power of money? The concrete polarity seems to imply the more abstract notion that money has power to reach the sacred and the profane *indiscriminately*, to ignore or transgress the distinction between them. We think of the tyrant using ritual and temple treasures to obtain and extend his secular power."

13. Agamben, *Kingdom*, 75, 76, 79.

14. Florence Dupont, "The Emperor-God's Other Body," in *Fragments for a History of the Human Body, Part 3*, ed. Michael Feher, Ramona Nadoff, and Nadia Tazi (New York: Zone Books, 1989), 396–419. Note also the extended engagement with this theme in Giorgio Agamben, *Homo Sacer: Sovereign Power and Bare Life*, trans. Daniel Heller-Roazen (Stanford: Stanford University Press, 1998), 91–103. The theme is a central discussion in political theology based on Ernst Kantorowicz, *The King's Two Bodies: A Study in Medieval Political Theology* (Princeton, NJ: Princeton University Press, 1957).

15. Clifford Ando, *Imperial Ideology and Provincial Loyalty in the Roman Empire* (Berkeley: University of California Press, 2000), 217, citing *Life of Constantine* 4.71. Drake, *In Praise*, 9 mentions the debate that persists around interpreting these specific coins, since certain coin finds bear the title *divus* for Constantine, in pagan fashion. If indeed they did, such a detail would naturally have been excluded by Eusebius and any pagan imagery, like in the Alexander *solidus*, reinterpreted.

16. As negative example, Herodotus's depiction of Darius as both tyrannical and "money-grubbing" takes dramatic form in the tale of his raiding of the tomb of Queen Nitokris of Babylon. Searching for treasure purportedly buried with her, he finds only her corpse and this inscription: "If you were not insatiate of money and greedy for base gain, you would not have opened the tombs of corpses" (Herodotus, *Histories* 1.187, cited in Leslie Kurke, *Coins, Bodies, Games, and Gold: The Politics of Meaning in Archaic Greece* [Princeton, NJ: Princeton University Press, 1999], 84). Tyrants have no regard for custom or propriety, wantonly violating sacred spaces. On the contrary, pious Constantine upholds tradition and marks the ritual crossing of boundaries upon his sanctified money.

17. On tyranny, money, and the political see, e.g., David M. Schaps, *The Invention of Coinage and the Monetization of Ancient Greece* (Ann Arbor: University of Michigan Press, 2004), ch. 9 and Kathryn A. Morgan, ed., *Popular Tyranny: Sovereignty and Its Discontents in Ancient Greece* (Austin: University of Texas Press, 2003). On tyranny and money in literature see, e.g., Richard Seaford, *Money and the Early Greek Mind: Homer, Philosophy, Tragedy* (Cambridge:

Cambridge University Press, 2004); Marc Shell, *The Economy of Literature* (Baltimore: Johns Hopkins University Press, 1978) and Kurke, *Coins, Bodies, Games, and Gold.*

18. P. N. Ure, *The Origin of Tyranny* (Cambridge: Cambridge University Press, 1922) argues more specifically that tyranny arose in ancient Greece *explicitly* in conjunction with the appearance of coinage. Kurke, *Coins, Bodies, Games, and Gold,* chs. 1–2 also surveys and problematizes the relation between tyrants and state coined money. We must note that not all depictions of tyranny in classical Greek thought were negative, and the term may be employed neutrally and at times with approbation; see, e.g., Mark Munn, *The Mother of the Gods, Athens, and the Tyranny of Asia: A Study of Sovereignty in Ancient Religion* (Berkeley: University of California Press, 2006), 16–19.

19. "Now the Lydians . . . were the first of men, so far as we know, who struck and used coin of gold or silver" (Herodotus, *Histories* 1.94). Although the ancient Greeks held a variety of opinions about its place of origin, there is some consensus among modern numismatists that Lydian origin is highly plausible; see, e.g., William Young, "The Fabulous Gold of the Pactolus Valley," *Boston Museum Bulletin* 70, no. 59 (1972): 8–9 and Schaps, *Invention,* 34, 93–96. Shell, *Economy,* 12 claims further: "As coinage was associated with the Lydians, so too was political tyranny . . . The very word *tyrannos* is Lydian in origin," citing Roberto Gusmani, *Lydisches Wörterbuch* (Heidelberg: Carl Winter Universitätsverlag, 1964).

20. For example, Shell, *Economy,* 20 cites the poem of Archilochus (Fragment 25), also recalled by Herodotus (*Histories* 1.12): "I care not for the wealth of golden Gyges, nor ever have I envied him; I am not jealous of the work of gods, and I have no desire for lofty tyranny, for such things are far beyond my sight." Shell notes the important convergence of money, the realm of the divine, tyranny, and the theme of vision.

21. Shell, *Economy,* 12–13.

22. Plato, *Republic* 360a–b.

23. As Seaford, *Money,* 118 notes, the ring's "power to make its wearer invisible expresses the invisibility of the magical power embodied in it, in particular the invisible power of the king (i.e. even where he is not personally present) to enforce his will throughout his kingdom."

24. Shell, *Economy,* 33–36. See also Seaford, *Money,* 109, 113, 117–18.

25. Shell, *Economy,* 21 draws out the connections between money, tyranny, and the theme of invisibility in the *Republic.* Socrates engages his interlocutors about the relationship between money and justice. Cephalus lauds the power of money, since it allows one to repay debts both "to men and gods." Equalizing power means that one can pass into the next life free from condemnation, having settled all accounts. Shell writes: "Like many other Greeks, Cephalus trusts that his wealth will save him from punishment or from committing the wrongs

that entail punishment. He hopes that it will make the vengeful Hades (*Haidês*) unable to see (*idein*) him, and he believes that his money is in this sense an agent of invisibility" (see Plato, *Republic* 330d–331b). Relatedly, Shell, *Economy*, 24–25 claims, "Money is one of two competing architectonic principles in the *Republic*; the other such principle is philosophy. Philosophy and money both order the 'other' arts and are about 'worth' (although in different senses). Wage-earning is the tyrant's substitute for philosophy. A man cannot be both philosopher and wage earner." Eusebius specifically cites Plato's praise of the pursuit of virtue and education in contradistinction to that of wealth and money in *Preparation for the Gospel* 12.18.

26. Shell, *Economy*, 31, citing Aristotle, *Politics* 1313–14.

27. Seaford, *Money*, 215.

28. As Kurt A. Raaflaub, "Stick and Glue: The Function of Tyranny in Fifth-Century Athenian Democracy," in *Popular Tyranny: Sovereignty and its Discontents in Ancient Greece*, ed. Kathryn A. Morgan (Austin: University of Texas Press, 2003), 60 notes, *tyrannos* did not originally demarcate illegitimate singular rule from legitimate: "'Tyranny' is an umbrella term used both in antiquity and by modern scholars for a variety of types of sole rule with different origins and characteristics. It was originally and could always be used indiscriminately with other terms for monarchy (especially *basileia*, kingship). A precise and strict functional separation, in which *basileia* was the term for legitimate and good forms, *tyrannis* that for illegitimate, violent and bad types of monarchy, is a late phenomenon, first occurring in Thucydides."

29. Friedrich Balke, "Derrida and Foucault on Sovereignty," *German Law Journal* 6, no. 1 (2005): 71–85, at 74 claims that "Greek political theory as well as political praxis knows the problem of tyranny as a liminal case of sovereign dominance, transforming the sovereign into an *outlaw*, with no contractual connection to the citizens, so that they can deal with him like a tyrant." As our exploration has noted, however, such a distinction is nominal rather than substantive, for sovereignty itself manifests radical exclusion from the sphere of rule, as an outlaw, as under the "ban." Compare Agamben, *Homo Sacer*, 104–11. Conversely, any ties that persist between sovereignty and the order can be ascribed to the tyrant as well, and it is significant that Balke describes the connection as "contractual." The tie that binds is one of debt and obligation, as manifested in law and money and, hence, contracts. The tyrant is rhetorically constructed as an *exceptional case* of sovereign rule and, as such, proves the norm.

30. Martin, *Inventing Superstition*, 222–23.

31. Paul Veyne, *Bread and Circuses: Historical Sociology and Political Pluralism*, trans. Brian Pearce (London: Allen Lane at The Penguin Press, 1990).

32. There is some irony in the fact that Eusebius draws on anti-tyrannical discourse in the service of glorifying Constantine's *monarchic* reign. Such discourse

in the classical Greek context was generally marshaled against models of centralized power. Indeed, a heroic figure was often presented as a tyrant killer. Almost paradoxically, Eusebius simultaneously employs anti-tyrannical tropes while exalting a *solitary* monarch. While not unprecedented, this represents one of his adaptations of tradition. His links from such discourse to Christian virtue and biblical leadership patterns are further evidence of his creative development. Eusebius also draws on the increasingly popular practice in his time of labeling many deposed and disgraced forbears as *tyranni*. For a survey of tyranny's application in Eusebius's time, but without attention to financial themes, see Timothy D. Barnes, "Oppressor, Persecutor, Usurper: The Meaning of 'Tyrannus' in the Fourth Century," in *Historiae Augustae Colloquium Barcinonense*, ed. G. Bonamente and M. Mayer (Bari: Edipuglia, 1996), 55–65.

33. Note that in this schema at least, the Son and monetary resources are structurally parallel. Rather than divine administrator and dispenser, the Son is here, as he is often construed, the wealth that is dispensed. Eusebius employs but qualifies the metaphor of the Son as ray of light from the Father, striving hard to maintain the unity-in-distinction between God and the Logos, and asserting that the Son is begotten as a result of the Father's will (e.g., Eusebius, *Demonstration of the Gospel* 4.3; 5.1).

34. For his crimes against the gods, Tantalus was condemned to thirst but never be quenched and reach for fruit that was always just out of reach, forever "tantalizing" him. Significantly, some ancient Greeks posited that he was of Lydian origin, and Strabo speaks of his vast wealth derived from the mines of Phrygia. He was also the founder of the house of Atreus, whose descendants included Agamemnon, Orestes, and Electra, luminaries of Greek tragedy itself concerned, among other things, with tyranny and abuse of wealth. Eusebius conveys much with this pointed reference.

35. Drake, *In Praise*, 167 n.3.

36. Ibid., 167 n.5.

37. See the illuminating discussion in Noel Lenski, *Constantine and the Cities: Imperial Authority and Civic Politics* (Philadelphia: University of Pennsylvania Press, 2016), 167–78.

38. Plato, *Republic* 612b. "This helmet renders the wearer invisible to the gods and so ensures him protection from punishment in Hades similar to the protection that Cephalus believed money made available to him. The Helmet of Hades, like money, can make wrong-doers invisible to a vengeful Hades" (Shell, *Economy*, 25–26).

Chapter 4

1. Georg Friedrich Knapp, *The State Theory of Money*, ed. H. M. Lucas and James Bonar, abr. ed. (London: Macmillan, 1924); Geoffrey K. Ingham, *The*

Nature of Money (Cambridge, UK: Polity, 2004); and Keith Hart, *Money in an Unequal World: Keith Hart and His Memory Bank* (New York: Texere, 2000).

2. Susanna Elm, "Inscriptions and Conversions: Gregory of Nazianzus on Baptism (*Or.* 38–40)," in *Conversion in Late Antiquity and the Early Middle Ages: Seeing and Believing*, ed. Kenneth Mills and Anthony Grafton (Rochester, NY: University of Rochester Press, 2003), 6.

3. Ibid., 9.

4. Ibid.

5. Harry O. Maier, "Dominion from Sea to Sea: Eusebius of Caesarea, Constantine the Great, and the Exegesis of Empire," in *The Calling of the Nations: Exegesis, Ethnography, and Empire in the Biblical-Historical Present*, ed. Mark Vessey et al. (Toronto: University of Toronto Press, 2011), 150.

6. Elm, "Inscriptions and Conversions," 10–11.

7. Ingham, *Nature*, 98.

8. As Mark S. Peacock, "The Origins of Money in Ancient Greece: The Political Economy of Coinage and Exchange," *Cambridge Journal of Economics* 30 (2006): 643 notes, generally in ancient context *coins were counted, not weighed*, suggesting their nominal as opposed to substantive significance: "What distinguishes Greek coinage from bullion is that, like today's money, its issuer, the state, stamped it. A stamp may originally have been nothing more than a mark of ownership on the part of the issuer; yet the state's stamp served as a sign of coin's 'redeemability': the state would accept coin in payments to itself."

9. Ronald S. Stroud, "An Athenian Law on Silver Coinage," *Hesperia* 43, no. 2 (1974): 157–88 discusses an ancient Athenian law allowing foreign-minted, "counterfeit" Athenian coins to circulate so long as they bore an acceptable Athenian stamp and were of adequate silver content. Rather than as a challenge to Athenian sovereignty, these "honest fakes" were seen as extending Athenian prestige. For discussion of the ideology of precious metals as reinforcing elite values in the ancient world, see Leslie Kurke, *Coins, Bodies, Games, and Gold: The Politics of Meaning in Archaic Greece* (Princeton, NJ: Princeton University Press, 1999), 41–64.

10. As Clifford Ando, *Imperial Ideology and Provincial Loyalty in the Roman Empire* (Berkeley: University of California Press, 2000), 221 notes, citing Suetonius, *Tiberius* 58: "The belief that a coin was legitimated, indeed, rendered sacrosanct, by the portrait of the emperor that it carried had its origins in the Julio-Claudian era. Already in that period Romans had begun to apply the law of *maiestas* [i.e., treason] to acts that infringed on the dignity of the imperial portrait. Suetonius associated this development with the reign of Tiberius: 'Gradually charges of this kind proceeded so far that even the following became capital offenses: to strike a slave near a statue of Augustus, to change one's clothes near such a statue, to bring his portrait, whether stamped on a coin or ring, into a bathroom or a brothel, or to attack any word or deed of his with some opinion.'"

11. Ando, *Imperial Ideology*, 221, citing *Codex Theodosianus*, 9.22.1.

12. Monetary value is tied to declarations of sovereignty, glimpsed here in the power of the image. See, e.g., C. H. V. Sutherland, *Coinage in Roman Imperial Policy 31 B.C.–A.D. 68* (London: Methuen, 1951).

13. See Eusebius, *Ecclesiastical Theology* 2.7, 2.23; Athanasius, *Against the Arians* 3.5; and Basil, *On the Holy Spirit* 18.45.

14. Translation from E. H. Gifford, *Eusebii Pamphili Evangelicae Praeparationis libri xv* (Oxford, 1903).

15. Translation from Alexander Roberts, James Donaldson, and A. Cleveland Coxe, eds., *Latin Christianity: Its Founder, Tertullian*, vol. 3, *Ante-Nicene Fathers* (Buffalo, NY: Christian Literature Publishing, 1885).

16. Elm, "Inscriptions and Conversions," 14.

17. On this dynamic of interaction broadly considered, see S. R. F. Price, *Rituals and Power: The Roman Imperial Cult in Asia Minor* (Cambridge: Cambridge University Press, 1984).

18. Despite debate about to what extent we can speak of a propagandistic role for coinage in the ancient world, there is general consensus that it played a crucial role in the communicative interaction between emperor and populace. See, e.g., A. H. M. Jones, *The Roman Economy: Studies in Ancient Economic and Administrative History*, ed. P. A. Brunt (Oxford: Blackwell, 1974), 61–81; Barbara Levick, "Propaganda and the Imperial Coinage," *Antichthon* 16 (1982): 104–16; M. H. Crawford, "Roman Imperial Coin Types and the Formation of Public Opinion," in *Studies in Numismatic Method Presented to Philip Grierson.*, ed. C. N. L. Brooke et al. (Cambridge: Cambridge University Press, 1983), 47–64; and Andrew Wallace-Hadrill, "Image and Authority in the Coinage of Augustus," *Journal of Roman Studies* 76 (1986): 66–87.

19. On the ambivalent and contested status of minters in late antiquity see Sarah Bond, "Currency and Control: Mint Workers in the Later Roman Empire," in *Work, Labour, and Professions in the Roman World*, ed. Koenraad Verboven and Christian Laes (Leiden: Brill, 2017), 227–45.

20. See, e.g., Ando, *Imperial Ideology*, ch. 7 and Wallace-Hadrill, "Image and Authority." Ando notes that "writers often attributed the conscious selection of types and legends to emperors and would-be emperors. What is more, their diction just as often indicates either that they regarded that responsibility as an imperial prerogative or, conversely, that they believed coins reflected the immediate political and propagandistic interests of the court" (216).

21. There is evidence that coinage could be employed strategically so as to target specific classes of subjects depending upon the denomination used; see Olivier Hekster, "Coins and Messages: Audience Targeting on Coins of Different Denominations?" in *The Representation and Perception of Roman Imperial Power: Proceedings of the Third Workshop of the International Network: Impact of Empire*

(*Roman Empire, c. 200 B.C.–A.D. 476) Rome, March 20–23, 2002*, ed. Lukas de Blois et al. (Leiden: Brill, 2003).

22. Arrian, *Discourses of Epictetus*, 4.5.15–18, cited in Wallace-Hadrill, "Image and Authority," 66.

23. Ando, *Imperial Ideology*, 225.

24. Ibid., 226.

25. After analyzing Tertullian's *Apology*, for instance, Ando (ibid., 242) notes that he "clearly associated the accession of a new emperor both with the arrival of a new portrait on the coinage and with the advertisement of a particular ceremonial act."

26. One of the most well-known and representative discussions of this need to restore the corrupted image in humanity is Athanasius, *On the Incarnation of the Word*. For an exploration of the centrality of the image of God in humanity as demonstrating its intrinsic relationship to God, and specifically to the Son as eternal Image, see Kathryn Tanner, *Christ the Key* (Cambridge: Cambridge University Press, 2010), ch. 1.

27. Cited in Ando, *Imperial Ideology*, 220. For the edition of Macarius, see A. J. Mason, ed., *Fifty Spiritual Homilies of St. Macarius the Egyptian* (New York: Macmillan, 1921).

28. Translation from Philip Schaff and Henry Wace, eds., *Gregory of Nyssa: Dogmatic Treatises, etc.*, vol. 5, *Nicene and Post-Nicene Fathers, Second Series* (Buffalo, NY: Christian Literature Publishing, 1893). The centrality and pivotal nature of this chapter are suggested by its location at the midpoint of the chiastic structure of the work. The opening and concluding chapters (1 and 23–24) favorably compare images and imaging over against the power of words. It is not that words or the Word are denigrated, but that the communicating, testifying, and sanctifying power of the image conveys elements on a level inaccessible to discourse. The pivotal chapter, coming as it were at the center of this chiasm (chapter 12), presents the book's most direct and extended exploration of the significance of the image.

29. Origen, *Homilies on Genesis and Exodus*, trans. Ronald Heine, Fathers of the Church 71 (Washington, DC: Catholic University of America Press, 1982).

30. Dotan Leshem, *The Origins of Neoliberalism: Modeling the Economy from Jesus to Foucault* (New York: Columbia University Press, 2016), 120–23.

31. The various levels of imaging are developed in the patristic principle of *transcription*; see ibid., 57–59.

32. Michael Peppard, "Archived Portraits of Jesus: Unorthodox Christological Images from John and Athanasius," in *Portraits of Jesus: Essays in Christology. Festschrift for Harold Attridge*, ed. Susan Myers, Wissenschaftliche Untersuchungen zum Neuen Testament 3 (Tübingen: Mohr Siebeck, 2012), 393–409.

33. Cited in and translated by Peppard, "Archived Portraits," 405.

34. In his reflections on Genesis cited above, Origen switches registers from coining to painting to claim that "the Son of God is the painter of this image" (*Genesis Homily* XIII.4). The logic is similar even though the metaphors are mixed, for Origen appears to describe God as painting, rather than stamping, the divine image on the coins of humanity. Of course, the agency here is altered as well, for the Son is active in this process as the artist rather than as the archetypal seal. The role of the Father here remains unstated.

35. Elm, "Inscriptions and Conversions."

36. Walter Benjamin, "Fragment 74: Capitalism as Religion," in *Religion as Critique: The Frankfurt School's Critique of Religion*, ed. Eduardo Mendieta, trans. Chad Kautzer (New York: Routledge, 2005), 260.

37. This connection is tellingly documented in Marc Shell, *Art & Money* (Chicago: University of Chicago Press, 1995).

38. Susan Buck-Morss, "Visual Empire," *Diacritics* 32:2–3 (2007): 182.

39. A thoroughgoing comparative examination of money and icons is outside the scope of this study. My points here are intentionally allusive. I certainly do not collapse monetary and iconic economies; rather, I highlight correspondences, however troubling, that invite further consideration. Icons certainly resist identification with money and coinage in various ways. For a brief consideration of resonances among coins, banknotes, and icons, see Shell, *Art & Money*, ch. 1. See also the important conceptual redeployment of the iconicity of money in Martijn Konings, *The Emotional Logic of Capitalism: What Progressives Have Missed* (Stanford: Stanford University Press, 2015), 15–52. Although the Eucharist is not an icon, important parallels exist, and for one exploration of relations between eucharistic economy and money see Gil Anidjar, "Christians and Money (The Economic Enemy)," *Ethical Perspectives: Journal of the European Ethics Network* 12, no. 4 (2005): 497–519.

40. Even oppositional construal of the imperial image and Christocentric image reveals the same continuum of relation between the two. As Gerhart B. Ladner, "The Concept of the Image in the Greek Fathers and the Byzantine Iconoclastic Controversy," *Dumbarton Oaks Papers* 7 (1958): 22 notes, in Origen's exegesis of the famous "render unto Caesar" passage (Matt 22:21), "the imperial image as a symbol of this world has become an analogue to man molded from earth according to Genesis 2:7, and the man of the heavenly or divine image is analogous to the image of Christ, which was not on the imperial coin—one might be tempted to add: not yet on the imperial coin. That Christ and the emperor *could* appear on Byzantine coins, first during the reigns of Justinian II (about 700) and then continuously from the end of the Iconoclastic Controversy to the end of the Empire—this was in a sense a fulfillment of Origen's allegory and a realization of patristic image doctrine in general." The eventual fusion of the two images in material, theopolitical practice speaks to their fundamental

conceptual relation, whether or not previous allegorical interpretation set them at odds in creative fashion.

41. See, e.g., Ando, *Imperial Ideology*, 206–76 and Dale B. Martin, *Inventing Superstition: From the Hippocratics to the Christians* (Cambridge, MA: Harvard University Press, 2004), 207–25.

42. Marie-José Mondzain, *Image, Icon, Economy: The Byzantine Origins of the Contemporary Imaginary*, trans. Rico Franses (Stanford: Stanford University Press, 2005), 157.

43. Theosterikos, *Vita Nicetae*, xxviii and Georgius Monachus, *Chronicle* II, 751, cited in Edward James Martin, *A History of the Iconoclastic Controversy* (London: SPCK, 1930), 62. See the discussion in Shell, *Art & Money*, 34.

44. Shell, *Art & Money*, 30 notes the persistence of such an analogy, citing the medieval handbook of anatomy *Auslegung und Beschreibung der Anathomy*, "Von der Mutter": "'The uterus,' so goes the traditional analogy, 'is a tightly sealed vessel, similar to a coin purse [*Seckel*].'" See also Thomas Laqueur, *Making Sex: Body and Gender from the Greeks to Freud* (Cambridge, MA: Harvard University Press, 1990), 63.

45. The ongoing historical linkage between Christ and gold is noteworthy. The myth of Danae—impregnated by Jupiter through a "golden shower" of coin, after which she gave birth to Perseus—provided conceptual backdrop for medieval theologians and artists to depict insemination of Mary by the Word. As Shell, *Art & Money*, 24 notes, such theologians "saw the parallel between the aurigenetic conception of Perseus and the mysterious conception of Jesus. 'If Danae conceived from Jupiter through a golden shower,' remarks Franz of Retz in the early fifteenth century, 'why should the Virgin not give birth when impregnated by the Holy Spirit?' The early fourteenth-century *Ovid Moralized* similarly emphasizes the ideas that the substance of God's semen is gold (which the French author calls both *or* and *aure*), that it enters Mary by the ear (*oreille*), and that Christ is an *aurigena* like Perseus. (Christian authorities had long pictured God's Word as a shower of gold entering the Gospel-writing Saint Matthew's ear and then issuing forth from his pen; see [e.g.,] Ebo Gospel . . .) And it was not difficult for artists to imagine God's golden semen entering the Virgin through the vagina: Titian's *Danae* thus displays a shower of gold streaming from a turbulent aureole toward Danae's lap. And the fifteenth-century Catalan artist Bernardo Martorell's panel *The Annunciation* shows Gabriel announcing the coming of the Lord even as God showers gold from a fertile halo."

46. Warwick William Wroth, *Catalogue of the Imperial Byzantine Coins in the British Museum*, 2 vols. (London: British Museum, 1908). For discussion of the reintroduction of the Christ image on coinage and in art as part of the imperial and ecclesial program, see Hans Belting, *Likeness and Presence: A History of the Image before the Era of Art* (Chicago: University of Chicago Press, 1994), ch. 9.

47. Ladner, "Concept," 32, n. 156.

48. Historical examples could be multiplied. In his *Apology for Christianity* before the caliph, the patriarch Timothy employs discourse of money and precious metals to explain the Trinity: "a piece of three gold denarii is called one and three, one in its gold, that is to say in its nature, and three in its persons, that is to say in the number of denarii. The fact that the above objects are one does not contradict and annul the other fact—that they are also three, and the fact that they are three does not contradict and annul the fact that they are also one. In the very same way the fact that God is one does not annul the other fact that He is in three persons, and the fact that He is in three persons does not annul the other fact that He is one God." Shell, *Art & Money*, 21 also notes that "Peter Abelard, for example, presents a nominalist doctrine of the Trinity through a complex image involving sealing or minting. In associating the Father, Son, and Holy Ghost with one another, Abelard distinguishes among the metal of a seal, the impression on the seal, and its productive use as a seal." On the wider material associations of gold with forms of Christian imagery, see Dominic Janes, *God and Gold in Late Antiquity* (Cambridge: Cambridge University Press, 1998).

49. Following the translation in Joseph T. Lienhard, *Contra Marcellum: Marcellus of Ancyra and Fourth-Century Theology* (Washington, DC: Catholic University of America Press, 1999), 115.

50. Richard Seaford, "Tragic Tyranny," in *Popular Tyrrany: Sovereignty and Its Discontents in Ancient Greece*, ed. Kathryn A Morgan (Austin: University of Texas Press, 2003), 100.

Chapter 5

1. The economy in the ancient and medieval worlds has typically been described as "embedded" and not construed as an isolated object of reflection or inquiry. See, e.g., M. I. Finley, *The Ancient Economy*, rev. ed. (Berkeley: University of California Press, 1999). On its modern "disembedding," see Karl Polanyi, *The Great Transformation* (New York: Rinehart, 1944).

2. On the following points, see Albert Hirschman, *The Passions and the Interests: Political Arguments for Capitalism before Its Triumph* (Princeton, NJ: Princeton University Press, 1977); David Singh Grewal, "The Political Theology of *Laissez-Faire*: From *Philia* to Self-Love in Commercial Society," *Political Theology* 17, no. 5 (2016): 417–33; Devin Singh, "Irrational Exuberance: Hope, Expectation, and Cool Market Logic," *Political Theology* 17, no. 2 (2016): 120–36.

3. Charles-Louis de Montesquieu, *Spirit of the Laws*, bk. 20, cited in Albert Hirschman, "Rival Interpretations of Market Society: Civilizing, Destructive, or Feeble?," *Journal of Economic Literature* 20 (1982): 1464. See also Marcel Hénaff, *The Price of Truth: Gift, Money, and Philosophy*, trans. Jean-Louis Morhange

and Anne-Marie Feenberg-Dibon (Stanford: Stanford University Press, 2010), 358–62.

4. Paul Oslington, ed., *Adam Smith as Theologian* (New York: Routledge, 2011) and Harvey Cox, *The Market as God* (Cambridge, MA: Harvard University Press, 2016), 142–75.

5. See Bill Maurer, "Repressed Futures: Financial Derivatives' Theological Unconscious," *Economy and Society* 31, no. 1 (2002): 15–36.

6. Attention to such themes appears in, e.g., H. E. W. Turner, *The Patristic Doctrine of Redemption: A Study of the Development of Doctrine during the First Five Centuries* (London: A. R. Mowbray, 1952); Hastings Rashdall, *The Idea of Atonement in Christian Theology*, The Bampton Lectures for 1915 (London: Macmillan, 1919); Darby Kathleen Ray, *Deceiving the Devil: Atonement, Abuse, and Ransom* (Cleveland, OH: Pilgrim Press, 1998); Marion Grau, *Of Divine Economy: Refinancing Redemption* (New York: T & T Clark, 2004); Eugene TeSelle, "The Cross as Ransom," *Journal of Early Christian Studies* 4, no. 2 (1996): 147–70.

7. Gary A. Anderson, *Sin: A History* (New Haven, CT: Yale University Press, 2009). Many circumstances in addition to debt peonage could lead to slavery in the ancient world, including capture and conquest in battle. Talk of ransom in Christian contexts need not indicate redemption from *debt* slavery per se.

8. Nathan Eubank, *Wages of Cross-Bearing and Debt of Sin: The Economy of Heaven in Matthew's Gospel* (Berlin: de Gruyter, 2013).

9. Translation here follows the New American Standard Bible for its clearer rendering of debt language.

10. Giorgio Agamben, *The Kingdom and the Glory: For a Theological Genealogy of Economy and Government*, trans. Lorenzo Chiesa and Matteo Mandarini (Stanford: Stanford University Press, 2011), 31.

11. Cited in Agamben, *Kingdom*, 33.

12. Neil Forsyth, *The Old Enemy: Satan and the Combat Myth* (Princeton, NJ: Princeton University Press, 1987).

13. Ibid., 331.

14. Here following the translation in Alexander Roberts, James Donaldson, and A. Cleveland Coxe, eds., *The Apostolic Fathers with Justin Martyr and Irenaeus*, vol. 1, *Ante-Nicene Fathers* (Buffalo, NY: Christian Literature Publishing, 1885).

15. The polemical use of blood to assert Christian ecclesial authority would come to characterize much of the Christian imperial project as it developed in Western thought and society, as recounted in Gil Anidjar, *Blood: A Critique of Christianity* (New York: Columbia University Press, 2014).

16. Forsyth, *Old Enemy*, 336.

17. Ibid., 326.

18. Ibid., 336

19. Ibid.

20. Dotan Leshem, *The Origins of Neoliberalism: Modeling the Economy from Jesus to Foucault* (New York: Columbia University Press, 2016), 136–51.

21. Giorgio Agamben, *Homo Sacer: Sovereign Power and Bare Life*, trans. Daniel Heller-Roazen (Stanford: Stanford University Press, 1998), 104–11. Schmitt, *Political Theology*, 36, we should recall, looked to the miracle as the theological analogue to exception: "The exception in jurisprudence is analogous to the miracle in theology." This reveals his own providential paradigm, since the miracle is the violation of cosmological laws governing nature set into place by God. Miraculous exception is God's decision, as cosmic sovereign and governor, to suspend such laws momentarily. Recentering the soteriological paradigm and importance of ransom provides the reminder that miracles on their own are insignificant. They exist to prove the identity of the Son of Man who came "to give his life as a ransom for many" (Matt 20:28; Mark 10:45). Miracles are subservient to the more primary soteriological economy centered on the redemptive exchange. Schmitt's focus on providence and his animosity toward the economic realm lead him to neglect this fundamental connection.

22. Erik Peterson, "Monotheism as a Political Problem: A Contribution to the History of Political Theology in the Roman Empire," in *Theological Tractates*, trans. and ed. Michael J. Hollerich (Stanford: Stanford University Press, 2011), 71–72.

23. As Grau, *Of Divine Economy*, 153 notes, "[t]he *commercium* [i.e., ransom] is part of Irenaeus's larger rhetorical economy in *Against Heresies*—that of creating a metanarrative of divine *oikonomia* that binds all history into the being of the preexistent Word—and emerges as a smaller *oikonomia* identified with the ransom through the incarnate Word's blood." We should keep in mind that Irenaeus wrote in Greek, although only a Latin translation survives.

24. Ibid., 154.

25. Hollis Phelps, "Overcoming Redemption: Neoliberalism, Atonement, and the Logic of Debt," *Political Theology* 17, no. 3 (2016): 264–82 and Adam Kotsko, *The Prince of this World* (Stanford: Stanford University Press, 2016).

26. Hirschman, *Passions* and Grewal, "Political Theology."

27. Cited in and translated by Rashdall, *Idea*, 259.

28. See, e.g., Gregory of Nazianzus, *Orations* 45.22; John of Damascus, On *the Orthodox Faith* 3.27; and Anselm, *Why God Became Man* 1.3–7. See also the discussion in Forsyth, *Old Enemy*, 337–38.

29. Following Origen, *Homilies on Genesis and Exodus*, trans. Ronald Heine, Fathers of the Church (Washington, DC: Catholic University of America Press, 1982).

30. Ibid.

31. For an exploration of this subsequent interpretive tradition see C. William Marx, *The Devil's Rights and the Redemption in the Literature of Medieval England* (Woodbridge, UK: D. S. Brewer, 1995).

32. Christopher A. Beeley, "Eusebius' *Contra Marcellum*. Anti-Modalist Doctrine and Orthodox Christology," *Zeitschrift für Antikes Christentum* 12 (2008): 433–52; Christopher A. Beeley, *The Unity of Christ: Continuity and Conflict in Patristic Tradition* (New Haven, CT: Yale University Press, 2012); Andrew Carriker, *The Library of Eusebius of Caesarea*, Supplements to Vigiliae Christianae 67 (Leiden: Brill, 2003). The status of Eusebius as standing within the tradition of Origen and the Cappadocians remains contested.

33. See the helpful excursus in Thanos Zartaloudis, *Giorgio Agamben: Power, Law and the Uses of Criticism*, Nomikoi: Critical Legal Thinkers (Abingdon, UK: Routledge, 2010), 64–65.

34. Leshem, *Origins*, 87–96.

35. Steven Runciman, *The Byzantine Theocracy*, The Weil Lectures 1973 (Cambridge: Cambridge University Press, 1977), 30.

36. Peterson, "Monotheism," 226, n. 136.

37. Runciman, *Byzantine Theocracy*, 30 claims that the Cappadocians "opposed the use of physical force in dealing with heretics," here apparently affirming the ideal set forth by Irenaeus. While Constantine, even as portrayed by Eusebius, in no way follows this model of noncoercive interaction with "barbarians," Eusebius's various portrayals of the emperor engaging in generous acts draw on this redemptive theme. This tension in Eusebius may even suggest in nascent form the pattern, so prevalent in developed Christendom, of attending with care to the souls of the vanquished while torturing and obliterating their bodies.

38. For chapters 19–24 of the *Address* I generally follow the translation in Anthony Meredith, *Gregory of Nyssa* (London: Routledge, 1999). Citations from other sections follow the translation in Edward R. Hardy, *Christology of the Later Fathers*, Library of Christian Classics 3 (Philadelphia: Westminster Press, 1954).

39. Meredith, *Gregory*, 152 n. 18 notes "the importance constantly attached by Gregory in all his writings to the idea of logical progression and order, expressed above all as *taxis* and *akolouthia* . . ."

40. See the discussion in Morwenna Ludlow, *Gregory of Nyssa: Ancient and (Post)Modern* (Oxford: Oxford University Press, 2007), 117.

41. See the discussion in Hénaff, *Price*, 27–76.

42. Clearly condemning usury and the state of debt bondage, Gregory, in his *Against Those Who Practice Usury*, proclaims: "Whoever lends money to a destitute person intensifies his misery instead of relieving distress." Translation and page numbers refer to Casimir McCambley, "Against Those Who Practice Usury by Gregory of Nyssa," *Greek Orthodox Theological Review* 36 (1991): 287–302, here at 295.

43. On the coimplication of money, law, and codes of recompense, see Devin Singh, "Speculating the Subject of Money: Georg Simmel on Human Value," *Religions* 7, no. 7 (2016): 1–15; Michael Hudson, "The Archaeology of Money: Debt versus Barter Theories of Money's Origins," in *Credit and State Theories of Money: The Contributions of A. Mitchell Innes*, ed. L. Randall Wray (Cheltenham, UK: Edward Elgar, 2004), 99–127; and David Graeber, *Debt: The First 5,000 Years* (Brooklyn, NY: Melville House, 2010), 73–88, 165–210.

44. "And by so doing he [i.e. God] benefited not only the one who had perished, but also the very one who had brought us to ruin [i.e., Satan]. For when death came into contact with life, darkness with light, corruption with incorruption, the worse of these things disappeared into a state of nonexistence, to the profit of him who was freed from these evils" (Gregory of Nyssa, *Address* 26).

45. Gregory's older brother Basil, reflecting on the term for interest (*tokos*), which could also mean childbirth, writes: "There is interest upon interest, the wicked offspring of wicked parents"; see "Homily Twelve. A Psalm of David Against Usurers (on Psalm 14)" in Basil, *Saint Basil: Exegetic Homilies*, trans. Agnes Way, Fathers of the Church 46 (Washington, DC: Catholic University of America Press, 1963), 187. As McCambley, "Against Those Who Practice," 290 notes, Gregory, in his *Commentary on Ecclesiastes*, also "contrasts the fertility of nature resulting from the union of man and woman in marriage with its opposite, the birth or *tokos* of greed through usury."

46. The trickster gift is explored in Lewis Hyde, *The Gift: Imagination and the Erotic Life of Property* (New York: Random House, 1983). The trickster as a subversive theological motif in ransom is examined in Grau, *Of Divine Economy.*

47. See, e.g., Marcel Mauss, *The Gift: The Form and Reason for Exchange in Archaic Societies*, trans. W. D. Halls (London: Routledge, 1990) and Pierre Bourdieu, *Outline of a Theory of Practice* (Cambridge: Cambridge University Press, 1977).

48. Following McCambley, "Against Those Who Practice," 299.

49. Furthermore, there is proximity between gifts, commodities, and money rather than simple opposition, as is so often construed in secondary literature. See the important intervention by Jonathan Parry, "On the Moral Perils of Exchange," in *Money and the Morality of Exchange*, ed. Jonathan P. Parry and Maurice Bloch (Cambridge: Cambridge University Press, 1989), 64–93. Such proximity can be glimpsed here as both monetary loans and gifts partake of giving, delay, and a return with added value. Gift economies can operate under pernicious constraints like loans, for the receiver may be culturally obligated to return the gift (plus interest) in order to maintain social bonds. Failing to do so can result in exclusion from the community and its exchanges, resulting in death. Remarkably, Gregory of Nyssa is aware of the elision of gift and loan relations. When exhorting the wealthy in his congregation to give alms without

expecting repayment (or, at least, not charging interest), he speaks of a double sense of gift and loan: "For my part, I loudly proclaim acts of charity. I first advocate making loans (in the second place, loaning is a form of giving) without profit through moneylending as the divine word has decreed" (*Against Those Who Practice Usury*, following McCambley, "Against Those Who Practice," 301). Basil, too, proclaims: "Whenever you have the intention of providing for a poor man for the Lord's sake, the same thing is both a gift and a loan, a gift because of the expectation of no repayment, but a loan because of the great gift of the Master who pays in his place" (*Homily 12* in Basil, *Saint Basil: Exegetic Homilies*, 190). This dynamic reemerges in the differences between Protestant and Catholic lending ethics during emergent capitalism. Some Catholic theologians resisted construing lending relations in terms of contract, configuring them instead in gift/countergift language; see Hénaff, *Price*, 282–86.

50. Modern aspersions cast upon Gregory's theory are reviewed in Ludlow, *Gregory*, 109–11.

51. Nicholas P. Constas, "The Last Temptation of Satan: Divine Deception in Greek Patristic Interpretations of the Passion Narrative," *Harvard Theological Review* 97, no. 2 (2004): 146–47.

52. Ibid., 147.

53. Following McCambley, "Against Those Who Practice," 296.

54. On this relationship and the theme of usury in Basil and Gregory, see Brenda Llewellyn Ihssen, "Basil and Gregory's Sermons on Usury: Credit Where Credit Is Due," *Journal of Early Christian Studies* 16, no. 3 (2008): 403–30.

55. Following McCambley, "Against Those Who Practice," 302.

56. Following Philip Schaff, ed., *St. Basil: Letters and Select Works*, vol. 8, *Nicene and Post-Nicene Fathers, Second Series* (Edinburgh: T & T Clark, 1895), 60.

57. Following Basil, *Saint Basil: Exegetic Homilies*, 186.

58. In addition to biblical references that refer to hooking the ancient dragon, one might explore to what extent the imagery used by the prophet Amos also informs the conceptual heritage: "Hear this word, you cows of Bashan who are on Mount Samaria, who oppress the poor, who crush the needy, who say to their husbands, 'Bring something to drink!' The Lord God has sworn by his holiness: The time is surely coming upon you, when they shall take you away with hooks, even the last of you with fishhooks" (Amos 4:1–2). This may provide an interesting contextual nexus of fishhook language with that of economic injustice and the excesses of desire. Gregory cites Amos in his sermon against usury.

59. Following McCambley, "Against Those Who Practice," 295

60. Following Basil, *Saint Basil Exegetic Homilies*, 183.

Chapter 6

1. Of the many possible examples in this vast literature, see, e.g., David Chidester, *Savage Systems: Colonialism and Comparative Religion in Southern Africa* (Charlottesville: University Press of Virginia, 1996); Willie James Jennings, *The Christian Imagination: Theology and the Origins of Race* (New Haven: Yale University Press, 2010); and Marion Grau, *Rethinking Mission in the Postcolony: Salvation, Society, and Subversion* (New York: Continuum, 2011).

2. Following Philip Schaff and Henry Wace, eds., *Select Orations of Saint Gregory Nazianzen*, vol. 8, *Nicene and Post-Nicene Fathers, Second Series* (Buffalo, NY: Christian Literature Publishing, 1894).

3. Cited in and translated by Hastings Rashdall, *The Idea of Atonement in Christian Theology*, The Bampton Lectures for 1915 (London: Macmillan, 1919), 259.

4. See the discussion in, e.g., C. William Marx, *The Devil's Rights and the Redemption in the Literature of Medieval England* (Woodbridge, UK: D. S. Brewer, 1995) and Adam Kotsko, *The Prince of this World* (Stanford: Stanford University Press, 2016). Although outside our present scope, such tensions persist in contemporary theology, which continues to grapple with the claim that God would demand a sacrifice or payment. Many writers find such an image offensive, as well as problematic in its social implications, because it is taken to serve a notion of divine surrogacy in which God requires the suffering of Christ and, by extension, Christ's disciples. A classic challenge in this regard is found in Delores S. Williams, *Sisters in the Wilderness: The Challenge of Womanist God-Talk* (Maryknoll, NY: Orbis Books, 1993), 161–70.

5. Following Schaff and Wace, *Select Orations*.

6. Augustine's reflections on redemption also take up the language of sacrifice, yet without rejecting an idea of payment and ransom to Satan. Rather than Nyssen's fishhook, Augustine speaks of a mousetrap baited with Christ's blood used to lure the devil to his demise (*muscipula diaboli*); see Augustine, *Sermons* 263 and the fascinating discussion of this interpretive tradition in Marx, *Devil's Rights*, 9–12. What we see in Augustine and ensuing tradition is sacrifice, debt, and ransom language combined into a set of interlocking concepts. Sacrifice as expiation and a means of reconciliation works together with repayment and debt cancellation, such that relations with God are restored and moral guilt is erased simultaneously as a sacrifice is made, debts are discharged, and the devil is defeated. Also noteworthy is that the very action that Nazianzen finds offensive—namely, Christ's payment for an *unjust* debt—is viewed by Augustine as an indicator of Christ's abundant grace. Speaking of his mother, he writes that "her debts are cancelled by Christ, who cannot be repaid the price which he paid for us when the debt was not his to pay"; see Augustine, *Confessions* 9.13.36,

cited in Eugene TeSelle, "The Cross as Ransom," *Journal of Early Christian Studies* 4, no. 2 (1996): 157. By entering into this exchange with unjust tyranny, and through the offense of a sacrifice of the righteous and debt-free Christ, God's payment demonstrates gratuity.

7. Cited in TeSelle, "Cross ," 170, n. 5.

8. Gustaf Aulén, *Christus Victor: An Historical Study of the Three Main Types of the Idea of the Atonement* (London: SPCK, 1965). See also Gustaf Aulén, "Chaos and Cosmos: The Drama of Atonement," *Interpretation* 4 (1950): 156–67.

9. Aulén, *Christus Victor*, 54.

10. I have no interest here in following Aulén's polemic of invoking this notion of simple fairness over against so-called Latin accounts of legal justice. Indeed, the later prominence of legal language in soteriology need not indicate any departure from ransom accounts or their monetized imaginary. Law and economy operate together in money, such that developing notions of legal exchange with God can be seen as an outworking of a sense of law already present in early exchange and payment scenarios. Rendering payment to God elides with tax and tribute requirements to uphold divine honor and commands. Payment to redeem a debt and satisfaction to enforce the law need not be mutually exclusive economies. See, e.g., Bernard E. Harcourt, *The Illusion of Free Markets: Punishment and the Myth of Natural Order* (Cambridge: Harvard University Press, 2011); David Graeber, *Debt: The First 5,000 Years* (Brooklyn, NY: Melville House, 2010), 43–88; and Devin Singh, "Speculating the Subject of Money: Georg Simmel on Human Value," *Religions* 7, no. 7 (2016): 1–15.

11. Aulén, *Christus Victor*, 54.

12. Ibid., 53.

13. Following Casimir McCambley, "Against Those Who Practice Usury by Gregory of Nyssa," *Greek Orthodox Theological Review* 36 (1991): 295.

14. Basil cautions the would-be debtor: "Do not endure, like a prey, to be hunted and tracked down" (*Homily* 12, following Basil, *Saint Basil Exegetic Homilies*, 184). While in our passages it is the fish, as prey, that bites the bait, Gregory elsewhere speaks of predatory lending as biting or consuming the poor. Such language draws on Judaic tropes of moneylending as consumption of the needy. As Brenda Llewellyn Ihssen, "Basil and Gregory's Sermons on Usury: Credit Where Credit is Due," *Journal of Early Christian Studies* 16, no. 3 (2008): 417 observes, "Taking a 'bite' out of one's brother is reminiscent of one of the Hebrew words for usury, *nèsèk*, meaning a literal 'bite,' as in the debtor being 'bitten' by the lender," citing Edward Neufeld, "Prohibitions against Loans at Interest in Ancient Hebrew Laws," *Hebrew Union College Annual* 26 (1955): 355.

15. Harvey Cox, *The Market as God* (Cambridge, MA: Harvard University Press, 2016), 69–84.

16. Granted, Jewish biblical teaching on moneylending was nuanced to allow it between Jews and outsiders (Deut 23:20–21). Money was neither to be lent within the community nor used to take advantage of the poor in its midst, whether native or stranger. But lending at interest to non-Jews was permitted, partly as a practical measure to deal with the uncertainty of lending money to those not beholden to Israel's communal standards of reciprocity and justice. Reconciled with broader admonitions against predatory lending, such external moneylending must still follow guidelines of justice and compassion. God might here be posited as simply lending to Satan as an outsider and not necessarily breaking with the ethics revealed in the Torah. This interpretation, however, appears insufficient, for Gregory implies that the lending acts involved in this drama of redemption are, in fact, predatory and aggressive.

17. Kotsko, *Prince*, 81–82.

18. As Roberto Esposito, *Communitas: The Origin and Destiny of Community*, trans. Timothy Campbell (Stanford: Stanford University Press, 2010) suggests, modern social contract theory suppresses the fundamental logic of debt relations that make community possible. They are still operative but erupt in insidious ways in the modern moment.

19. Following Origen, *Homilies on Genesis and Exodus*, trans. Ronald Heine, Fathers of the Church (Washington, DC: Catholic University of America Press, 1982).

20. Following McCambley, "Against Those Who Practice," 296. Note that the term "debtor" in this translation is used for the role that we are accustomed to labeling as "creditor." Recall that Basil also spoke of the "Master who pays in [the poor man's] place, and who, receiving trifling things through a poor man, will give great things in return for them" (*Homily 12*, following Basil, *Saint Basil Exegetic Homilies*, 190).

21. As Marc Shell, *Art & Money* (Chicago: University of Chicago Press, 1995), 49 notes, "the inscription on the cross [i.e., *IHS* or *INRI*] eventually found its way onto the tax coins and coinlike medals of Roman Christendom. It is as if the crucified God who cancels all debts were to become his own redemption money."

22. A. Mitchell Innes, "The Credit Theory of Money," *The Banking Law Journal* (1914): 160–61.

23. Charles Goodhart, "The Two Concepts of Money: Implications for the Analysis of Optimal Currency Areas," *European Journal of Political Economy* 14 (1998): 416–17; C. A. Gregory, "Cowries and Conquest: Towards a Subalternate Quality Theory of Money," *Comparative Studies in Society and History* 38, no. 2 (1996): 195–217; and Matthew Forstater, "Taxation and Primitive Accumulation: The Case of Colonial Africa," *Research in Political Economy* 22 (2005): 51–62.

24. On mimicry in this sense, see Homi Bhabha, "Of Mimicry and Man: The Ambivalence of Colonial Discourse," *October* 28 (1984): 125–33 and Homi K. Bhabha, *The Location of Culture* (London: Routledge, 1994), 90.

25. Marion Grau, *Of Divine Economy: Refinancing Redemption* (New York: T & T Clark, 2004), 159. See also Darby Kathleen Ray, *Deceiving the Devil: Atonement, Abuse, and Ransom* (Cleveland, OH: Pilgrim Press, 1998)

26. Kotsko, *Prince*, 103–5.

27. J. Denny Weaver, *The Nonviolent Atonement*, 2nd ed. (Grand Rapids, MI: Eerdmans, 2011).

28. Harry O. Maier, "Dominion from Sea to Sea: Eusebius of Caesarea, Constantine the Great, and the Exegesis of Empire," in *The Calling of the Nations: Exegesis, Ethnography, and Empire in the Biblical-Historical Present*, ed. Mark Vessey et al. (Toronto: University of Toronto Press, 2011), 149–75.

29. Notably, Gregory of Nyssa had his own run-ins with sovereign power in relation to monetary matters. As Edward R. Hardy, *Christology of the Later Fathers*, The Library of Christian Classics (Philadelphia: Westminster Press, 1954), 237 recounts, Gregory was banished by the emperor Valens under "trumped-up Arian charges about the illegitimacy of his ordination and his misappropriation of Church funds." This most certainly sensitized him to the scope of political power and to the role of money and financial stewardship in the eyes of such authorities. This banishment happened prior to Basil's death, soon after which Gregory delivered his sermon on usury. See Ihssen, "Basil and Gregory's Sermons," 407.

30. Marx, *Devil's Rights*, 26.

31. Candida R. Moss, *The Other Christs: Imitating Jesus in Ancient Christian Ideologies of Martyrdom* (New York: Oxford University Press, 2010).

Conclusion

1. Michel Foucault, *Security, Territory, Population: Lectures at the Collège de France, 1977–1978*, ed. Michael Senellart and Arnold I. Davidson (New York: Palgrave Macmillan, 2007), 95.

2. Ibid., 168.

3. Ibid., 173.

4. Ibid., 183.

5. Michel Foucault, *The Birth of Biopolitics: Lectures at the Collège de France, 1978–79*, ed. Michael Senellart (New York: Palgrave Macmillan, 2008), 277–86.

6. Foucault, *Security, Territory, Population*, 129–30.

7. Ibid., 149–50.

8. Peter Brown, *Poverty and Leadership in the Later Roman Empire*, The Menahem Stern Jerusalem Lectures (Hanover, NH: University Press of New England, 2002), 76.

9. Charles Goodhart, "Two Concepts of Money: Implications for the Analysis of Optimal Currency Areas," *European Journal of Political Economy* 14 (1998): 415 and Geoffrey K. Ingham, *The Nature of Money* (Cambridge, UK: Polity, 2004), 110.

10. Ingham, *Nature*, 113–14, emphasis added.

11. L. Randall Wray, "Conclusion: The Credit Money and State Money Approaches," in *Credit and State Theories of Money : The Contributions of A. Mitchell Innes*, ed. L. Randall Wray (Cheltenham, UK: Edward Elgar, 2004), 223–62.

12. Ingham, *Nature*, 97, emphasis added. Ingham also claims that "Roman social structure was inimical to such development" (104). Here he draws on the claims of Max Weber, *Economy and Society: An Outline of Interpretive Sociology*, ed. Guenther Roth and Claus Wittich, 2 vols. (Berkeley: University of California Press, 1978), 2:682, who notes that as "a result of the highly personalized character of the debt relationship, instruments payable to the order of the payee or to the bearer, which served for the transfer of claims, especially monetary claims, and of powers of disposition over commercial goods and membership rights in commercial enterprises . . . had been utterly unknown in Roman law."

13. Foucault, *Security, Territory, Population*, 215.

14. Ibid., 209–11. One exploration of eucharistic power in relation to the money economy is found in Gil Anidjar, "Christians and Money (The Economic Enemy)," *Ethical Perspectives: Journal of the European Ethics Network* 12, no. 4 (2005): 497–519; see also Gil Anidjar, *Blood: A Critique of Christianity* (New York: Columbia University Press, 2014), 136–54.

15. Jacques Le Goff, *Your Money or Your Life: Economy and Religion in the Middle Ages*, trans. Patricia Ranum (New York: Zone Books, 1998), 22. Shakespeare's *The Merchant of Venice* reflects this medieval view as commonsensical. Antonio, defending his antisemitism while nevertheless entreating Shylock to lend him money, declares: "If thou wilt lend this money, lend it not as to thy friends, for when did friendship take a breed for barren metal of his friend? But lend it, rather, to thine enemy, who, if he break, thou mayst with better face exact the penalty" (1.3.142–47). Antonio acknowledges that charging interest is antagonistic and that to lend at interest is to declare or reaffirm enmity.

16. The discourse on the devil and economic indebtedness gets taken up explicitly in colonial context to capture the structural and cultural violence in the colonial extraction of resources and subjugation of indigenous labor. See the classic Michael T. Taussig, *The Devil and Commodity Fetishism in South America*, 2nd ed. (Chapel Hill: University of North Carolina Press, 2010). For an exploration of

late medieval primitive accumulation in terms of gender and the use of demonic discourse to police women's bodies and labor, see Silvia Federici, *Caliban and The Witch: Women, the Body and Primitive Accumulation* (New York: Autonomedia, 2003). On early modern primitive accumulation as occluded by religious tropes of liberation from the "Egyptian bondage" and "demonic" oppression of earlier modes of production, see Jordana Rosenberg, *Critical Enthusiasm: Capital Accumulation and the Transformation of Religious Passion* (New York: Oxford University Press, 2011).

17. Paul Gilroy, *The Black Atlantic: Modernity and Double Consciousness* (Cambridge, MA: Harvard University Press, 1993); J. Kameron Carter, *Race: A Theological Account* (New York: Oxford University Press, 2008); Jennings, *Christian Imagination*. Our exploration of the debt logic in Gregory of Nyssa's account needs to be squared with Carter's depiction of Nyssen as an "abolitionist intellectual" (Carter, *Race*, 229–51). These need not be irreconcilable, and part of the paradoxical legacy of such thought may stem from Gregory's capacity to condemn usury, predatory lending, and related forms of slavery while using the logic of debt domination to vindicate God's toppling and subjugation of Satan.

18. See, e.g., Kate Bowler, *Blessed: A History of the American Prosperity Gospel* (New York: Oxford University Press, 2013). Prosperity theology may also be radicalizing the Calvinist impulse described by Weber of striving for economic success as a sign of election; see Max Weber, *The Protestant Ethic and the Spirit of Capitalism*, trans. Stephen Kalberg, rev. ed. (New York: Oxford University Press, 2011). Of course, Weber's Calvinists need to be revisited for the ways they, too, may be taking up this patristic trope of cosmic economic victory, putting to use newly rekindled language of God as divine creditor in their theological formulations, and attempting to discern the outworking of God's coin in their own entrepreneurial endeavors.

19. E.g., Craig L. Blomberg, *Neither Poverty nor Riches: A Biblical Theology of Material Possessions* (Grand Rapids, MI: Eerdmans, 1999).

20. See William E. Connolly, *Capitalism and Christianity, American Style* (Durham, NC: Duke University Press, 2008) and Harvey Cox, *The Market as God* (Cambridge, MA: Harvard University Press, 2016).

21. Concrete historical studies that explore the merger of American Christianity and the corporate business model include Bethany Moreton, *To Serve God and Wal-Mart: The Making of Christian Free Enterprise* (Cambridge, MA: Harvard University Press, 2009); George J. González, *Shape-Shifting Capital: Spiritual Management, Critical Theory, and the Ethnographic Project* (Lanham, MD: Lexington Books, 2015); and Kevin Kruse, *One Nation Under God: How Corporate America Invented Christian America* (New York: Basic Books, 2015).

Bibliography

Adorno, Theodor W. *Prisms.* Translated by Samuel Weber and Shierry Weber. Studies in Contemporary German Social Thought. Cambridge, MA: MIT Press, 1981.

Agamben, Giorgio. *Die Beamten des Himmels: Über Engel.* Translated by Andreas Hiepko. Berlin: Verlag der Weltreligionen im Insel Verlag, 2007.

———. *Homo Sacer: Sovereign Power and Bare Life.* Translated by Daniel Heller-Roazen. Stanford: Stanford University Press, 1998.

———. *The Kingdom and the Glory: For a Theological Genealogy of Economy and Government.* Translated by Lorenzo Chiesa and Matteo Mandarini. Stanford: Stanford University Press, 2011.

———. *The Signature of All Things: On Method.* Translated by Luca D'Isanto and Kevin Attell. Cambridge, MA: Zone Books, 2009. Distributed by MIT Press.

———. *State of Exception.* Translated by Kevin Attell. Chicago: University of Chicago Press, 2005.

———. *"What is an Apparatus?" and Other Essays.* Translated by David Kishik and Stefan Pedatella. Stanford: Stanford University Press, 2009.

Anderson, Gary A. *Charity: The Place of the Poor in the Biblical Tradition.* New Haven, CT: Yale University Press, 2013.

———. *Sin: A History.* New Haven, CT: Yale University Press, 2009.

Ando, Clifford. *Imperial Ideology and Provincial Loyalty in the Roman Empire.* Berkeley: University of California Press, 2000.

Anidjar, Gil. *Blood: A Critique of Christianity.* New York: Columbia University Press, 2014.

———. *"Christians and Money (The Economic Enemy)." Ethical Perspectives: Journal of the European Ethics Network* 12, no. 4 (2005): 497–519.

Appadurai, Arjun. *Modernity At Large: Cultural Dimensions of Globalization.* Minneapolis: University of Minnesota Press, 1996.

Asad, Talal. *Formations of the Secular: Christianity, Islam, Modernity.* Stanford: Stanford University Press, 2003.

———. *Genealogies of Religion: Discipline and Reasons of Power in Christianity and Islam.* Baltimore: Johns Hopkins University Press, 1993.

Aulén, Gustaf. "Chaos and Cosmos: The Drama of Atonement." *Interpretation* 4 (1950): 156–67.

———. *Christus Victor: An Historical Study of the Three Main Types of the Idea of the Atonement.* London: SPCK, 1965.

Auvinen, Tero. "At the Intersection of Sovereignty and Biopolitics: The Di-Polaric Spatializations of Money." *Foucault Studies* 9 (2010): 5–34.

Ayres, Lewis. *Nicaea and its Legacy: An Approach to Fourth-Century Trinitarian Theology.* Oxford: Oxford University Press, 2004.

Balke, Friedrich. "Derrida and Foucault on Sovereignty." *German Law Journal* 6, no. 1 (2005): 71–85.

Banaji, Jairus. *Agrarian Change in Late Antiquity: Gold, Labour, and Aristocratic Dominance.* Oxford: Oxford University Press, 2001.

———. "Economic Trajectories." In *The Oxford Handbook of Late Antiquity,* edited by Scott Fitzgerald Johnson, 597–624. Oxford: Oxford University Press, 2012.

Barnes, Timothy D. *Constantine and Eusebius.* Cambridge, MA: Harvard University Press, 1981.

———. "Oppressor, Persecutor, Usurper: The Meaning of 'Tyrannus' in the Fourth Century." In *Historiae Augustae Colloquium Barcinonense,* edited by G. Bonamente and M. Mayer, 55–65. Bari: Edipuglia, 1996.

Basil. *Saint Basil Exegetic Homilies.* Translated by Agnes Way. Fathers of the Church 46 Washington, DC: Catholic University of America Press, 1963.

Beeley, Christopher A. "Eusebius' *Contra Marcellum.* Anti-Modalist Doctrine and Orthodox Christology." *Zeitschrift für Antikes Christentum* 12 (2008): 433–52.

———. *The Unity of Christ: Continuity and Conflict in Patristic Tradition.* New Haven, CT: Yale University Press, 2012.

Behr, John. *The Nicene Faith.* 2 vols. Crestwood, NY: St. Vladimir's Seminary Press, 2004.

Bell, Daniel M. *The Economy of Desire: Christianity and Capitalism in a Postmodern World.* Grand Rapids, MI: Baker Academic, 2012.

Bellah, Robert N. *Religion in Human Evolution: From the Paleolithic to the Axial Age.* Cambridge, MA: Belknap Press of Harvard University Press, 2011.

Belting, Hans. *Likeness and Presence: A History of the Image before the Era of Art.* Chicago: University of Chicago Press, 1994.

Benjamin, Walter. "Fragment 74: Capitalism as Religion." In *Religion as Critique: The Frankfurt School's Critique of Religion,* edited by Eduardo Mendieta, translated by Chad Kautzer, 259–62. New York: Routledge, 2005.

Bernal, Martin. *Black Athena: The Afroasiatic Roots of Classical Civilization.* 3 vols. New Brunswick, NJ: Rutgers University Press, 1987.

Bernasconi, Robert. "African Philosophy's Challenge to Continental Philosophy." In *Postcolonial African Philosophy: A Critical Reader*, edited by Emmanuel Chukwudi Eze, 183–196. London: Blackwell, 1997.

Bhabha, Homi K. "Of Mimicry and Man: The Ambivalence of Colonial Discourse." *October* 28 (1984): 125–33.

———. *The Location of Culture.* London: Routledge, 1994.

Blomberg, Craig L. *Neither Poverty Nor Riches: A Biblical Theology of Material Possessions.* Grand Rapids, MI: Eerdmans, 1999.

Blumenberg, Hans. *The Legitimacy of the Modern Age.* Translated by Robert M. Wallace. Cambridge, MA: MIT Press, 1983.

Bond, Sarah. "Currency and Control: Mint Workers in the Later Roman Empire." In *Work, Labour, and Professions in the Roman World*, edited by Koenraad Verboven and Christian Laes, 227–45. Leiden: Brill, 2017.

Bourdieu, Pierre. *Outline of a Theory of Practice.* Cambridge: Cambridge University Press, 1977.

Bowler, Kate. *Blessed: A History of the American Prosperity Gospel.* New York: Oxford University Press, 2013.

Bratich, Jack Z., Jeremy Packer, and Cameron McCarthy. *Foucault, Cultural Studies, and Governmentality.* Albany: State University of New York Press, 2003.

Brown, Peter. *Poverty and Leadership in the Later Roman Empire.* The Menahem Stern Jerusalem Lectures. Hanover, NH: University Press of New England, 2002.

———. *The Ransom of the Soul: Afterlife and Wealth in Early Eastern Christianity.* Cambridge, MA: Harvard University Press, 2015.

———. *Through the Eye of a Needle: Wealth, the Fall of Rome, and the Making of Christianity in the West, 350–550 AD.* Princeton, NJ: Princeton University Press, 2012.

Buck-Morss, Susan. "Visual Empire." *Diacritics* 32, nos. 2–3 (2007): 171–98.

Burchell, Graham, Colin Gordon, and Peter Miller, eds. *The Foucault Effect: Studies in Governmentality.* Chicago: University of Chicago Press, 1991.

Bussolini, Jeffrey. "What is a Dispositive?" *Foucault Studies* 10 (November 2010): 85–107.

Capener, Sean. "Being and Acting: Agamben, Athanasius, and the Trinitarian Economy." *Heythrop Journal* 57 (2016): 950–63.

Carriker, Andrew. *The Library of Eusebius of Caesarea.* Supplements to Vigiliae Christianae. Leiden: Brill, 2003.

Carter, J. Kameron. *Race: A Theological Account.* New York: Oxford University Press, 2008.

Casanova, José. *Public Religions in the Modern World*. Chicago: University of Chicago Press, 1994.

Chakrabarty, Dipesh. *Provincializing Europe: Postcolonial Thought and Historical Difference*. Princeton, NJ: Princeton University Press, 2000.

Cheng, William. *Just Vibrations: The Purpose of Sounding Good*. Ann Arbor: University of Michigan Press, 2016.

Chidester, David. *Savage Systems: Colonialism and Comparative Religion in Southern Africa*. Charlottesville: University Press of Virginia, 1996.

Coffee, Neil. *Gift and Gain: How Money Transformed Ancient Rome*. New York: Oxford University Press, 2016.

Comaroff, Jean, and John Comaroff. "Millennial Capitalism: First Thoughts on a Second Coming." *Public Culture* 12, no. 2 (2000): 291–343.

Connolly, William E. *Capitalism and Christianity, American Style*. Durham, NC: Duke University Press, 2008.

Constas, Nicholas P. "The Last Temptation of Satan: Divine Deception in Greek Patristic Interpretations of the Passion Narrative." *Harvard Theological Review* 97, no. 2 (2004): 139–63.

Countryman, L. Wm. *The Rich Christian in the Church of the Early Empire: Contradictions and Accommodations*. New York: Edwin Mellen Press, 1980.

Cox, Harvey. *The Market as God*. Cambridge, MA: Harvard University Press, 2016.

Crawford, M. H. "Roman Imperial Coin Types and the Formation of Public Opinion." In *Studies in Numismatic Method Presented to Philip Grierson*, edited by C. N. L. Brooke, B. H. Stewart, J. G. Pollard, and T. R. Volk, 47–64. Cambridge: Cambridge University Press, 1983.

Crockett, Clayton. *Radical Political Theology: Religion and Politics after Liberalism*. Insurrections: Critical Studies in Religion, Politics, and Culture. New York: Columbia University Press, 2011.

Davis, Creston, John Milbank, and Slavoj Žižek, eds. *Theology and the Political: The New Debate*. Durham, NC: Duke University Press, 2005.

Dean, Mitchell. *Governmentality: Power and Rule in Modern Society*. 2nd ed. London: SAGE, 2010.

Dodd, Nigel. *The Social Life of Money*. Princeton, NJ: Princeton University Press, 2014.

Drake, H. A. *In Praise of Constantine: A Historical Study and New Translation of Eusebius' Tricennial Orations*. University of California Publications in Classical Studies 15. Berkeley: University of California Press, 1976.

Duncan-Jones, Richard. *Money and Government in the Roman Empire*. Cambridge: Cambridge University Press, 1994.

———. *Structure and Scale in the Roman Economy*. Cambridge: Cambridge University Press, 1990.

Dupont, Florence. "The Emperor-God's Other Body." In *Fragments for a History of the Human Body, Part 3*, edited by Michael Feher, Ramona Nadoff, and Nadia Tazis 396–419. New York: Zone Books, 1989.

Durantaye, Leland de la. *Giorgio Agamben: A Critical Introduction*. Stanford: Stanford University Press, 2009.

Dussel, Enrique. *The Invention of the Americas: Eclipse of "The Other" and the Myth of Modernity*. Translated by Michael Barber. New York: Continuum, 1995.

———. *Las metáforas teológicas de Marx*. Estella: Editorial Verbo Divino, 1993.

———. *Postmodernidad y transmodernidad: Diálogos con la filosofía de Gianni Vattimo*. Mexico City: Universidad Iberamericana Plantel Golfo Centro, 1999.

Elm, Susanna. "Inscriptions and Conversions: Gregory of Nazianzus on Baptism (*Or.* 38–40)." In *Conversion in Late Antiquity and the Early Middle Ages: Seeing and Believing*, edited by Kenneth Mills and Anthony Grafton, 1–35. Rochester, NY: University of Rochester Press, 2003.

Erskine, Andrew. *Roman Imperialism*. Edinburgh: Edinburgh University Press, 2010.

Esposito, Roberto. *Communitas: The Origin and Destiny of Community*. Translated by Timothy Campbell. Stanford: Stanford University Press, 2010.

Eubank, Nathan. *Wages of Cross-Bearing and Debt of Sin: The Economy of Heaven in Matthew's Gospel*. Berlin: de Gruyter, 2013.

Eusebius of Caesarea. "Against Hierocles." In *The Life of Apollonius of Tyana, the Epistles of Apollonius and the Treatise of Eusebius*, translated by F. C. Conybeare, 404–605. Loeb Classical Library. New York: Macmillan, 1912.

———. *Demonstratio Evangelica*. Translated by W. J. Ferrar. London: SPCK, 1920.

———. *Life of Constantine*. Edited and translated by Averil Cameron and Stuart George Hall. Oxford: Oxford University Press, 1999.

———. *On Ecclesiastical Theology*. Translated by Markus Vinzent and Kelley Spoerl. Fathers of the Church. Washington, DC: Catholic University Press of America, forthcoming.

Federici, Silvia. *Caliban and The Witch: Women, the Body and Primitive Accumulation*. New York: Autonomedia, 2003.

Finley, M. I. *The Ancient Economy*. Rev. ed. Berkeley: University of California Press, 1999.

Fletcher, Paul. *Disciplining the Divine: Toward an (Im)political Theology*. Farnham, UK: Ashgate, 2009.

Forstater, Matthew. "Taxation and Primitive Accumulation: The Case of Colonial Africa." *Research in Political Economy* 22 (2005): 51–62.

Forsyth, Neil. *The Old Enemy: Satan and the Combat Myth*. Princeton, NJ: Princeton University Press, 1987.

Foucault, Michel. *Archaeology of Knowledge.* London: Routledge, 2002.

———. *The Birth of Biopolitics: Lectures at the Collège de France, 1978–79.* Edited by Michael Senellart. New York: Palgrave Macmillan, 2008.

———. "Nietzsche, Genealogy, History." In *The Foucault Reader,* edited by Paul Rabinow, 76–100. New York: Pantheon, 1984.

———. *Politics, Philosophy, Culture: Interviews and Other Writings, 1977–1984.* Edited by Lawrence D. Kritzman. Translated by Alan Sheridan et al. New York: Routledge, 1988.

———. *Security, Territory, Population: Lectures at the Collège de France, 1977–1978.* Edited by Michel Senellart and Arnold I. Davidson. New York: Palgrave Macmillan, 2007.

Fradinger, Moira. *Binding Violence: Literary Visions of Political Origins.* Stanford: Stanford University Press, 2010.

Friedman, Thomas. *The Lexus and the Olive Tree.* New York: Anchor Books, 2000.

Geréby, György. "Political Theology versus Theological Politics: Erik Peterson and Carl Schmitt." *New German Critique* 105, no. 3 (2008): 7–33.

Giardina, Andrea. "The Transition to Late Antiquity." In *The Cambridge Economic History of the Greco-Roman World,* edited by Walter Scheidel, Ian Morris, and Richard Saller, 743–68. New York: Cambridge University Press, 2007.

Gifford, E. H. *Eusebii Pamphili Evangelicae Praeparationis libri xv.* Oxford, 1903.

Gillespie, Michael. *The Theological Origins of Modernity.* Chicago: University of Chicago Press, 2008.

Gilroy, Paul. *The Black Atlantic: Modernity and Double Consciousness.* Cambridge, MA: Harvard University Press, 1993.

González, George J. *Shape-Shifting Capital: Spiritual Management, Critical Theory, and the Ethnographic Project.* Lanham, MD: Lexington Books, 2015.

Goodchild, Philip. *Capitalism and Religion: The Price of Piety.* London: Routledge, 2002.

———. *Theology of Money.* Durham, NC: Duke University Press, 2009.

Goodhart, Charles. "The Two Concepts of Money: Implications for the Analysis of Optimal Currency Areas." *European Journal of Political Economy* 14 (1998): 407–32.

Goodman, Martin. *The Roman World: 44 BC–AD 180.* London: Routledge, 1997.

Gorski, Philip S. *The Protestant Ethic Revisited.* Philadelphia: Temple University Press, 2011.

Goux, Jean-Joseph. *Symbolic Economies: After Marx and Freud.* Translated by Jennifer Curtiss Gage. Ithaca, NY: Cornell University Press, 1990.

Graeber, David. *Debt: The First 5,000 Years.* Brooklyn, NY: Melville House, 2010.

Grau, Marion. *Of Divine Economy: Refinancing Redemption.* New York: T & T Clark, 2004.

————. *Rethinking Mission in the Postcolony: Salvation, Society, and Subversion*. New York: Continuum, 2011.

Gregory, Brad S. *The Unintended Reformation: How a Religious Revolution Secularized Society*. Cambridge, MA: Belknap Press of Harvard University Press, 2012.

Gregory, C. A. "Cowries and Conquest: Towards a Subalternate Quality Theory of Money." *Comparative Studies in Society and History* 38, no. 2 (1996): 195–217.

Grewal, David Singh. "The Political Theology of *Laissez-Faire*: From *Philia* to Self-Love in Commercial Society." *Political Theology* 17, no. 5 (2016): 417–33.

Grillmeier, Alois. *From the Apostolic Age to Chalcedon*. Vol. 1, *Christ in Christian Tradition*. Translated by John Bowden. 2nd rev. ed. Atlanta: John Knox Press, 1975.

Gusmani, Roberto. *Lydisches Wörterbuch*. Heidelberg: Carl Winter Universitätsverlag, 1964.

Hanson, R. P. C. *The Search for the Christian Doctrine of God: The Arian Controversy 318–381*. Edinburgh: T & T Clark, 1988.

Harcourt, Bernard E. *The Illusion of Free Markets: Punishment and the Myth of Natural Order*. Cambridge, MA: Harvard University Press, 2011.

Hardy, Edward R. *Christology of the Later Fathers*. Library of Christian Classics 3. Philadelphia: Westminster Press, 1954.

Harl, Kenneth W. *Civic Coins and Civic Politics in the Roman East, A.D. 180–275*. The Transformation of the Classical Heritage 12. Berkeley: University of California Press, 1987.

————. *Coinage in the Roman Economy, 300 B.C. to A.D. 700*. Baltimore: Johns Hopkins University Press, 1996.

Harries, Jill. *Law and Empire in Late Antiquity*. Cambridge: Cambridge University Press, 1999.

Harrison, Evelyn B. "The Constantinian Portrait." *Dumbarton Oaks Papers* 21 (1967): 81–96.

Hart, Keith. *Money in an Unequal World: Keith Hart and His Memory Bank*. New York: Texere, 2000.

Hekster, Olivier. "Coins and Messages: Audience Targeting on Coins of Different Denominations?" In *The Representation and Perception of Roman Imperial Power: Proceedings of the Third Workshop of the International Network Impact of Empire (Roman Empire, c. 200 B.C.–A.D. 476), Rome, March 20–23, 2002*, edited by Lukas de Blois, Paul Erdkamp, Olivier Hekster, Gerda de Kleijn and Stephan Mols. Leiden: Brill, 2003.

Hénaff, Marcel. *The Price of Truth: Gift, Money, and Philosophy*. Translated by Jean-Louis Morhange and Anne-Marie Feenberg-Dibon. Stanford: Stanford University Press, 2010.

Hinsley, F. H. *Sovereignty.* 2nd ed. Cambridge: Cambridge University Press, 1982.

Hirschman, Albert. *The Passions and the Interests: Political Arguments for Capitalism before Its Triumph.* Princeton, NJ: Princeton University Press, 1977.

———. "Rival Interpretations of Market Society: Civilizing, Destructive, or Feeble?" *Journal of Economic Literature* 20 (1982): 1463–84.

Hollander, David B. *Money in the Late Roman Republic.* Leiden: Brill, 2007.

Hollerich, Michael J. "Myth and History in Eusebius's 'De vita Constantini': 'Vit. Const. 1.12' in Its Contemporary Setting." *Harvard Theological Review* 82, no. 4 (October 1989): 421–45.

———. "Religion and Politics in the Writings of Eusebius: Reassessing the First 'Court Theologian'." *Church History* 59, no. 3 (1990): 309–25.

Hopkins, Dwight N. "The Religion of Globalization." In *Religions/Globalizations: Theories and Cases,* edited by Dwight N. Hopkins, Lois Ann Lorentzen, Eduardo Mendieta, and David Batstone, 7–32. Durham, NC: Duke University Press, 2001.

Hopkins, Keith. "Taxes and Trade in the Roman Empire (200 B.C.–A.D. 400)." *Journal of Roman Studies* 70 (1980): 101–25.

Howgego, Christopher. *Ancient History from Coins.* London: Routledge, 1995.

———. "Coin, Circulation and the Integration of the Roman Economy." *Journal of Roman Archaeology* 7 (1994): 5–21

Hudson, Michael. "The Archaeology of Money: Debt versus Barter Theories of Money's Origins." In *Credit and State Theories of Money: The Contributions of A. Mitchell Innes,* edited by L. Randall Wray, 99–127. Cheltenham, UK: Edward Elgar, 2004.

Hyde, Lewis. *The Gift: Imagination and the Erotic Life of Property.* New York: Random House, 1983.

Ihssen, Brenda Llewellyn. "Basil and Gregory's Sermons on Usury: Credit Where Credit Is Due." *Journal of Early Christian Studies* 16, no. 3 (2008): 403–30.

Ingham, Geoffrey K. *The Nature of Money.* Cambridge, UK: Polity, 2004.

Innes, A. Mitchell. "The Credit Theory of Money." *The Banking Law Journal* (1914): 151–68.

Jameson, Fredric. *The Political Unconscious: Narrative as a Socially Symbolic Act.* Ithaca, NY: Cornell University Press, 1981.

Janes, Dominic. *God and Gold in Late Antiquity.* Cambridge: Cambridge University Press, 1998.

Jennings, Willie James. *The Christian Imagination: Theology and the Origins of Race.* New Haven, CT: Yale University Press, 2010.

Johnson, Aaron P. *Ethnicity and Argument in Eusebius' "Praeparatio Evangelica".* Oxford: Oxford University Press, 2006.

Jones, A. H. M. *The Roman Economy: Studies in Ancient Economic and Administrative History.* Edited by P. A. Brunt. Oxford: Blackwell, 1974.

Kallet, Lisa. "Demos Tyrranos: Wealth, Power, and Economic Patronage." In *Popular Tyranny: Sovereignty and its Discontents in Ancient Greece,* edited by Kathryn A. Morgan, 117–54. Austin: University of Texas Press, 2003.

Kantorowicz, Ernst. *The King's Two Bodies: A Study in Medieval Political Theology.* Princeton, NJ: Princeton University Press, 1957.

Keane, Webb. *Christian Moderns: Freedom and Fetish in the Mission Encounter.* Berkeley: Unversity of California Press, 2007.

Kelly, Christopher. *Ruling the Later Roman Empire.* Cambridge, MA: Belknap Press of Harvard University Press, 2004.

Keynes, John Maynard. *The General Theory of Employment, Interest, and Money.* New York: Harcourt Brace, 1936.

Knapp, Georg Friedrich. *The State Theory of Money.* Edited by H. M. Lucas and James Bonar. Abr. ed. London: Macmillan, 1924.

Konings, Martijn. *The Emotional Logic of Capitalism: What Progressives Have Missed.* Stanford: Stanford University Press, 2015.

Kotsko, Adam. *The Prince of this World.* Stanford: Stanford University Press, 2016.

Kraay, Colin M. "Hoards, Small Change and the Origin of Coinage." *Journal of Hellenic Studies* 84 (1964): 76–91.

Kruse, Kevin. *One Nation Under God: How Corporate America Invented Christian America.* New York: Basic Books, 2015.

Kurke, Leslie. *Coins, Bodies, Games, and Gold: The Politics of Meaning in Archaic Greece.* Princeton, NJ: Princeton University Press, 1999.

Ladner, Gerhart B. "The Concept of the Image in the Greek Fathers and the Byzantine Iconoclastic Controversy." *Dumbarton Oaks Papers* 7 (1958): 1–34.

Lakoff, George, and Mark Johnson. *Metaphors We Live By.* Chicago: University of Chicago Press, 2003.

Laqueur, Thomas. *Making Sex: Body and Gender from the Greeks to Freud.* Cambridge, MA: Harvard University Press, 1990.

Le Goff, Jacques. *Your Money or Your Life: Economy and Religion in the Middle Ages.* Translated by Patricia Ranum. New York: Zone Books, 1998.

Lee, Samuel. *Eusebius Bishop of Caesarea, On the Theophaneia or Divine Manifestation of Our Lord and Saviour Jesus Christ.* Cambridge: Cambridge University Press, 1843.

Lenski, Noel. *Constantine and the Cities: Imperial Authority and Civic Politics.* Philadelphia: University of Pennsylvania Press, 2016.

Leshem, Dotan. "Oikonomia in the Age of Empires." *History of the Human Sciences* 26, no. 1 (2013): 29–51.

———. "Oikonomia Redefined." *Journal of the History of Economic Thought* 35, no. 1 (2013): 43–61.

———. *The Origins of Neoliberalism: Modeling the Economy from Jesus to Foucault.* New York: Columbia University Press, 2016.

Levick, Barbara. "Propaganda and the Imperial Coinage." *Antichthon* 16 (1982): 104–16.

Lienhard, Joseph T. *Contra Marcellum: Marcellus of Ancyra and Fourth-Century Theology.* Washington, DC: Catholic University of America Press, 1999.

Lin, Yii-Jan. *The Erotic Life of Manuscripts: New Testament Textual Criticism and the Biological Sciences.* New York: Oxford University Press, 2016.

Lloyd, Vincent W. *The Problem with Grace: Reconfiguring Political Theology.* Stanford: Stanford University Press, 2011.

Lo Cascio, Elio. "The Early Roman Empire: The State and the Economy." In *The Cambridge Economic History of the Greco-Roman World*, edited by Walter Scheidel, Ian Morris and Richard Saller, 619–47. New York: Cambridge University Press, 2007.

Long, D. Stephen. *Divine Economy: Theology and the Market.* London: Routledge, 2000.

Long, D. Stephen, and Nancy Ruth Fox. *Calculated Futures: Theology, Ethics, and Economics.* Waco, TX: Baylor University Press, 2007.

Löwith, Karl. *Meaning in History.* Chicago: University of Chicago Press, 1957.

Ludlow, Morwenna. *Gregory of Nyssa: Ancient and (Post)Modern.* Oxford: Oxford University Press, 2007.

Maier, Harry O. "Dominion from Sea to Sea: Eusebius of Caesarea, Constantine the Great, and the Exegesis of Empire." In *The Calling of the Nations: Exegesis, Ethnography, and Empire in the Biblical-Historical Present*, edited by Mark Vessey, Sharon V. Betcher, Robert A. Daum, and Harry O. Maier, 149–75. Toronto: University of Toronto Press, 2011.

Maraval, Pierre. *Eusèbe de Césarée. La théologie politique de l'empire chrétien: louanges de Constantin (Triakontaétérikos).* Sagesses chrétiennes. Paris: Les Éditions du Cerf, 2001.

Martin, Dale B. *Inventing Superstition: From the Hippocratics to the Christians.* Cambridge, MA: Harvard University Press, 2004.

———. *Slavery as Salvation: The Metaphor of Slavery in Pauline Christianity.* New Haven, CT: Yale University Press, 1990.

Martin, Edward James. *A History of the Iconoclastic Controversy.* London: SPCK, 1930.

Marx, C. William. *The Devil's Rights and the Redemption in the Literature of Medieval England.* Woodbridge, UK: D. S. Brewer, 1995.

Marx, Karl. *Selected Writings.* Edited by Lawrence Hugh Simon. Indianapolis, IN: Hackett, 1994.

Mason, A. J., ed. *Fifty Spiritual Homilies of St. Macarius the Egyptian.* New York: Macmillan, 1921.

Masuzawa, Tomoko. *In Search of Dreamtime: The Quest for the Origin of Religion.* Chicago: University of Chicago Press, 1993.

———. *The Invention of World Religions, or, How European Universalism was Preserved in the Language of Pluralism.* Chicago: University of Chicago Press, 2005.

Maurer, Bill. "Repressed Futures: Financial Derivatives' Theological Unconscious." *Economy and Society* 31, no. 1 (2002): 15–36.

Mauss, Marcel. *The Gift: The Form and Reason for Exchange in Archaic Societies.* Translated by W. D. Halls. London: Routledge, 1990.

McCambley, Casimir. "Against Those Who Practice Usury by Gregory of Nyssa." *Greek Orthodox Theological Review* 36 (1991): 287–302.

McFague, Sallie. *Metaphorical Theology: Models of God in Religious Language.* Philadelphia: Fortress Press, 1982.

Meeks, M. Douglas. *God the Economist: The Doctrine of God and Political Economy.* Minneapolis, MN: Fortress Press, 1989.

Meredith, Anthony. *Gregory of Nyssa.* London: Routledge, 1999.

Mignolo, Walter. *The Darker Side of the Renaissance: Literacy, Territoriality, and Colonization.* Ann Arbor: University of Michigan Press, 1995.

———. *The Darker Side of Western Modernity: Global Futures, Decolonial Options.* Durham, NC: Duke University Press, 2011.

———. "Delinking." *Cultural Studies* 21, no. 2 (2007): 449–514.

———. "The Geopolitics of Knowledge and the Colonial Difference." *South Atlantic Quarterly* 101, no. 1 (2002): 56–97.

Milbank, John. *Theology and Social Theory: Beyond Secular Reason.* 2nd ed. Oxford: Blackwell, 2006.

Millar, Fergus. *The Emperor in the Roman World (31 BC–AD 337).* Ithaca, NY: Cornell University Press, 1977.

Momigliano, Arnaldo. "The Disadvantages of Monotheism for a Universal State." *Classical Philology* 81, no. 4 (1986): 285–97.

Mondzain, Marie-José. *Image, Icon, Economy: The Byzantine Origins of the Contemporary Imaginary.* Translated by Rico Franses. Stanford: Stanford University Press, 2005.

Moreton, Bethany. *To Serve God and Wal-Mart: The Making of Christian Free Enterprise.* Cambridge, MA: Harvard University Press, 2009.

Morgan, Kathryn A., ed. *Popular Tyranny: Sovereignty and Its Discontents in Ancient Greece.* Austin: University of Texas Press, 2003.

Moss, Candida R. *The Other Christs: Imitating Jesus in Ancient Christian Ideologies of Martyrdom.* New York: Oxford University Press, 2010.

Munn, Mark. *The Mother of the Gods, Athens, and the Tyranny of Asia: A Study of Sovereignty in Ancient Religion*. Berkeley: University of California Press, 2006.

Nelson, Robert H. *Economics as Religion: From Samuelson to Chicago and Beyond*. University Park: Pennsylvania State University Press, 2001.

———. *Reaching for Heaven on Earth: The Theological Meaning of Economics*. Savage, MD: Rowman & Littlefield, 1991.

Neufeld, Edward. "Prohibitions against Loans at Interest in Ancient Hebrew Laws," *Hebrew Union College Annual* 26 (1955): 355–412.

Nietzsche, Friedrich. *On the Genealogy of Morals and Ecce Homo*. Translated and edited by Walter Kaufman. New York: Random House, 1967.

———. "On Truth and Lying in an Extra-Moral Sense (1873)." In *Friedrich Nietzsche on Rhetoric and Language*, translated and edited by Sander L. Gilman, Carole Blair, and David J. Parent, 246-57. New York: Oxford University Press, 1989.

Origen. *Homilies on Genesis and Exodus*. Translated by Ronald Heine. Fathers of the Church. Washington, DC: Catholic University of America Press, 1982.

Oslington, Paul, ed. *Adam Smith as Theologian*. New York: Routledge, 2011.

Overbeck, Franz. *Werke und Nachlaß*. Vol. 6.1, *Kirchenlexicon. Materialien. "Christentum und Kultur."* Edited by Barbara von Reibnitz. Stuttgart: J. B. Metzler, 1996.

Pabst, Adrian. "Modern Sovereignty in Question: Theology, Democracy and Capitalism." *Modern Theology* 24, no. 4 (2010): 570–602.

Parry, Jonathan. "On the Moral Perils of Exchange." In *Money and the Morality of Exchange*, edited by Jonathan P. Parry and Maurice Bloch, 64–93. Cambridge: Cambridge University Press, 1989.

Peacock, Mark S. "The Origins of Money in Ancient Greece: The Political Economy of Coinage and Exchange." *Cambridge Journal of Economics* 30 (2006): 637–50.

Pemberton, Jo-Anne. *Sovereignty: Interpretations*. Basingstoke, UK: Palgrave Macmillan, 2009.

Peppard, Michael. "Archived Portraits of Jesus: Unorthodox Christological Images from John and Athanasius." In *Portraits of Jesus: Essays in Christology. Festschrift for Harold Attridge*, edited by Susan Myers, Wissenschaftliche Untersuchungen zum Neuen Testament 2, 393–409. Tübingen: Mohr Siebeck, 2012.

Peterson, Erik. "Monotheism as a Political Problem: A Contribution to the History of Political Theology in the Roman Empire." In *Theological Tractates*, translated and edited by Michael J. Hollerich, 68–105. Stanford: Stanford University Press, 2011.

Phelps, Hollis. "Overcoming Redemption: Neoliberalism, Atonement, and the Logic of Debt." *Political Theology* 17, no. 3 (2016): 264–82.

Polanyi, Karl. *The Great Transformation.* New York: Rinehart, 1944.

―――. *Trade and Market in the Early Empires.* Glencoe, IL: Free Press, 1957.

Prestige, G. L. *God in Patristic Thought.* 2nd ed. London: SPCK, 1969.

Price, S. R. F. *Rituals and Power: The Roman Imperial Cult in Asia Minor.* Cambridge: Cambridge University Press, 1984.

Raaflaub, Kurt A. "Stick and Glue: The Function of Tyranny in Fifth-Century Athenian Democracy." In *Popular Tyranny: Sovereignty and its Discontents in Ancient Greece,* edited by Kathryn A. Morgan, 59–94. Austin: University of Texas Press, 2003.

Rashdall, Hastings. *The Idea of Atonement in Christian Theology.* The Bampton Lectures for 1915. London: Macmillan, 1919.

Ray, Darby Kathleen. *Deceiving the Devil: Atonement, Abuse, and Ransom.* Cleveland, OH: Pilgrim Press, 1998.

Reumann, John. "'Jesus as Steward': An Overlooked Theme in Christology." In *Studia Evangelica V: Papers Presented to the Third International Congress on New Testament Studies Held at Christ Church, Oxford, 1965,* edited by F. L. Cross., 21–29. Berlin: Akademie Verlag, 1968.

―――. "Οἰκονομία as 'Ethical Accommodation' in the Fathers, and its Pagan Backgrounds." In *Studia Patristica III,* edited by F. L. Cross, 370–79. Berlin: Akademie Verlag, 1961.

―――. "Oikonomia-Terms in Paul in Comparison with Lucan *Heilsgeschichte.*" *New Testament Studies* 13, no. 2 (1967): 147–67.

―――. "'Stewards of God': Pre-Christian Religious Application of Oikonomos in Greek." *Journal of Biblical Literature* 77, no. 4 (1958): 339–49.

―――. *Stewardship and the Economy of God.* Grand Rapids, MI: Eerdmans, 1992.

―――. "The Use of Οἰκονομία and Related Terms in Greek Sources to about A.D. 100, as a Background for Patristic Applications." Ph.D. diss., University of Pennsylvania, 1957.

Rhee, Helen. *Loving the Poor, Saving the Rich: Wealth, Poverty, and Early Christian Formation.* Grand Rapids, MI: Baker Academic, 2012.

Richter, Gerhard. *Oikonomia: Der Gebrauch des Wortes Oikonomia im Neuen Testament, bei den Kirchenvätern und in der theologischen Literatur bis ins 20. Jahrhundert.* Arbeiten zur Kirchengeschichte 90. Berlin: de Gruyter, 2005.

Ricœur, Paul. *Figuring the Sacred: Religion, Narrative, and Imagination.* Translated by David Pellauer. Edited by Mark I. Wallace. Minneapolis, MN: Fortress Press, 1995.

―――. *The Rule of Metaphor: The Creation of Meaning in Language.* Translated by Robert Czerny. London: Routledge, 2003.

Roberts, Alexander, James Donaldson, and A. Cleveland Coxe, eds. *Apostolic*

Fathers, Justin Martyr, Irenaeus. Vol. 1, *Ante-Nicene Fathers.* Buffalo, NY: Christian Literature Publishing, 1885.

———, eds. *Latin Christianity: Its Founder, Tertullian.* Vol. 3, *Ante-Nicene Fathers.* Buffalo, NY: Christian Literature Publishing, 1885.

Robinson, Cedric. *An Anthropology of Marxism.* London: Ashgate, 2001.

Rosenberg, Jordana. *Critical Enthusiasm: Capital Accumulation and the Transformation of Religious Passion.* New York: Oxford University Press, 2011.

Runciman, Steven. *The Byzantine Theocracy.* The Weil Lectures 1973. Cambridge: Cambridge University Press, 1977.

Schaff, Philip, ed. *St. Basil: Letters and Select Works.* Vol. 8, *Nicene and Post-Nicene Fathers, Second Series.* Edinburgh: T & T Clark, 1895.

Schaff, Philip, and Henry Wace, eds. *Gregory of Nyssa: Dogmatic Treatises, etc.* Vol. 5, *Nicene and Post-Nicene Fathers, Second Series.* Buffalo, NY: Christian Literature Publishing, 1893.

Schaff, Philip and Henry Wace, eds. *Select Orations of Saint Gregory Nazianzen.* Vol. 7, *Nicene and Post-Nicene Fathers, Second Series.* Buffalo, NY: Christian Literature Publishing, 1894.

Schaps, David M. *The Invention of Coinage and the Monetization of Ancient Greece.* Ann Arbor: University of Michigan Press, 2004.

Schmitt, Carl. *The Concept of the Political.* Translated by George Schwab. Rev. ed. Chicago: University of Chicago Press, 2007.

———. *Political Theology: Four Chapters on the Concept of Sovereignty.* Translated by George Schwab. Chicago: University of Chicago Press, 2005.

———. *Political Theology II: The Myth of the Closure of Any Political Theology.* Translated by Michael Hoelzl and Graham Ward. Cambridge, UK: Polity, 2008.

———. *Roman Catholicism and Political Form.* Translated by G. L. Ulmen. Westport, CT: Greenwood Press, 1996.

Seaford, Richard. *Money and the Early Greek Mind: Homer, Philosophy, Tragedy.* Cambridge: Cambridge University Press, 2004.

———. "Tragic Tyranny." In *Popular Tyranny: Sovereignty and Its Discontents in Ancient Greece,* edited by Kathryn A. Morgan, 95–116. Austin: University of Texas Press, 2003.

Shell, Marc. *Art & Money.* Chicago: University of Chicago Press, 1995.

———. *The Economy of Literature.* Baltimore: Johns Hopkins University Press, 1978.

———. *Money, Language, and Thought: Literary and Philosophical Economies from the Medieval to the Modern Era.* Berkeley: University of California Press, 1982.

Singh, Devin. "Anarchy, Void, Signature: Agamben's Trinity among Orthodoxy's Remains." *Political Theology* 17, no. 1 (2016): 27–46.

———. "Disciplining Eusebius: Discursive Power and Representation of the Court Theologian." In *Studia Patristica LXII.10*, edited by Markus Vinzent, 89–102. Leuven: Peeters, 2013.

———. "Eusebius as Political Theologian: The Legend Continues." *Harvard Theological Review* 108, no. 1 (2015): 129–54.

———. "Incarnating the Money-Sign: Notes on an Implicit Theopolitics." *Implicit Religion* 14, no. 2 (2011): 129–40.

———. "Irrational Exuberance: Hope, Expectation, and Cool Market Logic." *Political Theology* 17, no. 2 (2016): 120–36.

———. "Monetized Philosophy and Theological Money: Uneasy Linkages and the Future of a Discourse." In *The Future of Continental Philosophy of Religion*, edited by Clayton Crockett, B. Keith Putt, and Jeffrey W. Robbins, 140–53. Bloomington: Indiana University Press, 2014.

———. "Provincializing Christendom: Reviewing John Milbank's *Beyond Secular Order*." *Syndicate: A New Forum for Theology* 2, no. 6 (2015): 177–83.

———. "Speculating the Subject of Money: Georg Simmel on Human Value." *Religions* 7, no. 7 (2016): 1–15.

Smithin, John N., ed. *What is Money?* London: Routledge, 2000.

Stroud, Ronald S. "An Athenian Law on Silver Coinage." *Hesperia* 43, no. 2 (1974): 157–88.

Sutherland, C. H. V. *Coinage in Roman Imperial Policy 31 B.C.–A.D. 68*. London: Methuen, 1951.

Tanner, Kathryn. *Christ the Key*. Cambridge: Cambridge University Press, 2010.

———. *Economy of Grace*. Minneapolis, MN: Fortress Press, 2005.

———. "Is Capitalism a Belief System?" *Anglican Theological Review* 92, no. 4 (2010): 617–35.

———. "Trinity." In *The Blackwell Companion to Political Theology*, edited by Peter Scott and William T. Cavanaugh, 319–32. Malden, MA: Blackwell, 2004.

Taussig, Michael T. *The Devil and Commodity Fetishism in South America*. 2nd ed. Chapel Hill: University of North Carolina Press, 2010.

Taylor, Charles. *A Secular Age*. Cambridge, MA: Belknap Press of Harvard University Press, 2007.

Taylor, Mark C. *Confidence Games: Money and Markets in a World without Redemption*. Chicago: University of Chicago Press, 2004.

Teall, John L. "The Age of Constantine: Change and Continuity in Administration and Economy." *Dumbarton Oaks Papers* 21 (1967): 11–36.

Temin, Peter. *The Roman Market Economy*. Princeton, NJ: Princeton University Press, 2013.

TeSelle, Eugene. "The Cross as Ransom." *Journal of Early Christian Studies* 4, no. 2 (1996): 147–70.

Tillich, Paul. *Theology of Culture.* Edited by Robert C. Kimball. New York: Oxford University Press, 1959.

Tooley, Wilfred. "Stewards of God: An Examination of the Terms OIKONO-MOS and OIKONOMIA in the New Testament." *Scottish Journal of Theology* 19 (1966): 74–86.

Turner, H. E. W. *The Patristic Doctrine of Redemption: A Study of the Development of Doctrine during the First Five Centuries.* London: A. R. Mowbray, 1952.

Tyrell, George. *Christianity at the Crossroads.* London: Longmans, 1910.

Ure, P. N. *The Origin of Tyranny.* Cambridge: Cambridge University Press, 1922.

Vanhoozer, Kevin J. *Biblical Narrative in the Philosophy of Paul Ricoeur: A Study in Hermeneutics and Theology.* Cambridge: Cambridge University Press, 1990.

Veyne, Paul. *Bread and Circuses: Historical Sociology and Political Pluralism.* Translated by Brian Pearce. London: Allen Lane at The Penguin Press, 1990.

Vidal-Naquet, Pierre. *The Black Hunter: Forms of Thought and Forms of Society in the Greek World.* Translated by Andrew Szegedy-Maszak. Baltimore: Johns Hopkins University Press, 1998.

Vries, Hent de. "On General and Divine Economy: Talal Asad's Genealogy of the Secular and Emmanuel Levinas's Critique of Capitalism, Colonialism, and Money." In *Powers of the Secular Modern: Talal Asad and His Interlocutors,* edited by David Scott and Charles Hirschkind, 113–33. Stanford: Stanford University Press, 2006.

Vries, Hent de, and Lawrence Eugene Sullivan, eds. *Political Theologies: Public Religions in a Post-Secular World.* New York: Fordham University Press, 2006.

Wallace-Hadrill, Andrew. "Image and Authority in the Coinage of Augustus." *Journal of Roman Studies* 76 (1986): 66–87.

Wariboko, Nimi. *God and Money: A Theology of Money in a Globalizing World.* Lanham, MD: Lexington Books, 2008.

Weaver, J. Denny. *The Nonviolent Atonement.* 2nd ed. Grand Rapids, MI: Eerdmans, 2011.

Webb, Stephen H. "Providence and the President (or, The New Eusebius)." *Reviews in Religion and Theology* 15, no. 4 (2008): 622–29.

Weber, Cynthia. *Simulating Sovereignty: Intervention, the State, and Symbolic Exchange.* Cambridge: Cambridge University Press, 1995.

Weber, Max. *Economy and Society: An Outline of Interpretive Sociology.* Edited by Guenther Roth and Claus Wittich. 2 vols. Berkeley: University of California Press, 1978.

———. *The Protestant Ethic and the Spirit of Capitalism.* Translated by Stephen Kalberg. Rev. ed. New York: Oxford University Press, 2011.

Weber, Samuel. *Institution and Interpretation.* Rev. ed. Stanford: Stanford University Press, 2002.

Williams, Delores S. *Sisters in the Wilderness: The Challenge of Womanist God-Talk*. Maryknoll, NY: Orbis Books, 1993.

Woodmansee, Martha, and Mark Osteen, eds. *The New Economic Criticism: Studies at the Intersection of Literature and Economics*. London: Routledge, 1999.

Wray, L. Randall. "Conclusion: The Credit Money and State Money Approaches." In *Credit and State Theories of Money: The Contributions of A. Mitchell Innes*, edited by L. Randall Wray, 223–62. Cheltenham, UK: Edward Elgar, 2004.

———, ed. *Credit and State Theories of Money: The Contributions of A. Mitchell Innes*. Cheltenham, UK: Edward Elgar, 2004.

Wroth, Warwick William. *Catalogue of the Imperial Byzantine Coins in the British Museum*. 2 vols. London: British Museum, 1908.

Young, William. "The Fabulous Gold of the Pactolus Valley." *Boston Museum Bulletin* 70, no. 359 (1972): 4–13.

Yuran, Noam. *What Money Wants: An Economy of Desire*. Stanford: Stanford University Press, 2014.

Zartaloudis, Thanos. *Giorgio Agamben: Power, Law and the Uses of Criticism*. *Nomikoi*: Critical Legal Thinkers. Abingdon, UK: Routledge, 2010.

Index

Abelard, Peter, 238n48

Acts 17:29, 122

Acts of Thomas, Peter, and Philip, 71

Adamantius, 170

Aesop's fable of dog chasing reflection, 152, 153, 154

Agamben, Giorgio, 14, 132, 143, 213nn31,32, 218n28; on analogy, 21; on angels, 61–62, 68, 77, 223n11; *The Kingdom and the Glory*, 31, 223n11, 227n4; on *oikonomia*, 16, 22, 28–29, 31, 32, 35, 58, 60–61, 68–69, 136, 141–42, 196, 215n4, 216n7; on pastoral exclusion, 142; on Son's anarchy, 223n10; on sovereignty vs. governance, 15–16, 17, 28–29, 30, 35, 61–62, 85, 196, 227n4

almsgiving, 63, 84, 223n17, 224n20, 242n49; by civic benefactors/ *euergetai*, 64–65, 97, 223nn16,17; role in salvation, 66–68, 79, 135, 181–82

Ambrose, St.: on war and usury, 203

Amos 4:1–2, 243n58

analogies: Christ as gold and Mary as coin purse, 128, 237n44; between Christian theology and money, 4, 6, 17, 121; between God and Roman monarchy, 54–55; vs. homologies, 17–19, 21

Anidjar, Gil, 236n39, 239n15, 248n14

Ando, Clifford, 109, 115, 233n10

annexation, under Constantine, 185–87

Anselm, St., 145, 171, 184

archaeology, 8, 9, 193, 212n27

Aristotle: on money, 33–34, 152; on *oikonomia*, 32, 33–34; *Politics*, 152; on tyrants, 95

Athanasius, 161; *Against the Arians*, 228n9; *On the Incarnation of the Word*, 235n26

Augustine, St.: *City of God*, 48, 221n57; *Confessions*, 244n6; on humanity as coins of God, 120–21, 122, 124; on redemption and sacrifice, 161, 244n6; *Sermon* 9.8.9, 120; on Son of God, 120–21, 122, 123, 157

Aulén, Gustaf: on God and salvation, 171, 172; on justice, 171–72, 245n10; on salvation as ransom, 171–74; *Christus Victor*, 245n8

Axial Age, 53–54

Babylon, 53

Balke, Friedrich, 231n29

Basil I, 129

Basil the Great, St., 148, 241nn32,37, 247n29; on almsgiving, 243n49; on God and salvation, 174; on God as manager (*oikonomos*), 71; on moneylending, 162–63, 245n14

Benjamin, Walter: on capitalism as religion, 126, 127, 130

bills of exchange, 198–99

Blumenberg, Hans, 12

Bourdieu, Pierre, 208n6

Brown, Peter, 197, 226n50; on almsgiving, 66–67; on the poor, 64–66; on provision for the poor, 79, 80,

images of God, 118, 236n34, 236n40;
on Roman Empire, 41, 149, 218n29;
on salvation as ransom, 145–47, 148–
49; on wages of sin, 159
Orosius, Paulus: *History against
the Pagans*, 48–49, 221n57; on
incarnation and Augustan tax
census, 49–50, 107, 221n61
Ovid Moralized, 237n45

Pabst, Adrian, 208n5
papal authority vs. imperial authority,
30
pastorate: bishops, 23, 30, 40, 56, 59,
62, 64, 65–66, 67, 68, 78, 79, 84,
142, 224n20; care for the poor,
62–66, 81, 82, 84, 224n20; ecclesial
authority, 139, 143–44; Foucault
on, 59–60, 60, 78, 194, 196, 200,
201; management of financial
resources by, 62–66, 84; pastoral
economy and governmentality,
58–59, 68, 77, 78–79, 130, 135, 142,
143, 191–92, 196, 200; pastoral
exception, 142–45, 189; pastoral vs.
imperial governance, 78–82; role in
salvation, 79, 142, 194–95, 199, 200,
202; as shepherds, 58, 60–61, 69,
71–72, 78–79, 194–96, 199–201
patristic thought: authority of, 3; God
and monetary economy in, 7, 8,
9; humanity as image of God in,
111, 120; incarnation and Roman
Empire in, 47–48; money in, 105;
oikonomia in, 37, 90, 137–38, 141,
161; salvation in, 24, 134, 137, 141,
144, 169, 170, 173, 189; theology and
politics in, 40. *See also* Augustine,
St.; Basil the Great, St.; Chrysostom,
John; Eusebius of Caesarea;
Gregory of Nazianzus; Gregory of
Nyssa; Irenaeus of Lyon; Origen
of Alexandria; Orosius, Paulus;
Tertullian
Paul, St., 112, 136–37

payment, 18, 25, 134, 136, 144–45; to
God, 131, 145, 169, 245n10; as in-kind
payment, 47; Jesus Christ as, 28, 29,
38, 39, 56, 82, 105, 124, 131, 135, 137,
141, 143, 157–58, 160, 168–69, 174–
76, 179–80, 183, 187, 190, 191, 199,
200, 202, 244nn4,6
Peppard, Michael, 120
1 Peter 1:19, 226n47
Peterson, Erik: on Eusebius, 44, 47–48,
85, 215n3, 217n28, 220n46, 227n4; on
gnosticism, 76–77; on monotheism,
220n44; on Orosius and Augustine,
48–49, 221n57
philanthropy, 68, 80, 84, 97, 99, 142,
191, 223n17
Philippians 2:7, 72
Philo, 71, 110–11, 113, 114, 115, 118, 122,
225n32
Philodemus's *Peri Oikonomias*, 34
Plato, 32, 117, 148; *Cratylus*, 77; on the
demiurge, 76, 77–78, 92; on Gyges,
94–95; on money and desire, 152;
on money and invisibility, 230n25;
Republic, 152, 230n25, 232n38;
Timaeus, 77–78, 225n47
Polanyi, Karl: *The Great
Transformation*, 238n1
poor, the, 180, 197, 204, 226n52, 245n14;
almsgiving, 63, 64–65, 66–68, 79–
80, 84, 135, 181–82, 223n17, 224n20,
242n49; imperial care for, 68, 79–
80, 81, 82, 84, 89–90, 96–97, 226n51;
pastoral care for, 62–66, 81, 82, 84,
224n20
poststructuralism, 4
Presocratic philosophy, 53–54
Procopius, 115
prosperity gospel, 204–5, 249n18
Protestantism, 66, 200, 201, 243n49
Proverbs: 19:17, 66, 180; 31:10–31, 90
Psalm 104:26, 161

Raaflaub, Kurt, 231n28
Radical Orthodoxy, 208n5

Cultural Memory in the Present

Jonathan Culler, *The Literary in Theory*

Michael G. Levine, *The Belated Witness: Literature, Testimony, and the Question of Holocaust Survival*

Jennifer A. Jordan, *Structures of Memory: Understanding German Change in Berlin and Beyond*

Christoph Menke, *Reflections of Equality*

Marlène Zarader, *The Unthought Debt: Heidegger and the Hebraic Heritage*

Jan Assmann, *Religion and Cultural Memory: Ten Studies*

David Scott and Charles Hirschkind, *Powers of the Secular Modern: Talal Asad and His Interlocutors*

Gyanendra Pandey, *Routine Violence: Nations, Fragments, Histories*

James Siegel, *Naming the Witch*

J. M. Bernstein, *Against Voluptuous Bodies: Late Modernism and the Meaning of Painting*

Theodore W. Jennings Jr., *Reading Derrida / Thinking Paul: On Justice*

Richard Rorty and Eduardo Mendieta, *Take Care of Freedom and Truth Will Take Care of Itself: Interviews with Richard Rorty*

Jacques Derrida, *Paper Machine*

Renaud Barbaras, *Desire and Distance: Introduction to a Phenomenology of Perception*

Jill Bennett, *Empathic Vision: Affect, Trauma, and Contemporary Art*

Ban Wang, *Illuminations from the Past: Trauma, Memory, and History in Modern China*

James Phillips, *Heidegger's Volk: Between National Socialism and Poetry*

Frank Ankersmit, *Sublime Historical Experience*

István Rév, *Retroactive Justice: Prehistory of Post-Communism*

Paola Marrati, *Genesis and Trace: Derrida Reading Husserl and Heidegger*

Krzysztof Ziarek, *The Force of Art*

Marie-José Mondzain, *Image, Icon, Economy: The Byzantine Origins of the Contemporary Imaginary*

Cecilia Sjöholm, *The Antigone Complex: Ethics and the Invention of Feminine Desire*

Jacques Derrida and Elisabeth Roudinesco, *For What Tomorrow . . . : A Dialogue*

Elisabeth Weber, *Questioning Judaism: Interviews by Elisabeth Weber*

Jacques Derrida and Catherine Malabou, *Counterpath: Traveling with Jacques Derrida*

Martin Seel, *Aesthetics of Appearing*

Nanette Salomon, *Shifting Priorities: Gender and Genre in Seventeenth-Century Dutch Painting*

Jacob Taubes, *The Political Theology of Paul*

Jean-Luc Marion, *The Crossing of the Visible*

Eric Michaud, *The Cult of Art in Nazi Germany*

Anne Freadman, *The Machinery of Talk: Charles Peirce and the Sign Hypothesis*

Stanley Cavell, *Emerson's Transcendental Etudes*

Stuart McLean, *The Event and Its Terrors: Ireland, Famine, Modernity*

Beate Rössler, ed., *Privacies: Philosophical Evaluations*

Bernard Faure, *Double Exposure: Cutting Across Buddhist and Western Discourses*

Alessia Ricciardi, *The Ends of Mourning: Psychoanalysis, Literature, Film*

Alain Badiou, *Saint Paul: The Foundation of Universalism*

Gil Anidjar, *The Jew, the Arab: A History of the Enemy*

Jonathan Culler and Kevin Lamb, eds., *Just Being Difficult? Academic Writing in the Public Arena*

Jean-Luc Nancy, *A Finite Thinking*, edited by Simon Sparks

Theodor W. Adorno, *Can One Live after Auschwitz? A Philosophical Reader*, edited by Rolf Tiedemann

Patricia Pisters, *The Matrix of Visual Culture: Working with Deleuze in Film Theory*

Andreas Huyssen, *Present Pasts: Urban Palimpsests and the Politics of Memory*

Talal Asad, *Formations of the Secular: Christianity, Islam, Modernity*

Dorothea von Mücke, *The Rise of the Fantastic Tale*

Marc Redfield, *The Politics of Aesthetics: Nationalism, Gender, Romanticism*

Emmanuel Levinas, *On Escape*

Dan Zahavi, *Husserl's Phenomenology*

Rodolphe Gasché, *The Idea of Form: Rethinking Kant's Aesthetics*

Michael Naas, *Taking on the Tradition: Jacques Derrida and the Legacies of Deconstruction*

Herlinde Pauer-Studer, ed., *Constructions of Practical Reason: Interviews on Moral and Political Philosophy*

Jean-Luc Marion, *Being Given That: Toward a Phenomenology of Givenness*

Theodor W. Adorno and Max Horkheimer, *Dialectic of Enlightenment*

Ian Balfour, *The Rhetoric of Romantic Prophecy*

Martin Stokhof, *World and Life as One: Ethics and Ontology in Wittgenstein's Early Thought*

Gianni Vattimo, *Nietzsche: An Introduction*

Jacques Derrida, *Negotiations: Interventions and Interviews, 1971–1998*, edited by Elizabeth Rottenberg

Brett Levinson, *The Ends of Literature: The Latin American "Boom" in the Neoliberal Marketplace*

Timothy J. Reiss, *Against Autonomy: Cultural Instruments, Mutualities, and the Fictive Imagination*

Hent de Vries and Samuel Weber, eds., *Religion and Media*

Niklas Luhmann, *Theories of Distinction: Re-Describing the Descriptions of Modernity*, edited and introduced by William Rasch

Johannes Fabian, *Anthropology with an Attitude: Critical Essays*

Michel Henry, *I Am the Truth: Toward a Philosophy of Christianity*

Gil Anidjar, *"Our Place in Al-Andalus": Kabbalah, Philosophy, Literature in Arab-Jewish Letters*